Typing
First Course
Fourth Edition

Archie Drummond,
Matthew Boulton Technical College, Birmingham

Anne Coles-Mogford,
Matthew Boulton Technical College, Birmingham

with

Ida Scattergood

McGraw-Hill Book Company (UK) Limited
London · New York · St Louis · San Francisco · Auckland · Bogotá · Guatemala · Hamburg
Johannesburg · Lisbon · Madrid · Mexico · Montreal · New Delhi · Panama · Paris · San Juan
São Paulo · Singapore · Sydney · Tokyo · Toronto

Part One

Part One of TYPING FIRST COURSE, fourth edition, deals exclusively with BLOCKED STYLE and OPEN PUNCTUATION. The contents of Part Two are shown on page 109.

CONTENTS

Index

Index

Index

Index

PREFACE

When Sholes and Glidden decided on the layout of the typewriter keyboard, they could not possibly have envisaged that the skill of operating the keyboard would become so very important to business, science and society in the 1980s. The typewriter is still the most commonly used business machine, but now we have word processing machines, computer terminals, accounting machines—all with a typewriter keyboard. In the future many clerical workers will be concerned with data entry and retrieval and, no matter how sophisticated an automated data handling system may be, the more efficiently a person can use a keyboard, the better the results. Furthermore, if you wish to operate a word processor, then the conventional typing skills—accuracy, speed, correct presentation (layout), ability to proof-read and use the English language—are essential.

Typing First Course, fourth edition, offers you a keyboard course which has been tried and tested and used to train thousands of typists. In addition, this text includes the best features from 3 prior editions and, at the same time, it introduces significant new features which will help you become a more efficient typist.

Typing First Course will take you beyond the standard required for the

(a) competent copy typist;
(b) elementary stage of any typewriting examination;
(c) trainee word processor operator.

The purpose of **Typing First Course** is to help you

(a) acquire smooth and correct finger movement;
(b) raise the level and broaden the foundation of the skills and techniques practised in (a); and
(c) apply the skills and techniques to practical work.

If you play a musical instrument, swim, or play tennis, you will know that it takes patience to master the skills involved in any of these activities, and, also, that the more expert you wish to become, the harder and longer you must practise. The same applies when learning to type. At first your fingers will not move very quickly but, before long you will find that they will move faster and faster as your control of the keys becomes more and more automatic, provided good work habits and correct techniques are maintained from the beginning and practised continuously.

The book has been divided into 2 parts and you will welcome these special features of Part One:

all blocked and with open punctuation
simplicity of presentation
consistency in styles of display and layout
standardisation on vertical and horizontal spacing
theory points easily distinguishable as the shaded areas
greater emphasis on proof-reading
greater emphasis on basic production techniques
greater emphasis on efficient manipulation of the machine

for ease of reference, a note of the contents of each page is printed at the bottom of the page.

Part Two gives continued emphasis on the points covered in Part One with exercises in open and full punctuation, blocked and centred styles.

We are convinced that it is easier for you to start with open punctuation and, when you are competent in its uses, to then transfer to full punctuation.

Consistency in display has been followed because we felt it was unfair to expect students, in the learning stage, to change frequently from one style to another and thus become confused. Therefore, in Part One, all exercises (display, tabulation, enumerated items, memoranda, business letters, forms) are in open punctuation and blocked style.

The simplicity of presentation will help learners eliminate errors because doubts about correct display have been removed and, therefore, you can concentrate on accurate typing and efficient manipulation of the machine.

Further, in order to give you more confidence in the operation of the typewriter, display and tabulation are introduced immediately the keyboard has been completed.

Because proof-reading is such an important part of your training, we have included special exercises which will give you concentrated practice in this essential skill.

In order that you may identify the theory points more easily and quickly, these are printed on a blue background.

We have standardised on vertical and horizontal spacing; for example:

Vertical—one clear space only after*
(a) headings
(b) sub-headings

* The one exception is blocked exercises in double spacing.

(c) all parts of the business letter except after the complimentary closing.

Horizontal—2 clear spaces only after

(a) Numbers, full stops and brackets in enumerated items
(b) Paragraph headings (where applicable)

NOTE: *For the attention of ...* has always been typed before the name of the organisation on the envelope; therefore, in this edition *for the attention of* has been typed before the name of the organisation in the business letters.

In addition, this textbook retains all the popular features of the previous editions that students and teachers found helpful:

large typeface for keyboard drills

where desired, quicker completion of the keyboard

twenty-minute lessons—in the keyboard learning stage, each unit can be covered in 20 minutes

up-to-date content

two colours to enable a 'visual' presentation of all new keys

the second colour also emphasizes styling and display both in the text and in the form of marginal reminders

skill-building drills, accuracy and speed practice are a built-in, essential part of the course

explanations, points of theory, and specimens of all new work are short and simple to understand

specimens are displayed as they should appear when typed

all production work (there are 67 Production Jobs) has a timed target based on the average times taken by students of varying ability

flexibility is provided by the separation of keyboard techniques, accuracy/speed practice, new work, and office production typing

back-spacing method of centring

six consolidation units—each unit contains exercises on all the work covered up to that particular unit

test material—10 Production Jobs—covering all aspects of office- and examination-style typing.

Keyboard coverage

Alphabet keys. Because it has proved successful and popular, the keyboard approach given in the third edition has been retained with minor adjustments. To cover the needs of all learners, we have:

(a) Introduced only 2 alphabet keys in each unit. After the introduction of the home keys, only one new key is presented at a time.
(b) Given only 2 lines of drills on each new key. These drills are very easy, consisting mainly of words of 3 letters.
(c) After introducing the 2 new keys, given a further 2 lines of WORD FAMILY drills on these keys.
(d) At the beginning of each keyboard unit, given 3 lines of REVIEW THE KEYS YOU KNOW and at the end of each unit 3 lines of APPLY THE KEYS YOU KNOW.
(e) For students who prefer to spend a little more time on the alphabet keys, included 3 IMPROVEMENT PRACTICE UNITS—8, 12, and 18—each with 2 pages of drills on the keys introduced prior to the particular unit.

Twenty-minute modules. A number of schools and colleges have now switched to computer scheduling, open-plan classrooms, individualized instruction etc., and to meet the needs of the old and the new, the units covering the keyboard learning stages have been planned so that each unit can be completed in 20 minutes—the exceptions are the IMPROVEMENT PRACTICE UNITS. This means that, if you do not need to use the IMPROVEMENT PRACTICE UNITS, you will complete the alphabet keyboard in 5 hours.

Large typeface. All drills covering the alphabet keyboard are printed in large typeface which is easily read letter by letter at arm's length.

Figures and special characters. The figures and special characters are presented in Units 26–33: the special characters are introduced immediately after the presentation of the relevant figure key. In these 8 Units there is a sequence of:

(a) Alphabet reviews which provide ample keyboard revision and practice.
(b) Intensive drills on figures and special characters.
(c) Accuracy and speed practice.
(d) Introduction of, and intensive practice on, display work, tabulation, headings, manuscript, measurements, decimals, sums of money and enumerated items.

Skill Building and Technique Development

From Unit 34 onwards, accuracy, speed, new work and production work are developed in a carefully balanced sequence of activities:

(a) Skill building
 i. Keyboard Techniques
 ii. Accuracy/Speed Practice
 iii. Record Your Progress
(b) Technique Development (New work)
(c) Production Typing

Skill Building Units

i. *Keyboard Technique.* Each unit starts with an alphabetic sentence which is an excellent warm-up drill and at the same time gives intensive practice on the alphabet keys: this in turn improves accuracy. There then follow keyboard reviews which include the following drills: fluency, phrase, hyphen, line-end division, one-hand word, space bar, figure, punctuation, word family, shift key, special character, carriage return, vowel, prefix, suffix, double letter, etc.

ii. *Accuracy/speed practice.* **Typing First Course** contains a complete programme of accuracy/speed practice. The passages start in Unit 19 at 19 wpm (one-minute timing) and progress in easy stages to 30 wpm (one-minute timing) in Unit 42. From Unit 42, the length of the 30 wpm passages is graduated in $\frac{3}{4}$ minutes to 2 minutes in Unit 45. From Unit 46, the length of the 30 wpm *accuracy* passages is graduated in $\frac{3}{4}$ minutes to a maximum of 5 minutes in Units 53 and 54. Because it is easier to build speed on short (2 minutes or less) easy passages, the *speed* building material is given separately from Unit 46. In this unit the speed passages start at 35 wpm for one minute and move in easy stages to 45 wpm for one minute in Unit 54. Whether you practise for accuracy or speed is a very personal matter and can only be decided by you or on advice from your teacher. Accuracy is the result of correct practice combined with good techniques, good posture, and correct reading of copy. Speed, without any thought of accuracy, will lead only to fast but inaccurate typing. As a guide, we suggest that you work for accuracy if you have more than one error for each minute typed. If you have one error or less for each minute typed, then you may aim for a slight increase in speed. You should work up to the desired speed gradually and, having reached the speed, practice should continue at that speed until the required standard of accuracy is reached.

iii. *Record Your Progress.* There are 28 Record Your Progress exercises. The object is to let you know how you are progressing when typing from straight copy. A Record Your Progress Chart is given in the Handbook and Solutions Manual.

Syllabic Intensity (Copy control). We believe that a controlled but random and unselected vocabulary is the most effective way of building typing skills and, therefore, the difficulty of the copy in Accuracy, Speed, and Record Your Progress exercises has been graded according to the syllabic intensity. Syllabic intensity means the average number of syllables in the words of a passage. Thus in Accuracy/Speed Practice A/S 4 (page 28) SI 1.09 means that there is an average of 1.09 syllables per word.

Technique development units introduce new work in small and easy specific steps. The first exercise on all new work is set out clearly, and the essential features are emphasized in the second colour.

Production Typing. **Typing First Course** is as much concerned with applying typing skill as with building it. Production typing is introduced only when your speed and accuracy standards and the machine techniques necessary for reasonably fast output have been acquired. The inclusion of timed production targets emphasizes the importance of accuracy, speed, theory, and good machine techniques in all typing.

In addition to **Typing First Course**, there are 2 complementary books that you will find helpful: they are:

Practical Typing Exercises—Book One. This book contains further examples of exercises introduced in **Typing First Course**. Many of these exercises give the exact layout of typed documents and, therefore, are very easy to follow. Reference is made in **Typing First Course** to the relevant pages in **Practical Typing Exercises.**

Loose-leaf Handbook and Solution Manual.

Part I contains:

1. A brief explanation how **Typing First Course** was planned so that it incorporates a complete and systematic skill-building plan. There are also hints on how to use the textbook.

2. A brief but concise review of the basic principles of how typing skill is acquired and developed.

3. Syllabuses and Schemes of Work for full- and part-time courses, and helpful suggestions on how to plan a lesson.

4. Ideas on the presentation of a lesson.

Part II contains:

1. Each unit of **Typing First Course** is reviewed and suggestions given for lesson presentation.

2. All exercises not set out in the main text are displayed as they should look when

typed. These examples give margin and tab stops together with calculations for horizontal and vertical display.

3. As the book is loose-leaf, students' record sheets (Technique Check List, Record Your Progress Chart, etc.) and printed letter headings, invoice forms, form letters, etc., may be copied and duplicated.

4. Learning Guides—these will not only train students to type accurately and quickly, but also train them in

(a) the efficient use of the complete machine; and

(b) the automatic application of typing theory which is essential to all typists.

Also available are:

Keyboard Instruction Tapes—a series of tapes covering the presentation of the keyboard. These are suitable for

(a) individual practice at home or in the classroom;

(b) class teaching;

(c) reinforcement of keys previously practised.

For all information concerning price and availability, please contact: reach-a-teacha Ltd, 2 Hastings Court, Collingham, Wetherby, Yorkshire LS22 5JL.

Acknowledgments

The exercises in the book have been tested under practical conditions over the past few years by many teachers to whom we are indebted for their suggestions and criticisms concerning the suitability of the material included and the timing of production exercises. We also wish to thank our colleagues for the help given in copying the manuscript exercises.

We sincerely hope that you have enjoyed working through the first series of books and aids and that you will now proceed to

Second Series:

Applied Typing presents a systematic and comprehensive programme for perfecting and applying typing skill up to the standard of the intermediate and advanced stages of any typing examination.

Loose-Leaf Solutions Manual gives solutions to all exercises not displayed in APPLIED TYPING and headed paper and forms which can be copied easily.

Practical Typing Exercises—Book Two. This book contains further examples of exercises introduced in **Applied Typing**. Many of these exercises give the exact layout of typed documents and, therefore, are easy to follow. Reference is made in **Applied Typing** to the relevant pages in **Practical Typing Exercises**.

Note:

References in this book to the **Handbook and Solutions Manual** are to the **fourth edition**, and to **Practical Typing Exercises, Book One**, to the **second edition**, both of which are published at the same time as this, the **fourth edition** of **Typing First Course**.

Archie Drummond
Anne Coles-Mogford

The manufacturer always supplies a handbook with a new typewriter, and a diagram showing the different parts of your typewriter. As the position of the parts listed below can vary considerably, study the manufacturer's diagram carefully.

1 Paper rest
The paper rests on it ... so does the paper guide.

2 Carriage release
Frees carriage so it can be moved easily by hand to right or left ... one at each end of the carriage. When you depress it, hold the adjacent cylinder knob firmly.

3 Line-space selector
Controls the distance that the paper turns up when the carriage is returned by key or lever.

4 Cylinder or Platen knob
The large knob at each end of the cylinder.

5 Carriage return
Used to return the carriage and to space up the paper for the start of a new line of typing. On electrics, it is a large key at the right-hand side of the keyboard instead

6 Margin sets
Devices used to adjust the margin stops that control the width of the margin on each side of the paper.

7 Alignment guide
Close to the cylinder behind the ribbon on each side of the printing point. Indicates the exact writing line.

8 Paper guide
Used to guide the paper uniformly into the carriage.

9 Paper bail
Clamps the paper against the cylinder ... must be raised or pulled forward when you insert or straighten your paper.

10 Printing point
The V-shaped slot where the type bars come up to strike and print on the paper.

11 Printing-point indicator
A line or mark or arrowhead pointing to the space on the carriage-position scale to which the carriage has moved and at which the machine is ready to print.

12 Carriage-position scale
Counts the spaces across the cylinder.

13 Paper release
Loosens the paper for straightening or removal.

14 Carriage
The top, movable part of the machine ... carries the paper ... moves horizontally to right and left.

15 Cylinder or Platen
The long roller in the carriage around which the paper turns ... paper and cylinder turn each time you return the carriage or turn one of the cylinder knobs.

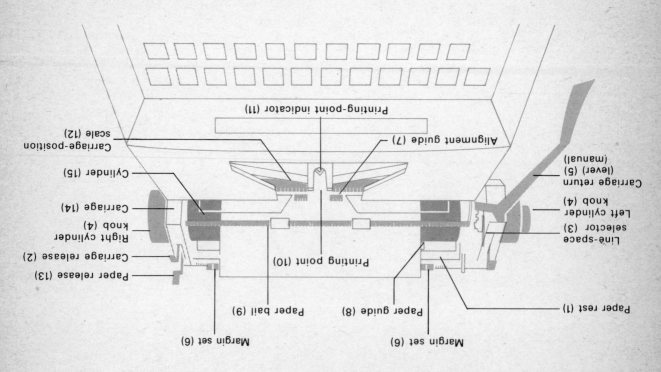

Learn the position and use of the following parts on your typewriter

Printing-point indicator (11)
Alignment guide (7)
Carriage-position scale (12)
Cylinder (15)
Carriage (14)
Right cylinder knob (4)
Carriage release (2)
Paper release (13)
Margin set (6)
Paper bail (9)
Printing point (10)
Paper guide (8)
Margin set (6)
Carriage return (lever) (5) (manual)
Left cylinder knob (4)
Line-space selector (3)
Paper rest (1)

1 Check the position of the paper guide

One of the marks on the paper rest shows where to set the paper guide so that the left edge of the paper will be '0' on the carriage-position scale. Check that the paper guide is set at that mark.

2 Set the line-space selector for single spacing

The line-space selector has a *1*, a *2*, and a *3* printed on or beside it. Adjust the selector so that it is in the *1* position. In addition, many machines are now fitted with half-line spacing to give $1\frac{1}{2}$ and $2\frac{1}{2}$ line-spaces. Examine your machine and check the line-spacing.

3 Set the margins as indicated in each unit or exercise

(a) On some machines you can see the margin stops on the front of the carriage, or behind the paper rest. On such machines: (1) press the button on top of the stop, (2) slide the stop to the point you wish, and (3) then release the button.

(b) On other machines you cannot see the margin stops. You must use a margin-set key. You may have a separate margin-set key at each end of the carriage, or you may have one key on the keyboard for use with both stops. On such machines: (1) move the carriage to the present setting of the stop, (2) press the margin-set key while you move the carriage to the point where you want the margin, and (3) then release the set key.

(c) In the keyboard learning stage (pages 5–44) only the left margin need be set. From page 45 onwards set margins at scale-points given.

As you progress through the textbook, you will find instructions such as 'Use suitable margins'—in such cases you must decide what margins to use. What is important is that, in the majority of exercises other than display and tabulation, your left margin must be wider than your right margin, e.g., Elite 22–82 (there are 21 clear spaces on the left and 18 clear spaces on the right).

In other cases you may be given measurements for your margins, e.g., 25 mm (one inch) on left and 13 mm (half an inch) on the right. This would mean that, when using A4 paper, you would have margins of Elite 13–94, Pica 11–77. With Elite type there are 12 spaces to 25 mm and with Pica type there are 10 spaces to 25 mm.

4 Get the paper bail out of the way

Pull the paper bail forward or up, temporarily away from the cylinder, so that you may insert paper without its bumping into the paper bail.

5 Insert a sheet of paper

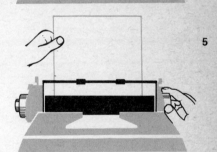

Hold the sheet in your left hand. Place the paper behind the cylinder, against the raised edge of the paper guide. Turn the right cylinder knob to draw the paper into the machine.

To prevent damage to the cylinder of the typewriter, use a backing sheet such as is usually supplied in boxes of carbon paper, or use a sheet of stout paper.

6 Check that the paper is straight

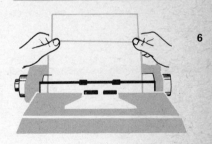

Push the top of the paper back. If the left side of the paper, at both top and bottom, fits evenly against the paper guide, your paper is straight. If it is not straight, loosen the paper (use the paper release), straighten it, and return the paper release to its normal position.

7 Place the paper bail against the paper

Slide the rubber rollers on the bail to the right or left to divide the paper into thirds. Then, set the bail back against the paper.

8 Adjust the paper for the top margin

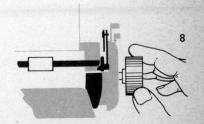

(a) When typing drills, turn the paper back, using the right cylinder knob, until only a small portion of paper shows above the paper bail.

(b) When typing production exercises (apart from display and tabulation) the majority of exercises typed on plain paper start on the seventh single-line space from the top edge of the paper, which means you leave 6 spaces (25 mm or one inch) clear. To do this proceed as follows:

i. Insert paper
ii. Check to see that paper is straight (see 6 above)
iii. Turn paper back so that top edge is level with top edge of alignment guide (See page 1 No. 7).
iv. Turn up 7 single-line spaces.

Type an original and two copies of the following. Use A4 paper, single spacing, and block paragraphs unless otherwise instructed.

At a meeting of Management & Staff Representatives held on 19th Aug., 1982, the following matters were discussed:

Annual Leave. It was agreed that entitlement to additional leave should be related to years of completed service whether or not there had been a break. *in the service* *after 10 years' service*

trs/
u.c.
np
Mileage Allowance. It was agreed that the mileage allowance as set out in Section IV of the handbook should be applied to all staff who used their cars for business purposes. Threshold Payments. The Secretary pointed out that these would be consolidated into the salary scales as from Sept 82. *payments*

Overtime. As from 1st Oct 1982, where any employee is required to work in excess of 35 hours a week, then the following options should apply:

(i) time off in lieu should be given wherever possible; or where this is not possible

(ii) payment should be made at the rate of time-and-a-half if the work was performed on week days, and *double time* if the work was carried out on Saturdays, Sundays, or during Statutory holidays.

Hanging paragraphs Please

Cost of living.
The staff representatives submitted that the increases in the cost of living was such that it had now eroded the increase given in January of this year and that a further increase was now necessary. Management replied that the cost of living index had not moved a sufficient number of points to have overtaken the increase, but promised to keep the Index under constant ~~super~~ revision. *to keep pace w. the cost of living*

#

Retirement. It was agreed that Management provide facilities to enable staff, within two years of their expected date of retirement, to make proper preparation for retirement. Employees are to be given special pay to attend courses organised by Local Colleges of Further Education. *leave with*

typist - Please insert main heading:
STAFF NOTICE (spaced caps)

SINGLE-ELEMENT TYPEWRITERS

There are now on the market many electric typewriters with single-element heads. These typewriters have no movable carriage, which also means that the platen roller is static, and there are no type bars. Instead, they have a printing head attached to a "carrier" that moves across the page from left to right, stroke by stroke. When you wish to return the carrier to the left margin, you press the return key as you would with the ordinary electric typewriter.

The printing head is the size and shape of a golf ball and it whirls and tilts to make an impression on the paper.

In previous editions of this textbook we have used phrases such as : RETURN CARRIAGE TO LEFT MARGIN, CENTRE CARRIAGE. In this edition we will use the expression CARRIAGE/CARRIER to cover both types of machines now in common usage.

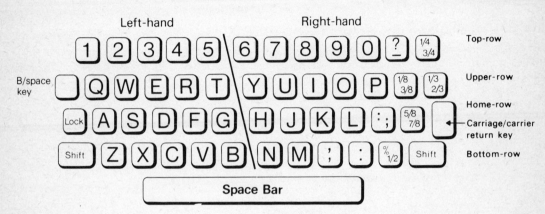

The ready-to-type position

1 Place your book on the right-hand side of your machine, or as indicated by your teacher.

2 Place your finger tips on the home keys: Left finger tips on A S D F and right finger tips on J K L ;. Check that you placed them correctly.

3 Keep your **left** thumb close to your left first finger.

4 Extend your right thumb so that it is slightly above the centre of the space bar.

5 Now, check your posture.
Your head—hold it erect, facing the book.
Your shoulders—hold them back, and relaxed.
Your body—centre yourself opposite the J-key a hand-span away from the machine.
Your back—straight, with your body sloping slightly forward from the hips.
Arms and elbows—let them hang loosely.
Wrists—keep them low, barely clearing the machine.
Hands—close together, low, flat across the backs.
Fingers—curved as though to grasp a handle bar.
Waist—sit back in the chair.
Feet—on the floor, one foot slightly in front of the other.

Finger Movement

1 Without typing, practise the finger movement for each exercise. During this preliminary practice you may look at your fingers. You will find it helpful to say the letters aloud. Continue this preliminary practice until your fingers 'know' where to move from the home key. Always return finger to its home key.

2 When you are confident that your fingers have acquired the correct movement, repeat this practice *without looking at your fingers*. Keep your eyes on the copy in your book, and do not strike the keys. If you hesitate in making the finger movement, repeat step one.

3 Practise the finger movement for each new key until your finger moves confidently and crisply to that key.

Correct Typing Posture

Job 65   Production Target—17 minutes

Type the following invoice on a suitable form.

FROM The Universal Supply Co Ltd, 84–114 High Street, Aberdeen. AB2 3HE

Invoice No 3843 dated 17 May 1982   VAT Reg No 992 3872 78

TO H Williamson & Co, 25 North Street, Montrose, Angus. DD10 8AA

Your Order No 7896/82   Terms: Nett 30 days   Tax Point: 17.5.82

Type of supply: Sale   VAT 15%

Goods supplied: 5 Lightweight Steam Irons @ £18.20 ea. £91.00 (VAT £13.65)
                   4 Electric Coffee Grinders @ £12.00 ea. £48.00 (VAT £7.20)
                   6 Electric Carpet Sweepers @ £122.00 ea. £732.00 (VAT £109.80)

Total goods £871.00   Total VAT £130.65   Total amount due £1001.65

Job 66   Production Target—16 minutes

Type the following memo on a printed A4 memo form. (a) Indented paragraphs. (b) Take 2 carbon copies: one for Ms F Jenkinson and the other for File.

To Company Secretary   REF PO/18T/82/PRE

From Purchasing Officer   DATE 29 Sept 1982

Further to our recent ~~talk~~ discussion abt power guillotines & duo punch binders, I give a short description of the machines available.

1   POWER GUILLOTINES

   (a) Model 200-A

   (b) Price - £1,983.00 plus VAT

   (c) Cuts 3" pile of paper 18" wide

   (d) Automatic blade return

   (e) Cuts cards/paper down to 1"

2   DUO PUNCH BINDER

   (a) Model DPB 82

caps (b) Price - £586.00 plus vat

   (c) Plastic ring binding

   (d) Binding thickness ¼" to 2"

20/ (e) Punches/sheets at a time

I also enc pamphlet abt the new offset-
uc/ litho machine you saw at the business
N.P./ Efficiency Exhibition. [Please let me know if you wd like to see a demonstration of these machines.

A Practise carriage return

1 MANUAL MACHINES

(a) Preliminary practice *without returning the carriage*. Look at the carriage return lever and raise your *left hand* and put the first finger and next finger or two against the lever. Practise the movement from the HOME KEYS to carriage return lever and back to HOME KEYS.

(b) Right- and left-hand fingers on HOME KEYS.

(c) Right-hand fingers remain on JKL;.

(d) With eyes on textbook
   (i) raise left hand and return carriage.
   (ii) return left hand so ASDF.

2 ELECTRIC MACHINES

(a) Preliminary practice *without returning the carriage/carrier*. Look at the carriage/carrier return key (on the right-hand side of the keyboard) and make the reach with your right-hand little finger from the semicolon to the return key and back to semicolon.

(b) All fingers remain just slightly above their HOME KEY except right-hand little finger.

(c) With eyes on textbook
   (i) raise the little finger of the right hand and lightly press the return key
   (ii) return little finger to semicolon key immediately.

B Set margins, line-space selector and insert paper

1 Set left margin at 30 Elite, 22 Pica

2 Set line-space selector at '1'

3 Set paper guide at '0'

4 Raise paper bail bar out of the way

5 (a) Take a sheet of A4 paper in your left hand
   (b) Place the paper behind the cylinder with the left edge against the raised edge of the paper guide
   (c) With your right hand turn the right cylinder knob clockwise to draw the paper into the machine

6 Check that paper is straight by pushing the top of the paper back. If top and bottom of paper do not fit evenly against the paper guide

   (a) Use paper release to loosen paper
   (b) Straighten paper
   (c) Return paper release lever to normal position

7 Return paper bail to normal position

8 Turn the paper back, using right cylinder knob, until only a small portion of paper shows above paper bail

Striking the keys

1 Let your finger bounce off each key and return to home key.

2 Reach with finger only; do *not* move wrist or arm.

3 For manual machines, strike key firmly and sharply; for electric machine, stroke key.

4 Strike keys, including space bar, evenly—one for each 'tick' and one for each 'tock' of the clock.

Examiner's Report (Centre in caps & u/score)

SHORTHAND 80 w.p.m.

;/ About a quarter of the candidates produced perfect scripts / a quarter failed; and of the remainder a ¼ passed in spite of their s'hand.

serious/ Spelling still causes/difficulty. Unfortunately candidates do not seem to realise th they

;/ cannot spell and / therefore, do not make use of the dictionaries provided. ⌐

Runon/ ⌐I must again point out th a sh-typist who cannot spell is a liability to any organisation.

TYPING (Stage II)

of Most candidates completed all the questions &,

most/ on the whole, the scripts ~~will~~ were very satisfactory. The/ common error was the omission of ballooned matter, & it was obvious th can-

carefully/ g/didates had not bothered to read the questions/ before typing. Candidates are advised to make full

now/ use of the 10 mins' "reading time" wh is/allowed before typing starts.

SECRETARIAL DUTIES (Stage II)

A surprising no of candidates failed to reach the req'd standard because:

(a) They did not answer the question. They answered a question given last yr on the same topic① ⊙

← Although this paper was a little more difficult than usual, there were some v.gd scripts.

uc/ (b) they were unable to apply their knowledge to specific situations.

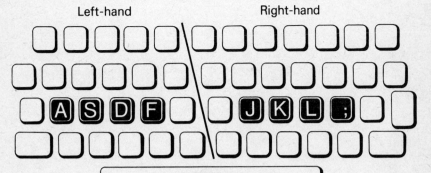

Left-hand   Right-hand

A S D F   J K L :

Space Bar

Left thumb close to first finger   Right thumb above space bar

C Ready-to-type position

1   Place book on right-hand side of machine

2   Feet—one foot slightly in front of the other

3   Arms and elbows—let them hang loosely

4   Fingers: (a) place left-hand fingers on ASDF
              (b) right-hand fingers on JKL;
              (c) curve fingers as though to grasp a handle bar
              (d) look at the keyboard and place your fingers on the HOME KEYS—ASDF JKL;
              (e) *never* type while looking at the keyboard

5   Sit back and relax

D Exercise 1

(a) See that carriage/carrier is at left margin

(b) Look at the keyboard and place your left-hand fingers on ASDF and right-hand fingers on JKL;

(c) Copy the following lines exactly as they stand—keeping eyes on textbook

fffjjjfffjjjfffjjjfffjjjfffjjjfffjjjfffjjjfffj   return carriage/carrier

fffjjjfffjjjfffjjjfffjjjfffjjjfffjjjfffjjjfffj   return carriage/carrier twice

(d) Sit back and relax and look at what you have typed.

E Space Bar

A clear space is left between each group of letters or words. This is done by striking the space bar with the *right thumb*. Keep your other fingers on the home keys as you bounce the thumb off the space bar. Practise striking space bar with right thumb.

F Exercise 2

(a) See that carriage/carrier is at left margin

(b) Look at the keyboard and place your left-hand fingers on ASDF and right-hand fingers on JKL;

(c) Copy the following lines exactly as they stand—keeping eyes on textbook

fff jjj fff jjj fjf jfj fff jjj fff fjfj   return carriage/carrier

fff jjj fff jjj fjf jfj fff jjj fff fjfj   return carriage/carrier

fff jjj fff jjj fjf jfj fff jjj fff fjfj   return carriage/carrier twice

(d) Sit back and relax and look at what you have typed.

UNIT 1   Introduction to Home Keys   5

Type an original and one copy of the following. For date put month and year only.

Our ref. DP/LC

Dear Sir(s),   OFFICE SUPPLIES   (Typist: Please insert current year)

Our catalogues will be ready for mailing at the end of this month. There are 4 catalogues, ea. covering one of the following sections:

OFFICE MACHINES   OFFICE FURNITURE
FILING EQUIPMENT   STATIONERY & ACCESSORIES

Because of rising inflation, many organisations now lease
u.c./ machines, equipment and furniture. ~~and~~ lease of
rentals do not fluctuate as these are fixed for the
N.P./ period of the lease, and leasing periods vary between
stet/ 3 and 6 years. [Please ~~complete~~ the tear-off portion of
this letter and send it to us. We shall be happy to send
y. complete details of and, should you wish it, our
rep. will be pleased to call and see y.
Yrs. ffy.   (at the bottom)

THE UNIVERSAL SUPPLY CO. LTD.

- -

      To: The Universal Supply Co. Ltd.,
27/14/   84 ~~88~~/ High Street, Aberdeen. AB2 3HE
      NAME _ _ _ _ _ _ _ _ _ _ _ _ _ _ _ _ _
      ADDRESS _ _ _ _ _ _ _ _ _ _ _ _ _ _ _ _
                                   POSTCODE _ _ _ _ _ _ _
me / Please send / the following catalogues.
      (Underline the ones you require.)
        OFFICE MACHINES   OFFICE FURNITURE
        FILING EQUIPMENT   STATIONERY & ACCESSORIES

Left-hand   Right-hand

Space Bar

Type each line or sentence 3 times, saying the letters to yourself. If time permits, complete your practice by typing each group of lines as it appears. Keep your eyes on the copy while you type and also when returning the carriage/carrier. The carriage/carrier must be returned IMMEDIATELY after the last character in the line has been typed. Set left margin stop at 30 Elite, 22 Pica, and use single spacing with double between exercises.

A Practise **F** and **J** keys—First fingers

Keep other fingers on home keys

1   fff jjj fjf jfj fjf jfj fff jjj fff fjfj

Always turn up TWICE between exercises

B Practise **D** and **K** keys—Second fingers

Raise first fingers slightly. Keep little fingers on home keys

2   ddd kkk dkd kdk dkd kdk ddd kkk dkd dkdk

3   fff jjj ddd kkk fkf kfk jdj djd fjk fdjk

Use an even stroke for space bar

C Practise **S** and **L** keys—Third fingers

Raise little fingers over home keys. Keep first fingers on home keys

4   sss lll sls lsl sls lsl sss lll sls slsl

5   fff jjj ddd kkk sss lll fds jkl fds jklj

Feet firmly on floor

D Practise **A** and **;** keys—Little fingers

Keep first fingers on home keys

6   aaa ;;; a;a ;a; a;a ;a; aaa ;;; ;a; a;a;

7   f;f jaj d;d kak a;s lal aaa ;;; a;a a;a;

E Word-building

8   aaa lll all lll aaa ddd lad ddd aaa dad;

9   fff aaa ddd fad sss aaa ddd sad fad lad;

F Apply the keys you know

10   all sad lads; a sad lass; a lad asks dad

One space after semicolon

11   all sad lads ask a dad; a sad lass falls

12   as a lass falls dad falls; all lads fall

UNIT 2   **Home Keys**   **6**

Type a copy of the following exercise on A4 paper. (a) Where items are numbered in small roman numerals, use hanging paragraphs where appropriate.

DUPLICATING PROCESSES

I   STENCIL

The master is cut by typewriter or in longhand by means of a stylus pen.

Advantages

easily

i   Corrections are made (correction fluid is used)
ii   Good quality reproduction
iii Up to 7,000 copies can be run off from one master.
iv   Masters may be stored and used again.
v   Masters may be made by photographic process.

II SPIRIT

or written

A special type of paper backed by a carbon is used ~~to prepare~~ in preparing the master, which may be typed in the usual way.

Advantages

i   One or several colours may be included in the same master.
     (by using different coloured carbons)
be ii   Masters may very easily prepared.
iii Paper for copies is of better quality than that in stencil duplicating.

III OFFSET LITHOGRAPHY

Master may be typed or written but a special grease-based ribbon (or pencil) must be used.

Advantages

1 Quality of reproduction is very high.
2 Much cheaper than printing & results almost as good.
3 Any type of paper may be used f copies.
4 A good quality master will produce up to 50,000 copies.
5 Masters are often prepared by photographic process.

Please use small Roman numerals

Left-hand   Right-hand

Space Bar

Type each line or sentence 3 times, saying the letters to yourself. If time permits, complete your practice by typing each group of lines as it appears. Keep your eyes on the copy while you type and also when returning the carriage/carrier. The carriage/carrier must be returned IMMEDIATELY after the last character in the line has been typed. Set left margin stop at 30 Elite, 22 Pica, and use single spacing with double between exercises.

A   Review the keys you know

1 aaa ;;; sss lll ddd kkk fff jjj asd jkl;

2 ask a lad; ask all lads; ask a sad lass;

3 all lads fall; dad falls; dad asks a lad

Return carriage/carrier without looking up

Turn up TWICE between exercises

B   Practise E key—D finger

Practise D to E back to D. Keep other fingers on home keys

4 ddd eee ded ded see ded lee ded fee ded;

5 ded sea ded lea ded led ded fed ded eke;

C   Practise H key—J finger

Practise J to H back to J. Keep other fingers on home keys

6 jjj hhh jhj jhj has jhj had jhj she jhj;

7 jhj has jhj had jhj she jhj ash jhj dash

D   Practise word-building

8 hhh eee lll ddd held jjj aaa fff jaffas;

9 sss hhh aaa lll shall fff eee ddd feeds;

E   Apply the keys you know

10 a lass has had a salad; dad sees a lake;

11 a jaffa salad; she held a sale; he shall

12 she feeds a lad; dad has a hall; a shed;

Use right thumb and even stroke for space bar

Type an original and two copies of the following letter. Mark the letter for the attention of Mrs. P. G. Barker. On the top left-hand corner of the first carbon copy type: Mr. J. R. Nicholson—for information. Type a C6 envelope.

Your Ref. PGB/PB
Our Ref. WM/BC
19th May 1982

R. MacGregor & Co. Ltd.,
18 Commercial Str,
PETERHEAD, Aberdeenshire.   AB4 6AA

Dear Sirs,
PRINTING CALCULATORS, 1

Thank you for yr enquiry dated 16th May.

The following is our quotation of the 2 calculators abt which y enquired:

(Electronic)

1021 J Printing Calculator, 10 digit capacity, constant & memory - - - - - - - - - - - £104.00

1033 J Electronic Printing Calculator, of 12 digit capacity, constant & 2 memories and % key - - - - - - - - - £130.00

N.P. The above prices are subject to VAT, & delivery will be ex stock.

Please do not hesitate to telephone if you require further information.

Yrs ffy
THE UNIVERSAL SUPPLY CO. LTD.

N.P. These machines are guaranteed for twelve months - 3 months labour, 12 months parts.

W. Mills
Sales Dept.

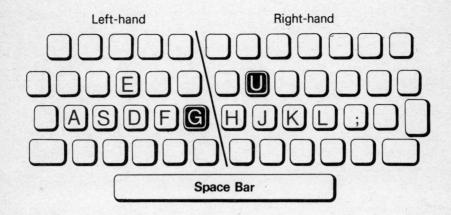

Left-hand   Right-hand

Space Bar

Type each line or sentence 3 times, saying the letters to yourself. If time permits, complete your practice by typing each group of lines as it appears. Keep your eyes on the copy while you type and also when returning the carriage/carrier. The carriage/carrier must be returned IMMEDIATELY after the last character in the line has been typed. Set left margin stop at 30 Elite, 22 Pica, and use single spacing with double between exercises.

A Review the keys you know

1 asd ;lk ded jhj def khj fed has lee had;

2 add salads; a sea lake; lads feed seals;

3 add leeks; she had leeks; he has a hall;

Wrists and arms straight

Turn up TWICE between exercises

B Practise G key—F finger

Practise F to G back to F. Keep other fingers on home keys

4 fff ggg fgf fgf fag fgf lag fgf sag fgf;

5 fgf jag fgf gag fgf hag fgf keg fgf leg;

C Practise U key—J finger

Practise J to U back to J. Keep little fingers on home keys

6 jjj uuu juj juj due juj sue juj hue juj;

7 juj sug juj jug juj dug juj hug juj lug;

D Practise word-building

8 uuu sss eee ddd use uses used useful us;

9 jjj uuu ddd ggg eee judge judges judged;

E Apply the keys you know

10 he had a dull glass; a judge has a flag;

11 see she has a full jug; she used jaffas;

12 dad had a full keg; he shall guess; use;

Feet firmly on floor

Type a copy of the following exercise on A4 paper. (a) Single spacing with double between paragraphs. (b) Use suitable margins.

Centre and underscore

↘General Hints and Examination Reminders

sl 1. Always read carefully all instruction/for/*each* exercise before you begin to type.

3 7. Mark in pencil the points at which any insertions are to be
ℋ   made so that you do not forget them ~~when you reach these points.~~

in/ 4 5. Use common-sense in deciphering manuscript and also/the arrange-
     ment of matter when this has to be continued on a second page.

of the original 5 4. If you are not sure how to set out any manuscript/it is a good
     ℋ   plan to follow the setting/~~given~~ unless, of course, other
     N.P. instructions are given [5 6 When typing a document in double *or tabulated matter*
     'l spacing with blocked paras/remember to turn up 2 double
         between the paragraphs.

⌒ 2. Do not be satisfied with slipshod work; correct neatly a͡ny
     typing errors before removing your paper from the machine.
     Never in any circumstances shd you overtype.

7. When deciding on margins, remember that the right margin should
   never be greater than the left margin.

        it may be necessary
8. In tabular work, ~~take care~~/to centre the matter vertically as well
ℋ   as horizontally; ~~and~~ also see that the columns are of a suitable
    width for the matter to be inserted.

                              a date
9. It is absolutely essential that you should be consistent. If the
'l date is typed first as 4th June/1982, and i͡t occurs again in the
    same piece of work, then it must be typed in the same way/not *, i.e.,*
Run on. June 2 or 2 June.⌐

ℋ Consistency also applies to spelling. A word like "realise" may
   be spelt with an "s" or a "z"; be consistent through/out any one
   exercise.

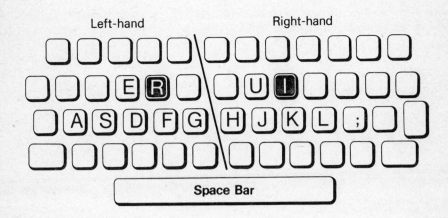

Left-hand   Right-hand

Space Bar

Type each line or sentence 3 times, saying the letters to yourself. If time permits, complete your practice by typing each group of lines as it appears. Keep your eyes on the copy while you type and also when returning the carriage/carrier. The carriage/carrier must be returned IMMEDIATELY after the last character in the line has been typed. Set left margin stop at 30 Elite, 22 Pica, and use single spacing with double between exercises.

A   Review the keys you know

1   fds jkl ded juj fgf jhj hag jug dug leg;

Eyes on copy always

2   a lass uses a flask; all lads had a jug;

3   sell us a full keg; see she has a glass;

B   Practise R key—F finger

Practise F to R back to F. Keep other fingers on home keys

4   fff rrr frf frf jar frf far frf rag frf;

5   frf are frf ark frf red frf fur frf rug;

C   Practise I key—K finger

Practise K to I back to K. Keep other fingers on home keys

6   kkk iii kik kik kid kik lid kik did kik;

7   kik dig kik fig kik rig kik jig kik gig;

D   Practise word families

8   fill hill rill drill grill skill frills;

9   ark lark dark hark; air fair hair lairs;

E   Apply the keys you know

10   she likes a fair judge; he has dark hair

Sharp, brisk strokes

11   his lad fills a jug; she has rare skills

12   she is sure; ask her here; he likes figs

UNIT 5   **New Keys R and I**   9

Type a copy of the following on A4 paper. Use suitable margins and type in single spacing. Use figures for all numbers except at the beginning of a sentence or the figure one on its own.

APPLICATION FOR
UNITED KINGDOM PASSPORT } All on one line please.

Applicants under the age of 16 yrs should complete Form "B" and those sixteen + over shd complete Form "A". The present fee for a 10-year passport is £11.

The following important points shd be noted:

(a) A family passport is available to a wife + husband, + children under the age of 16.

(b) Applicants over 16 and under eighteen years of age shd hv the consent of a parent (or guardian) who must sign the Application Form "A."

u.c. (c) All application forms must be countersigned by a British subject who has known the - applicant(s) personally for at least two years + who is a Member of Parliament, Justice of the Peace, or person of similar standing.

l.c./u.c. (d) 2 Photographs of yourself must be enclosed w the application form. The Photographs shd not be larger than 63 mm x 50 mm + the person countersigning yr. application form in (c) below shd endorse the reverse side of the photographs with the words " I certify that this is a true likeness of Mr (Mrs or Miss) . . . " + add his/her signature.

← (3 spaced dots, please)

Display the following on paper of suitable size.

AUCTION SALE ← spaced caps

at the
Closed caps → Morecambe Hotel } Single
North Promenade } spacing
BLACKPOOL

on
Thurs., 19th June, at 7.00 pm

u.c.   Over 200 Oil and watercolour paintings

Large collection of:

Please type sh 3 Jewellery (Diamond, Emerald & Sapphire)
in order   4 Precious Stone Rings
indicated.   2 Ladies'+ Gentlemen's Watches
Do not   5 Silverplate
type   1 Glass Tableware
numbers.

Closed caps → Many unusual + interesting objets d'art

Left-hand   Right-hand

Space Bar

Type each line or sentence 3 times, saying the letters to yourself. If time permits, complete your practice by typing each group of lines as it appears. Keep your eyes on the copy while you type and also when returning the carriage/carrier. The carriage/carrier must be returned IMMEDIATELY after the last character in the line has been typed. Set left margin stop at 30 Elite, 22 Pica, and use single spacing with double between exercises.

A   Review the keys you know

1   fgf jhj frf juj ded kik aid did her rug;

2   his full fees; she likes a dark red rug;

3   his girl is here; he is glad she is sure

Practise F to T
back to F. Keep
other fingers on
home keys

B   Practise T key—F finger

4   fff ttt ftf ftf fit ftf kit ftf lit ftf;

5   ftf sit ftf hit ftf sat ftf hat ftf fat;

Check your
posture

Practise L to O
back to L. Keep
other fingers on
home keys

C   Practise O key—L finger

6   lll ooo lol lol lot lol got lol hot lol;

7   lol rot lol dot lol jot lol tot lol sot;

D   Practise word families

8   old hold sold gold; look rook hook took;

9   let set jet get ret; rate late hate date

E   Apply the keys you know

Back straight

10   get her a set; he took a full jar to her

11   he had sold the gold; at this late date;

12   that old dress looks just right for her;

Job 57   Production Target—5 minutes

The aim of this test is to see how much of the following exercise you type in 5 minutes with not more than 6 errors.

(a) Use double spacing. (b) Margins: Elite 22–82, Pica 12–72. (c) Follow the line-endings as given in the copy. (d) Erasers or other means of rectifying mistakes must NOT be used.

Office equipment and machinery can cost a great deal of   11

money — £3,000 would just cover a typist's basic needs, such   23

as desk, chair, typewriter and filing cabinet. If you have   35

an electric typewriter, that alone will cost your employer   46

£1,000; or, if it is an electric with proportional spacing,   58

then £1,300 would be nearer the price.   65

Your employer, therefore, expects you to look after the   76

machinery and equipment that you use. He also expects the   87

typist not to waste paper, carbon paper, etc., because these   100

are also expensive. Office supplies used — and wasted —   111

amount to huge sums of money over a year, and your contribu-   123

tion towards economy is essential.   130

Work that is badly done is a sheer waste of time and   140

money. For example, a letter with finger marks on it, or   152

carelessly corrected errors will, if sent out, undermine a   163

customer's confidence in your Company.   171

Left-hand   Right-hand

Space Bar

Type each line or sentence 3 times, saying the letters to yourself. If time permits, complete your practice by typing each group of lines as it appears. Keep your eyes on the copy while you type and also when returning the carriage/carrier. The carriage/carrier must be returned IMMEDIATELY after the last character in the line has been typed. Set left margin stop at 30 Elite, 22 Pica, and use single spacing with double between exercises.

A   Review the keys you know

1   ftf lol frf juj ded kik tot out rot dot;
2   this is a red jet; the lad took the gold
3   he asked a just fee; the old folk agree;

Return carriage/carrier without looking up

Practise S to W back to S. Keep F finger on home key—

B   Practise W key—S finger

4   sss www sws sws low sws sow sws row sws;
5   sws hew sws few sws dew sws sew sws tew;

Practise J to N back to J. Keep little finger on home key

C   Practise N key—J finger

6   jjj nnn jnj jnj fan jnj ran jnj tan jnj;
7   jnj sin jnj kin jnj din jnj lin jnj tin;

D   Practise word families

8   end send lend tend fend rend wend trend;
9   low sow how row tow saw law daw jaw raw;

E   Apply the keys you know

10   we saw her look at the new gate; we knew
11   he sent us a gift of red jeans last week
12   we had left a jade silk gown and the rug

Wrist and arms straight, fingers curved

FORMS

Always type forms in double spacing. Use continuous dots or the underscore for the blank spaces where details are to be inserted later. Remember that there must be one clear space between the last typed character and the first dot; and one clear space between the last dot and the next typed character, if there is one.

7   Type the following exercise on A4 paper in double spacing. Take a carbon copy. Leave a left and right margin of 1½″ (38 mm). On the carbon copy complete the form with your own name, address and other details required.

COURSE APPLICATION FORM

Surname ....

Christian name(s) ....

Address ....

   ....

Age .... Date of birth ....

Qualifications ....

   ....

   ....

Last school attended ....

Course code ....

Aim of course ....

Examinations to be taken ....

   ....

   ....

KEYS TO SPOT THE ERRORS

JOB 15, PAGE 70: line 1—There; line 2—2 spaces after a full stop; line 3—pro-; line 4—computer; line 5—Off-line; line 6—space after comma; line 7—one space after punched; line 8—no space before and

JOB 26, PAGE 89: line 1—John; line 2—2 spaces after full stop; line 3—cir-; line 4—full stop after action; line 5—permissible; line 6—clerks; line 7—benefited; line 8—you

JOB 35, PAGE 108: line 1—processing; line 2—tables; line 3—edit-; line 4—and,; line 5—and; line 6—accuracy; line 7—a high degree; line 8—typewriter

JOB 45, PAGE 128: line 1—today's; line 2—ribbon; line 3—ribbons; line 4—insufficient space for indentation of paragraph; line 5—separate; line 6—may be; line 7—space after comma; line 8—error – the; line 9—Switch

JOB 56, PAGE 155: line 1—efficiency; line 2—perform-; line 3—space after comma; line 4—no space at beginning of the line; line 5—day-; line 6—firm's; line 7—performance; line 8—its; line 9—they

Keys to Spot the Errors

See **Practical Typing Exercises, Book One**, page 64, for further exercises on

IMPROVEMENT PRACTICE

Set left margin stop at 30 Elite, 22 Pica

A Improve control of carriage/carrier return

1 Type the following lines exactly as shown. Repeat the exercise twice.

Return carriage/carrier without looking up

```
as a lass

as a lass falls

as a lass falls dad falls
```

In the following exercises type each line three times, saying the letters to yourself.

B Improve control of [T] and [H] keys

```
2  the then than that this thus these there

3  she thus feels that this is rather good;

4  these lads are there for the third week;
```

C Improve control of space bar

Use right thumb and even stroke

```
5  a s d f j k l ; g h w e r t u i o a s d;

6  at it we he go to as are not for did ask

7  we are sure he did not ask us for these;
```

D Improve control of [R] and [O] keys

```
8  our for road work word offer order other

9  she works near our road; the other word;

10 he wrote the order; sort out our offers;
```

E Improve control of paper insertion

By means of the paper release, take out the sheet of paper you are using. Put it back quickly in the machine, so that the left edge is at 0 on the carriage-/carrier-position scale, and see that the paper is straight. Repeat this drill several times daily.

SUBDIVIDED COLUMN HEADINGS–BLOCKED STYLE

If you use blocked-style tabulation, then it is not necessary to centre subdivided headings vertically or horizontally. Starting points for headings will be the left margin and the tab stops for each column. All headings will start on the same horizontal line which will be the starting point for the deepest heading. Exercise 6 below is an example of blocked style with subdivided headings blocked—compare the layout with that in Exercise 5 on page 170.

Practise typing tabulation with subdivided column headings

6   Type the following table on A4 paper in double spacing. Centre the whole table vertically and horizontally on the paper. Use blocked style. Leave 3 spaces between columns.

WEEKLY METAL PRICE CHANGES

Metal	Latest price per ton	Change on week	Year ago	1980–1981	
				High	Low
	£	£	£	£	£
Aluminium ..	378.60	–	272.50	378.60	272.50
Antimony ...	1660.00	–	1035.00	1660.00	865.00
Copper	527.65	22.25*	950.00	1380.00	498.75
Nickel	1950.00	–	1596.00	1797.00	1414.00
Wolfram	42.00	–	21.75	48.00	21.00
Zinc	330.50	6.00*	655.00	910.00	302.60

* In both cases this was an increase in prices.

FOOTNOTES

In the table above you will notice an asterisk after the figures 22.25 and 6.00. This refers to the footnote after the last horizontal line. The footnote reference in the body is always a superior character (superscript)—see page 132—and may be a figure or sign (asterisk, etc). In the body of the document there is NO SPACE BEFORE the figure or sign. At the bottom (in the footnote) there is ONE SPACE AFTER the figure or sign. If there is no asterisk on your typewriter, make one with x and hyphen (combination characters—see page 130).

See **Practical Typing Exercises, Book One**, page 63, for further exercises on

F Improve control of E and N keys

11 en end tend new keen then when need near;

12 then she went; he knew the news was sent

13 we need the new jugs; near here; the end

Feet firmly on floor

G Improve control of W and I keys

14 win wish wife with will wait writ while;

15 his wife will wait with us; the wise lad

16 we will wish to write while we are there

H Improve control of U key

17 our hour sour dull lull full hull gulls;

18 all our dull hours; he ruled for a week;

19 use our usual rules; let us rush out now

I Improve control of G key

20 go got good goods sigh sight light right

21 urge her to get a rug; the girl is right

22 go on the green light; the night is long

J Improve control of suffix ING

23 ing going taking selling dealing heating

24 he is going; we are selling; owing to us

25 ask if she is dealing with that heating;

K Apply the keys you know

26 now that joke is not good; our old safe;

Shoulders back and relaxed

27 for fun ask if the jars she got were old

28 do join us; walk to that green fir tree;

Practise centring subdivided column headings

5 Study the following table and the notes given below. Then display the table on A4 paper in double-line spacing. Centre vertically and horizontally and insert leader dots.

CANAL TRAFFIC — 1981

Commodity	Canal Traffic '000 tons		
	Atlantic to Pacific	Pacific to Atlantic	Total
Wheat	2,901	100	3,001
Coarse Grain	13,000	353	13,353
Sugar	1,934	3,536	5,470
Soya Beans	5,237	---	5,237
Pulp and Paper	815	2,475	3,290
Iron and Steel Manufacturing	1,650	7,248	8,898
Miscellaneous Ores	710	3,050	3,760
Coal	14,500	200	14,700
Chemicals	2,700	655	3,355

Centring of subdivided column headings horizontally and vertically

In the above table, the heading 'Canal Traffic '000 tons' must be centred over the second, third and fourth columns. To do this, first find the centre point to these 3 columns as explained on page 135 (Centring of Headings over Columns) and then proceed as follows:

(a) Along the first horizontal line, mark only the scale points for the vertical lines which extend to the top horizontal line.
(b) Centre and type the heading 'Canal Traffic '000 tons'.
(c) Type the horizontal line underneath this heading, and along this line mark the scale-points for the vertical lines for each of the 3 columns beneath.
(d) Type the headings for these 3 columns.
(e) Centre the heading for the first column vertically on the headings already typed. Do this by counting the number of lines and spaces in the headings typed—in this case 5—and from this number take the number of lines to be typed, e.g., 1 line from 5 lines = 4. Divide by 2 = 2. With the alignment scale on 'Canal Traffic '000 tons' turn up 2 spaces and type the heading 'Commodity'.
(f) Type the horizontal line below the deepest headings.
(g) The items in the first column (usually descriptive) all start at the same scale-point.
(h) In the figure columns, the longest line of figures is centred and other figures typed so that units are under units, tens under tens, etc.

Note: When ruling vertical lines for the subdivided columns, only extend these as far as the mark you have made on the second horizontal line as shown above. Always type the deepest heading first.

See **Practical Typing Exercises, Book One,** page 62, for further exercises on

Left-hand   Right-hand

Space Bar

Type each line or sentence 3 times, saying the letters to yourself. If time permits, complete your practice by typing each group of lines as it appears. Keep your eyes on the copy while you type and also when returning the carriage/carrier. The carriage/carrier must be returned IMMEDIATELY after the last character in the line has been typed. Set left margin stop at 30 Elite, 22 Pica, and use single spacing with double between exercises.

A Review the keys you know

1 sws jnj ftf lol frf jhj won win new now;   *Eyes on copy*

2 we do not like those jars she got for us

3 the red dogs will go for a walk just now

B Practise right shift key

To make capitals for letters typed by the left hand:
(a) With right hand little finger depress and hold right shift key well down.
(b) Strike left hand capital letter.
(c) Remove finger from shift key and return all fingers to home keys.

4 fF; dD; sS; aA; Ada; Sad; Dad; Fad; Wade

5 Gee; Reg; Ted; Sue; Flo; Ede; Dora; West

Practise L to . back to L. Keep first finger on home key

C Practise full stop key—L finger

6 lll ... l.l f.l j.l Good.   Dear.   Ellis.
TWO spaces after full stop at end of sentence

7 Ask her.   Ted is sad.   Do go.   She will.

D Practise word families

8 Wee; Weed; Feed; Reed; Seed; Deed; Greed

9 And; Sand; Wand; Rand; Send; Tend; Fend;

E Apply the keys you know

Check your posture

10 Ask Ed Reid if we should join the Swede.

11 She was right.   Dirk was jealous.   Fine.

12 Flora would like to go; just state when.

4 (a) Prepare the following skeleton letter, taking 2 carbon copies. Use A5 portrait paper and margins of Elite 12–62, Pica 5–55. A skeleton of the following letter is given in the HANDBOOK AND SOLUTIONS MANUAL and may be copied.

NOTE: DELETIONS. It is often necessary to delete letters or words in a form, form letter or a circular letter. For instance, in exercise (b) below you are writing to a man and, therefore, it will be necessary to delete /Madam in the salutation. To delete previously typed characters, use a small x aligned precisely with the characters previously typed.

J A RANKIN & CO LTD
Trinity Road
LUTON Bedfordshire LU4 5TJ
(Turn up 2 single spaces)

Our Ref

(Turn up 10 single spaces)

Dear Sir/Madam

We thank you for your order dated (leave blank)
and numbered (8 blanks). We have pleasure in advising you that delivery will be made in (3 blanks) weeks.

Yours faithfully
J A RANKIN & CO LTD

MANAGER

(b) Using the original prepared above, insert the following information:

Our Ref FE/your initials Today's date
Addressee Mr F L Wilkes 24–28 High Street Brierley Hill West Midlands DY3 1DE
Order dated insert suitable date and numbered S.2906 Delivery 4 weeks

(c) Using a carbon copy prepared in (a) above, insert the following information:

Our Ref FE/your initials Today's date
Addressee Mrs W Franklyn 20 Market Street Barnsley South Yorkshire S4 8EZ
Order dated insert suitable date and numbered P.3347 Delivery 2 weeks

(d) Using the remaining carbon copy, insert the following information:

Our Ref FE/your initials Today's date
Addressee Mr L Yates 73 Lionel Street Burton-on-Trent Staffs DE13 1NF
Order dated insert suitable date and numbered A.6834 Delivery 3 weeks

See **Practical Typing Exercises, Book One,** page 61, for further exercises on

Left-hand   Right-hand

Space Bar

Type each line or sentence 3 times, saying the letters to yourself. If time permits, complete your practice by typing each group of lines as it appears. Keep your eyes on the copy while you type and also when returning the carriage/carrier. The carriage/carrier must be returned IMMEDIATELY after the last character in the line has been typed. Set left margin stop at 30 Elite, 22 Pica, and use single spacing with double between exercises.

A Review the keys you know

1 aA; sS; dD; fF; wW; eE; rR; Red; Gee; As
2 Ask Flo. See Roger. Tell Fred. Go in.
3 Ede had gone. Write to us. A fake jug.

Two spaces after full stop at end of sentence

B Practise left shift key

To make capitals for letters typed by the right hand:
(a) With left hand little finger depress and hold left shift key well down.
(b) Strike right hand capital letter.
(c) Remove finger from shift key and return all fingers to home keys.

4 jJa kKa lLa jUj kIk Judd Kidd Lode Hoad;
5 Ida Ken Len Jude Owen Hilda Oakes Usual;

Eyes on copy

Practise F to B back to F. Keep little finger on home key

C Practise B key—F finger

6 fff bbb fbf fbf bud fbf bus fbf but fbf;
7 fbf rob fbf sob fbf fob fbf hob fbf job;

D Practise word families

8 Nib Jib Lib Job Lob Hob Hail Jail Nails;
9 Jill Hill Kill Lill Tall Ball Fall Wall;

E Apply the keys you know

10 She will be taking those salads to Jane.
11 Jill knows. Kit had to bluff Bob Green.
12 Fred will ask us to do those jobs again.

FILLING IN FORM LETTERS

The following steps should be taken when you fill in a form letter:

(a) Insert the form letter into the machine so that the first line of the body of the letter is just above the alignment scale.

(b) By means of the paper release, adjust the paper so that the base of the entire line is in alignment with the top of the alignment scale (this position may vary with certain makes of machines) and so that an 'i' or 'l' aligns up exactly with one of the guides on the alignment scale.

(c) Set margin stops and paper guide. The margin stops should be set to correspond to the margins already used in the duplicated letter.

(d) Turn the platen back 2 single spaces (4 notches for machines with half-spacing) and, if not already typed, insert salutation at the left margin.

(e) Turn the platen back a sufficient number of spaces and type the reference.

(f) Turn up 2 single spaces and type the date.

(g) Turn up 2 single spaces and type the name and address of addressee.

(h) Insert any details required in the body of the letter. Remember to leave one clear space after the last character before starting to type the 'fill in'.

(i) Check carefully.

2   Following the instructions given above, and using the original of the form letter prepared in Exercise 1 on page 167, insert the following details:

Your Ref. MAP/RES   Our Ref LDA/your initials   Today's date
Addressee: J. Ellis (Hardware) Ltd., 62 Ipswich Road, STOWMARKET, Suffolk. IP14 1AA
Invoice No. 5490   Dated (suitable date)   for £260.50

3   On the carbon copy of the form letter prepared in Exercise 1 on page 167, insert the following details:

Your Ref. SW/SP   Our Ref. LDA/your initials   Today's date
Addressee: Messrs. Barrett & Obrien, 17 Hanover Road, STRANRAER, Wigtonshire. DG9 7SA
Invoice No. 3572   Dated (suitable date)   for £945.74

Record your progress   Margins: Elite 22–82, Pica 12–72   5 minutes

R 28   Epsom is known all over the world as the place where   10
the great horse race, the Derby, is run each year, but it   22
has also given its name to the well-known Epsom Salts.   33

          The small village was not known outside the immediate   43
district until early in the seventeenth century, and it is   55
said that one day a herdsman, much to his joy, found on the   66
common a water-hole which he did not know was there. He   78
hoped to water his sheep there, but they refused to drink   89
because the water was so bitter. This was at a time when it   101
was a popular habit to drink spa waters for most human ail-   113
ments. This water was soon recognised as a healing water,   124
a great blood purifier, and named Epsom Water. Soon visitors   137
flocked in from all over Europe and it was not long before   148
the craze for taking spa water was in full spate at Epsom   160
as elsewhere. Fashions change, however, and this craze died.   172

                                        (SI 1.31)

   1 | 2 | 3 | 4 | 5 | 6 | 7 | 8 | 9 | 10 | 11 | 12 |

Left-hand   Right-hand

Space Bar

Type each line or sentence 3 times, saying the letters to yourself. If time permits, complete your practice by typing each group of lines as it appears. Keep your eyes on the copy while you type and also when returning the carriage/carrier. The carriage/carrier must be returned IMMEDIATELY after the last character in the line has been typed. Set left margin stop at 25 Elite, 18 Pica, and use single spacing with double between exercises.

A   Review the keys you know

1   fbf sws jnj ftf lol frf jhj Len Ken Hen Ian Win Go

2   Dan and Rob left.   He will go just now.   Ask Nell.

3   Lois and Earl will see June.   Go with Fred Bolton.

Two spaces after full stop at end of sentence

B   Practise M Key—J finger

4   jjj mmm jmj jmj jam jmj ham jmj dam jmj ram jmjmj;

5   jmj rum jmj hum jmj sum jmj mum jmj gum jmj strum;

Practise J to M back to J. Keep little finger on home key

C   Practise left and right shift keys

6   Ada Ben Dan East Fred Green Hilda Irwin James King

7   Lil Mark Nell Owen Rene Sara Todd Usher Wills Watt

Little fingers for shift keys

D   Practise word families

8   arm farm harm warm alarm art hart tart darts mart;

9   game name dame fame same lame home dome some foam;

E   Apply the keys you know

10   Most of the fame goes to John who had been working
     hard for his father but he has now left the works.
     I think he is now at home.

Technique development

FORM LETTERS

Many firms use duplicated letters, printed forms, or postcards to send to customers. Details for each customer have to be filled in. Such letters or forms are known as 'Form Letters'. If details have to be filled in on ruled lines, or over dotted lines, it is essential that you type slightly above these lines.

Preparation of a form letter

1 Prepare the skeleton letter below, taking one carbon copy. To do this take the following steps:

(a) Use A5 portrait paper.
(b) Centre and type the name and address of the sender, starting on the fourth single space from top edge of paper.
(c) Set margins at scale-points Elite 12–62, Pica 5–55.
(d) After last line of sender's address turn up 2 single spaces and type Your Ref.
(e) Turn up one single space and type Our Ref.
(f) To allow for date, name and address of addressee and for one clear space after last line of address, turn up 10 single spaces. Care should be taken to see that there is a clear space between last line of address and the salutation. If necessary, put more than one item of address on a line.
(g) Type Dear Sirs,
(h) Turn up 2 single spaces and type remainder of letter, leaving clear spaces as indicated to accommodate the details given in Exercises 2 and 3 on page 168.

NEWTOWN WHOLESALE STORES LTD.
New Street, Sheffield. S5 8UP
(Turn up 2 single spaces)

Your Ref.
Our Ref.

NOTE: A skeleton copy of this letter is given in the HANDBOOK AND SOLUTIONS MANUAL, and may be copied.

(Turn up 10 single spaces)

Dear Sirs,

Please send us a copy of your invoice No. (leave blank)
dated (leave 16 spaces) for (leave 9 spaces) the receipt
of which we cannot trace. Your prompt attention
will be appreciated.

Yours faithfully,
NEWTOWN WHOLESALE STORES LTD.

Secretary

Improvement Practice

Type each line or sentence 3 times, saying the letters to yourself. If time permits, complete your practice by typing each group of lines as it appears. Keep your eyes on the copy while you type and also when returning the carriage/carrier. The carriage/carrier must be returned IMMEDIATELY after the last character in the line has been typed. Set left margin stop at 25 Elite, 18 Pica, and use single spacing with double between exercises.

A Improve control of home row keys

1 add had jag gas ask ash sash dash glad flags flash

2 Dad has a flag. Sal had a sash. A lass asks dad.

3 A lass had had a jag. A glad lad. Ask a sad lad.

Two spaces after full stop at the end of sentence

B Improve control of O and U keys

4 to go now out our hour tour sour would house shout

5 Ask Ruth if she would like to go to our house now.

6 Tell Flo we will start out on our tour in an hour.

C Improve control of carriage/carrier return

7 I will go
I will go soon
I will go as soon as
I will go as soon as I get there.

D Improve control of W E R and T keys

8 we wet were west tree tell test where threw refers

9 We were all in here. I saw those trees last week.

10 She referred to the tests. Tell her to rest here.

E Improve control of shift keys

11 He Ask Jon Sara Kite Dale Lord Ford Hall Iris Tait

12 Ask Miss Ford if she will see Mrs Tait in an hour.

No full stop after Mrs

13 Owen Dale and Gerald Reid are going to Harrow now.

SKILL BUILDING

In exercises A and B, type each line or sentence 3 times. If time permits, complete your practice by typing each group of lines as it appears. Keep your eyes on the copy while you type and also when returning the carriage/carrier.

Margins: Elite 22–82, Pica 12–72

A Review alphabet keys

1   Marjorie had just come back from Africa and had altered considerably, being now quite unrecognisable, except for her voice.

B Build speed on alternate-hand words

2 island visit girls lamb worn paid she hay men for but the me
3 formal usual their lend lame work may pen dog got did and us
4 The girls and the men got paid for their work on the island.
5 The lamb and the lame dog lay by the pen. She may visit me.

Accuracy practice	30 wpm	5 minutes	Not more than 5 errors

A 55   Perhaps the most lovable and desirable quality which a   11
person can have is that of tolerance. It need not be inborn   23
but it can be acquired and developed. It can be described   35
as the quality which makes us able to see the point of view   47
of the other fellow and which makes us always keep in mind   59
the fact that, however correct we may think our own opinion   71
of a thing to be, we still may be wrong. It is the decency   83
in us that concedes to others the right to have their own   94
views. It prevents us from meddling with what is no con-   105
cern of ours, and enables us to let others seek their own   116
happiness and salvation in their own way. It is a good   127
thing if we have tolerance, but if we feel we have not, we   138
should quickly make an effort to acquire and cultivate it.   150

(SI 1.33)

1 | 2 | 3 | 4 | 5 | 6 | 7 | 8 | 9 | 10 | 11 | 12 |

Speed building	45 wpm	One minute	Not more than 2 errors

S 13   When you take your first job, make up your mind to save   11
a small sum, say 10 per cent, out of your salary each week.   23
In a few years you should have saved a large sum, and a time   35
may come when you will be glad you took my advice. (SI 1.07)   45

S 14   You must bear in mind that we all have to live and work   11
with other people and we should do our best not just for our   23
own good, but also for that of our neighbours. We should at   35
all times be ready to help those who are in need. (SI 1.11)   45

1 | 2 | 3 | 4 | 5 | 6 | 7 | 8 | 9 | 10 | 11 | 12 |

Record your progress—page 168

Accuracy—5 minutes at 30 wpm
Speed—One minute at 45 wpm

UNIT 54   Skill Building   166

F Improve control of I and N keys

14 an is in into line infer night noise injure inside

15 Irene infers Nina was injured one night this week.

16 The noise is inside the inn. Neither one will go.

G Improve control when typing phrases

Brisk, even
strokes

17 to go to us to see to ask to take to fill to write

18 I wish to see Wales. Ask her to fill in the date.

19 Leslie would like to take Jill to the new theatre.

H Improve control of B key

20 bid but bad best both able book begin about better

21 Both of us will be better off when he begins work.

22 Bob has been able to book a table for Bill and me.

I Improve control of M key

23 am me man seem make main must item them from might

24 I am making out a form for the main items we lost.

25 I must tell him that the amount seems to be right.

J Improve control of space bar

Use right
thumb and
even strokes

26 a w s e d r f t g b h j n u m k i o l f b j n m l.

27 is it if in as an at am on or of to go he me we be

28 He did go to tea. It is now time for us to go on.

CIRCULAR LETTER—TEAR-OFF PORTION

Sometimes a letter will have a tear-off portion at the foot so that a customer can fill in certain details and return the tear-off portion to the sender.

The typing on the tear-off section should end about an inch (25 mm) from the bottom of the page and any space not required for the tear-off portion should be left after the Complimentary Close or the name of the signatory if this is given.

The minimum space to be left after the Complimentary Close or signatory is 4 spaces. In other words, turn up a minimum of 5 single spaces and then type, from EDGE TO EDGE of the paper CONTINUOUS HYPHENS or CONTINUOUS DOTS; then turn up 2 single spaces and type the information on the tear-off portion.

When blank spaces are left for details to be filled in, use CONTINUOUS DOTS or the UNDERSCORE and DOUBLE SPACING. Remember to leave one clear space after the last character typed before starting the dots or underscore and one clear space at the end of the dots or underscore before the next typed character if there is one, eg,

```
             space      space            space
Surname↓ . . . . . . . . ↓Christian names↓ . . . . . . .
```

Practise typing letter with tear-off portion

2 Type the following letter on A4 paper in single spacing in blocked style. Margins: 1½″ (38 mm) and 1″ (25 mm). No name and address will be inserted at a later date.

Our Ref PW/SM

Month and year only

Dear Sir

HIGH INCOME INVESTMENT

l.c. In these days of inflation, a high yield from your Capital is not
trs enough; it is essential also to protect the real value of your
High capital. Our new Income Investment scheme has been designed to   *u.c.*
meet this requirement.

specially.
By investing in selected Ordinary Shares, we aim not only to provide an income which starts at a high level and which will go on
growing over the years, but also to provide the growth needed to
keep the value of your investment in line with ahead of inflation.
This is the advantage that our High Income Investment has over
other forms of investment which are not designed to combat infla-
N.P. tion or rising prices. [If you require any further information,
complete the form below and return it to us, when our representative
will make an appointment to see you. *suit your convenience.*

Yours faithfully,
20TH CENTURY INVESTMENT CO LTD

(Typist: type line from edge to edge of paper.)

Please send me full details of your High Income Investment Scheme.

SURNAME . . . . Christian Name(s) . . . .

ADDRESS . . . .

. . . .

See **Practical Typing Exercises, Book One**, page 60, for further exercises on

Check your work after each exercise

After returning the carriage/carrier at the end of an exercise, check your typescript carefully and circle any errors. ALWAYS check *before* removing the paper from the machine.

They have to leave early.

1 Each incorrect character is one error.
2 Each incorrect punctuation is one error.
3 An extra space is one error.
4 Omitting a space is one error.
5 When using a manual machine, a raised/lowered capital is one error.
6 When using a manual machine, an uneven left margin is one error.
7 Omitting a word is one error.
8 Inserting an extra word is one error.
9 Inserting an extra letter is one error.
10 Omitting a letter is one error.

1 The(u) have to leave early.
2 They have to leave early(?)
3 They(/)have to leave early.
4 They have(to) leave early.
5 (T)hey have to leave early.
6 (T)hey have to leave early.
7 They have(/)leave early.
8 They have to(to) leave early.
9 They have to leave(s) early.
10 They have to(a)ve early.

Half- or one-minute goals

1 Type the exercise. If any word causes you to hesitate, type that word three times.
2 Take a half- or one-minute timing.
3 If you reach the goal, or beyond, take another timing and see if you can type the same number of words but with fewer mistakes.
4 If you do not reach the goal after three tries, you need a little more practice on the key drills. Choose the previous exercise(s) that give intensive practice on the keys that caused difficulty.

Notes:
(a) There is little to be gained by typing any one drill more than three times consecutively. When you have typed it three times, go on to another drill; then, if necessary, go back to the original drill.
(b) At present, techniques (striking the keys evenly and sharply, good posture, eyes on copy, returning the carriage without looking up) are very important and you should concentrate on good techniques. If your techniques are right, then accuracy will follow. However, if you have more than two errors for each minute typed, it could mean that you have not practised the new keys sufficiently and that you should go back and do further intensive practice on certain key drills.

Measure your speed

Five strokes count as one 'standard' word. In a typing line of 50 spaces there are ten 'standard' words. The figures to the right of each exercise indicate the number of 'standard' words in the complete line, and the scale below indicates the number across the page. If in the exercise below you reach the word 'we' in one minute, your speed is $10+6=16$ words per minute. You will now be able to measure and record your speed.

Type the following exercise as instructed under Nos. 1–4 of 'Half- or one-minute goals'. Set left margin at 25 Elite, 18 Pica.

Goal—8 words in half a minute   16 words in one minute

We will take her to see our new house on the north   10

side of the new estates and we shall ask George to   20

join us at that time. (SI 1.04)   24

1 | 2 | 3 | 4 | 5 | 6 | 7 | 8 | 9 | 10 |

Measure Your Speed—16 wpm

Type the following circular letter on A4 paper in single-line spacing and blocked style. Follow layout and leave 7 clear spaces for insertion of the name and address of addressee. Margins: Elite 22–82, Pica 12–72.

Our Ref. AB/JCB

Date as postmark

(Turn up 8 single-line spaces)

Dear Sir,

We are introducing a new PLASTIC WALL COATING for external use. Not only will this improve the appearance of the walls of your house, but it will also provide the walls with a plastic raincoat and insulate against the winter cold, eliminate dampness, and seal cracks and holes. Also, future maintenance will be avoided, as it has a minimum guaranteed life expectancy of 15 years.

The type of property which you own appears to be very suitable for our new PLASTIC WALL COATING. If your house is suffering from any of the following problems:

1. BRICKWORK — pointing in bad condition, bricks fibrous or porous;

2. STUCCO AND PEBBLE DASH — cracked, sandy and soft, pebbles falling off;

3. CEMENT RENDER — cracked, hollow patches, breaking away;

4. DAMP IN THE WALLS — showing inside or out;

we can cure all or any of these defects and transform the appearance of your property by the application of this coating — which will not only beautify and protect your house but will also increase its value.

If this offer appeals to you, please complete and post the enclosed card to us. All estimates are entirely free.

Yours faithfully,
PLASTIC PRODUCTS LTD.

A. Boggan (Miss)

Marketing Manager

Enc.

See **Practical Typing Exercises**, Book One, page 59, for further exercises on

Circular Letter

Left-hand   Right-hand

Space Bar

Type each line or sentence 3 times, saying the letters to yourself. If time permits, complete your practice by typing each group of lines as it appears. Keep your eyes on the copy while you type and also when returning the carriage/carrier. The carriage/carrier must be returned IMMEDIATELY after the last character in the line has been typed. Set left margin stop at 25 Elite, 18 Pica, and use single spacing with double between exercises.

A Review the keys you know

1 jmj fmj kmk fmf lml am; Mat Tom Ham Sam Lamb Farm;   Eyes on copy

2 Mrs Lamb would like to take on the job we offered.

3 None of them would go with Job down the long road.

B Practise C key—D finger

Practise D to C back to D. Keep little finger on home key

4 ddd ccc dcd dcd cod dcd cot dcd cob dcd cog dcdcd;

5 dcd cut dcd cub dcd cur dcd cud dcd cab dcd cat cd

C Practise Y key—J finger

Practise J to Y back to J. Keep other fingers on home keys

6 jjj yyy jyj jyj jay jyj hay jyj lay jyj bay jyjyj;

7 jyj say jyj day jyj ray jyj may jyj gay jyj way jj

D Practise word families

8 sty try fry dry cry wry dice rice mice nice trice;   Brisk, even strokes

9 shy sky sly try sty slay stay fray gray dray stray

E Apply the keys you know

Goal—8 words in half a minute   16 words in one minute

10 He is not able to find a nice jacket which he says   10

    he lost on the way to your farm. He will send you   20

    his bill in a week or so. (SI 1.08)   25

    1 | 2 | 3 | 4 | 5 | 6 | 7 | 8 | 9 | 10 |

Measure Your Speed—16 wpm

UNIT 14   **New Keys C and Y**   **20**

Technique development

CIRCULAR LETTERS

Circulars or circular letters are letters (the contents of which are the same) which are sent to a number of customers or clients. The original is usually typed on a master sheet (stencil or offset litho) and a quantity is 'run off'.

Reference—in usual position

Date—typed in various ways; eg, 21st July, 1982

	July, 1982 (month and year only)
Follow instructions or layout	Date as postmark (these words are typed in the position where you normally type the date).

Name and address of addressee—

(a) Space may be left for this, and in that case the details are typed on individual sheets after they have been 'run off'. When preparing the master (or draft) turn up 8 single spaces after the date (leaving 7 clear) before typing the salutation.
(b) Very often the name and address of addressee are not inserted and, if this is so, no space need be left when the master is prepared. Turn up 2 single spaces after date.

Salutation—

(a) Dear—the remainder of the salutation is typed in when the name and address are inserted.
(b) Dear Sir, Dear Madam, Dear Sir(s), Dear Sir/Madam.

Signature—the person writing the letter may or may not sign it. If the writer is signing, type the complimentary close, etc, in the usual way. If the writer is not signing, type Yours faithfully and company's name* in the usual position, turn up 2 single spaces and type the name of the person writing the letter, then turn up 2 single spaces and type the designation.

* If the company's name is not being inserted, turn up 2 single spaces after Yours faithfully and type the name of the writer, then turn up 2 single spaces and type the writer's designation.

Record your progress　　　Margins: Elite 22–82, Pica 12–72　　　5 minutes

R 27
```
        A good dictionary is the most useful reference book you      11
can have.  It is a tool to help you to do your work well and        23
easily, but, like all tools, it must be handled correctly if        35
the best use is to be made of it.  All words are arranged in        47
alphabetical order of the first letter of the word, and then        59
according to the second, third, and remaining letters.  Thus        71
'band' will come before 'bay'.  A short word always appears         83
before a longer word; thus 'bind' will come before 'binder'         94
and 'found' before 'founder'.  You must be sure you know how        106
your dictionary shows and uses hyphens; take care not to mix        118
up the use of the hyphen to join compound words, and its use        130
for dividing words or syllables.  Remember to keep your dic-        142
tionary always at hand, ready for use, and, when you are            153
doubtful about the spelling or meaning of a word, look it up.       165
                                                        (SI 1.33)
```

1　|　2　|　3　|　4　|　5　|　6　|　7　|　8　|　9　|　10　|　11　|　12　|

Left-hand   Right-hand

Space Bar

Type each line or sentence 3 times, saying the letters to yourself. If time permits, complete your practice by typing each group of lines as it appears. Keep your eyes on the copy while you type and also when returning the carriage/carrier. The carriage/carrier must be returned IMMEDIATELY after the last character in the line has been typed. Set left margin stop at 25 Elite, 18 Pica, and use single spacing with double between exercises.

A   Review the keys you know

Eyes on copy

1   dcd jyj dcd fbf jhj fgf lol yet coy yes call come.

2   Her mother had brought a new kind of jersey cloth.

3   He sent us a ticket for the jumble sale on Monday.

B   Practise P key—; finger

Practise ; to P back to ;. Keep J finger on home key and other fingers curved

4   ;;; ppp ;p; ;p; cap ;p; lap ;p; rap ;p; jap p;p;p;

5   ;p; pip ;p; dip ;p; sip ;p; hip ;p; lip ;p; nip p;

C   Practise V key—F finger

Practise F to V back to F. Keep little finger on home key

6   fff vvv fvf fvf vow fvf van fvf vat fvf vet fvfvf;

7   fvf eve fvf vie fvf via fvf very fvf give fvf live

D   Practise word families

8   tup cup pup sup lop pop fop hop cop top tops mops;

9   live jive hive dive give rave pave save wave gave;

E   Apply the keys you know

Goal—9 words in half a minute   17 words in one minute

10   She moved a pink jug away from the very back shelf   10

where it had been hidden from sight.   It now shows   20

up better on that top shelf.   (SI 1.15)   26

1 | 2 | 3 | 4 | 5 | 6 | 7 | 8 | 9 | 10 |

SKILL BUILDING

Type exercises A and B 3 times. Keep your eyes on the copy while you type and also when returning the carriage/carrier.

A Review alphabet keys

Margins: Elite 22–82, Pica 12–72

1   His extra blazer was made of the finely woven jet black cloth, and a quaint colourful badge adorned the pocket.

B Improve control of figure keys

2 we 23 24 25 26 27 28 29 30 31 32 33 34 35 36 37 38 39 40 41.
3 Order Nos. 2981/82 & 2995/82 were sent on 31st August, 1982.
4 Cheque No. 021048 is for £536.97 and No. 021069 for £534.78.

Accuracy practice   30 wpm   5 minutes   Not more than 5 errors

A 54   For some reason, I have been unable to obtain any satis-   11
faction from you in connection with the clock I left with you   23
3 months ago to be repaired. At that time, I pointed out to   35
you that the clock was not in first-class condition when I   47
bought it. Right from the beginning, it has always lost about   59
8 minutes every day.   63

From time to time I have telephoned your company about   74
the clock, and I usually spoke to Mr. G. Slown. A week ago   85
Mr. Slown telephoned me and promised to let me know this   97
week, without fail, what could be done to settle this matter.   109

I do not wish to make the same complaint over and over   121
again, but I cannot understand why a firm as large as yours   133
should neglect to make some adjustments when one of its clocks   145
had not been satisfactory. (SI 1.33)   150

    1 | 2 | 3 | 4 | 5 | 6 | 7 | 8 | 9 | 10 | 11 | 12 |

Speed building   40 wpm   2 minutes   Not more than 4 errors

S 11   We learn from your wife that you hope to build a new   10
house soon. Before the work starts, be sure you know what   22
kind of wood will be used. Last week we sent you one of our   34
books, and we would like you to read the section on wood.   45
We feel sure you will find the book a great help. Do not   56
forget to let your agent know that you must have the kind   68
of wood we suggest, and that you insist on the best quality.   80
                                               (SI 1.10)

S 12   It is sad to think that it is so easy to believe false   11
tales about others, or what is known as scandal. Perhaps   22
there are few people who ever tell the real truth about   33
others, and when we seek to test the truth of a tale we have   45
heard we sometimes find it is not quite true. This may not   57
be because those who tell the tale mean harm. All they want   69
is to make life less humdrum and add some colour to it. (SI 1.17)   80

    1 | 2 | 3 | 4 | 5 | 6 | 7 | 8 | 9 | 10 | 11 | 12 |

Record your progress—page 163

Accuracy—5 minutes at 30 wpm
Speed—2 minutes at 40 wpm

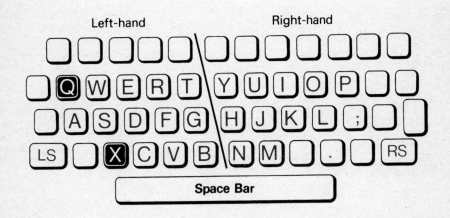

Left-hand   Right-hand

Space Bar

Type each line or sentence 3 times, saying the letters to yourself. If time permits, complete your practice by typing each group of lines as it appears. Keep your eyes on the copy while you type and also when returning the carriage/carrier. The carriage/carrier must be returned IMMEDIATELY after the last character in the line has been typed. Set left margin stop at 25 Elite, 18 Pica, and use single spacing with double between exercises.

A   Review the keys you know

1   ;p; fvf ftf jhj dpf apf kpf pot van cop map eve p;   Fingers curved

2   Jack was glad my family all moved to North Avenue.

3   Daniel may have to give back a few paper journals.

B   Practise X key—S finger

Practise S to X back to S. Keep first finger on home key

4   sss xxx sxs sxs tax sxs lax sxs pax sxs wax sxsxs;

5   sxs sex sxs hex sxs vex sxs rex sxs cox sxs vox sx

C   Practise Q key—A finger

Practise A to Q back to A. Keep first finger on home key

6   aaa qqq aqa aqa quad aqa aqua aqa equal aqa quick;

7   aqa quin aqa quit aqa quite aqa equal aqa query qa

D   Practise word families

8   qua quad squad quit quip quins quill quint quilts;

9   fox cox mix fix nix axe lax pax wax tax taxi taxed

E   Apply the keys you know

Goal—9 words in half a minute   17 words in one minute

10   Joe quickly moved the gross of new boxes for which   10

you had paid and then took an extra box of the red   20

quilts and sheets you wanted.   (SI 1.15)   26

1 | 2 | 3 | 4 | 5 | 6 | 7 | 8 | 9 | 10 |

POSTCARDS

Many firms send postcards (A6—148 × 105 mm) in acknowledgment of letters and orders. The name and address of the firm sending the card are usually printed across the top of the card. These formal acknowledgments are typed like memos with no salutation and no complimentary close. There are many different ways of setting out postcards: the following are just 2 examples.

Note the following points:

(a) Centre and type firm's name and address, starting 4 spaces from top of card.

(b) Use margins of 5 spaces on either side.

(c) Always use single spacing with double between paragraphs. Paragraphs may be indented or blocked.

(d) After typing address turn up 2 single spaces and at left-hand margin insert the reference. On the same line, backspace from right-hand margin and type date.

(e) Turn up 2 single spaces and type body.

Practise typing postcards

5 Following the above instructions and using postcard size paper, type the following postcard. On the reverse side, address the postcard to yourself.

RAYMOND DRESSES LTD.
59 Bryanston Street, London.   W1A 2AZ

(Turn up 2 single spaces)

BMT/FL   Today's date

Thank you for your order No. B/Sep/29 dated (insert date).

The various sizes of winter dresses your require are being sent by passenger train on Friday next, (insert date).

6 Using postcard size paper, type the following. Address it on the reverse side ready for despatch.

To: I. C. MacLean & Sons,   From: B. B. Manson & Co. Ltd.,
    Commercial Quay,   West Road,
    Aberdeen.   AB2 3HE   Newcastle-upon-Tyne.   NE5 2BJ

(Insert suitable date)

We have received your letter dated (insert date), and have telephoned the railway company who have promised to trace the packages despatched from our warehouse on (insert date). As soon as we have further news as to their whereabouts we will telephone you.

See **Practical Typing Exercises, Book One**, page 58, for further exercises on

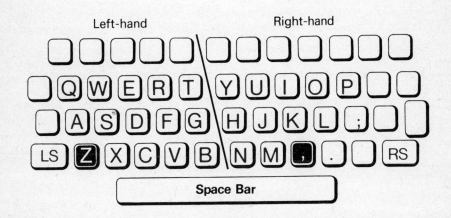

Left-hand | Right-hand

Space Bar

Type each line or sentence 3 times, saying the letters to yourself. If time permits, complete your practice by typing each group of lines as it appears. Keep your eyes on the copy while you type and also when returning the carriage/carrier. The carriage/carrier must be returned IMMEDIATELY after the last character in the line has been typed. Set left margin stop at 25 Elite, 18 Pica, and use single spacing with double between exercises.

A   Review the keys you know

1   axs aqa fxf fcf axs xaj sex vex tax quit aqua quad
2   Just have one box of new grey mats packed quickly.
3   With extra help Clive found many quite black jugs.

B   Practise Z key—A finger

Practise A to Z back to A. Keep first finger on home key

4   aaa zzz aza aza zoo aza zinc aza zeal aza azure za
5   aza zip aza zero aza size aza gaze aza jazz aza za

C   Practise , key—K finger

Practise K to , back to K. Keep little finger on home key

6   kkk ,,, k,k k,k l,k a,k s,k j,k d,k f,k hj,k g,f,k

One space after comma

7   at, it, is, or, if, one, can, yes, may, for, cross

D   Practise word families

8   daze haze gaze laze maze, lazy hazy crazy, puzzle.
9   zeal zero zest zone, size prize, buzz fuzz, azure.

E   Apply the keys you know
Goal—9 words in half a minute   18 words in one minute

10 We do hope the right size is in stock; yes, it is;   10

Feet apart, firmly on floor

    we have just a few boxes, but the colour, although   20

    quite pretty, is not the same. (SI 1.15)   26

    1 | 2 | 3 | 4 | 5 | 6 | 7 | 8 | 9 | 10 |

UNIT 17 **Measure Your Speed—18 wpm**
New Keys Z and Comma   23

DISPLAYED MATTER IN SEMI-BLOCKED LETTERS

The usual method for displaying matter in semi-blocked letters is to arrange for the longest line of the matter to be centred in the typing line. To do this

(a) Find the centre point of the body of the letter by adding together the points at which the left and right margins are set and divide by 2.

(b) Bring printing point to this scale point and backspace once for every 2 characters and spaces in the longest line of the displayed matter. This is the starting point for all items.

(c) ALWAYS leave one clear space above and below displayed matter.

Practise semi-blocked letter with displayed matter

4   Type the following letter on A4 paper in semi-blocked style. Use full punctuation, take a carbon copy and type a C6 envelope. Margins: Elite 20–86, Pica 11–77.

```
Ref. LAB/PAC                                    23rd August, 1982

FOR THE ATTENTION OF MR. H. W. WALKER

Atlas Wire Works Ltd.,
Farnborough Road,
Clifton,
NOTTINGHAM.
NG11 9AE

Dear Sirs,

                        CRIMPED WIRE

     We refer to your letter of the 24th June, 1982, enclosing
samples of nickel silver, phosphor bronze and brass wire.  We have
now tested the samples sent and find this material quite suitable
for our manufactures.
                    (Turn up 2 single spaces)
     Before passing you our trial order, we shall be glad if you
will submit us a quotation for the following quantities, bearing in
mind that we use minimum monthly quantities of 200 kg of each type:
                    (Turn up 2 single spaces)
          25 kg Crimped Brass Wire, nickel silver, 0.12 mm
          25 kg Phosphor Bronze Wire, 0.20 mm
          25 kg Brass Wire, 0.15 mm
                    (Turn up 2 single spaces)
     In your quotation please state the shortest delivery period
and your terms of payment.

                         Yours faithfully,
                         H. WILKINS & CO.




                         L. A. BUTLER
                         BUYING DEPARTMENT
```

IMPROVEMENT PRACTICE

Type each line or sentence 3 times, saying the letters to yourself. If time permits, complete your practice by typing each group of lines as it appears. Keep your eyes on the copy while you type and also when returning the carriage/carrier. The carriage/carrier must be returned IMMEDIATELY after the last character in the line has been typed. Set left margin stop at 25 Elite, 18 Pica, and use single spacing with double between exercises.

A Improve control of carriage/carrier return

1 Type the following lines exactly as shown.
  Repeat the exercise and see if you can type it in one minute

```
It was good
It was good to see
It was good to see you
It was good to see you today
```

Return carriage/carrier without looking up

B Improve control of B and M keys

2 mob bump brim Mabel blame bloom climb bombs became
3 Blame Mabel.   The mob climbed in through a window.
4 My rose bloom became well known.   I bumped my car.

TWO spaces after . at end of sentence

C Improve control of punctuation

5 I shall tell Wilfred.   No, he may be rather angry.
6 We are pleased to hear from you; but we cannot go.
7 John, Mary and Elsie are going.   You may come too.

ONE space after ; and ,

D Improve control of C and Y keys

8 cry city clay copy cozy carry yacht comply certify
9 I certify that this is a copy; it is quite correct
10 Cathy must comply with the order.   The yacht left.

E Improve control of space bar

11 at it up on to we an be go of so am by do as no he
12 Go to her.   It is up to us.   I am here.   Tell him.
13 If you go to the shop now, he will still be there.

Use right thumb and even strokes

SUBJECT HEADING IN SEMI-BLOCKED LETTERS

In a semi-blocked letter, turn up 2 single spaces after salutation and CENTRE the heading OVER THE BODY of the letter. To do this

(a) Add together the points at which the left and right margins are set and divide by 2.
(b) Bring the writing point to this scale point and backspace once for every

2 characters and spaces in the subject heading.
(c) Type heading.
(d) Turn up 2 single spaces before starting the body of the letter.

Practise typing semi-blocked letter with subject heading

3   Type the following letter on A4 paper in semi-blocked style. Use full punctuation. Margins: Elite 24–84, Pica 15–75.

Our Ref. HWW/ACF   24th June, 1982

FOR THE ATTENTION OF MR. L. A. BUTLER

Messrs. H. Wilkins & Co.,
Cradock Road,
SHEFFIELD.
S2 2IX

Dear Sirs,
↓   (Turn up 2 single spaces)   NOTE: Starting point for
                                                       heading: Elite 48, Pica 39
                    CRIMPED WIRE
↓   (Turn up 2 single spaces)

As requested in your letter of the 22nd June, we have pleasure in enclosing small samples of our crimped wire in nickel silver, phosphor bronze and brass. This material can be supplied in any dimension to suit your requirements.

We look forward to receiving a trial order from you when you are in need of further supplies, and shall be pleased to submit a quotation for your requirements.

Yours faithfully,

H. W. WALKER
SALES MANAGER

Enc.

F Improve control of P and V keys

14 pave prove vapour provide private prevent provoked
15 I will provide a private plane. We will prove it.
16 Prevent Peter from provoking Val and Victor Payne.

G Improve control of shift keys

17 Sal Joe Fay Ida Roy Lee Don Gay Bob Your Mary Hall
18 Tell Joe, Fay, Lee and Marie to call on Roy Young.
19 Edna Kelly and Nan Peters will visit Olive Walker.

Hold shift key
well down with
little finger

H Improve control of Q and X keys

20 mix tax vex exit next taxi; quay quiz quite quiet;
21 A taxi will be at the quay exit; expect him there.
22 Keep quite quiet in that queue for this next quiz.

I Improve control of phrases

23 to go, to ask, to see, to pay, to hear, to let him
24 I am pleased to hear that you are going to see me.
25 Remember to go and to ask her to pay for the flat.

J Improve control of Z and , keys

26 zip, size, lazy, zeal, zone, prize, dozen, amazed,
27 I was amazed, quite amazed, to see a dozen prizes.
28 We gazed at the zebra, also a gazelle, in the zoo.

K Apply the keys you know

Goal—9 words in half a minute   18 words in one minute

29 The whizzing of a jet plane across the sky had now   10

    become such a normal event that it won but a quick   20

    glance from the young boys in the crowd. (SI 1.14)   28

    1 | 2 | 3 | 4 | 5 | 6 | 7 | 8 | 9 | 10 |

SEMI-BLOCKED LETTERS WITH ATTENTION LINE AND ENCLOSURE

The ATTENTION LINE and ENCLOSURE are typed in the same position as in fully-blocked letters.

2   Type the following letter on A4 paper in semi-blocked style taking a carbon copy. Use open punctuation. Margins: Elite 22–82, Pica 12–72.

Our Ref LAB/PAC   22 June, 1982   NOTE: A comma may be
                                                                          inserted after the month

FOR THE ATTENTION OF MR H W WALKER

Atlas Wire Works Ltd
Farnborough Road
Clifton
NOTTINGHAM
NG11 9AE

Dear Sirs

      We thank you for your letter of 20 June, 1982, and note   NOTE: To be consistent,
your remarks with regard to your manufactures.   insert comma after the month

      We regret to inform you that we do not make tooth brushes.
On the other hand, as you will see from the brochure enclosed,
we do make brushes of all other kinds, and, although we have
at the moment a sufficient stock to cover our requirements for
the next 2 months, we should like to receive in the meantime
a small sample showing the quality of your products.

      As soon as we are in need of further supplies of any of
the material we use, we shall not fail to give you an opportunity of quoting us.

                              Yours faithfully
                              H WILKINS & CO

                              L A BUTLER
                              BUYING DEPARTMENT

Enc

| Record your progress | Margins Elite 22–82, Pica 12–72 | 4½ minutes |

R 26   Before your employer leaves on a business trip, obtain   11
       from him clear instructions as to the kind of letters to be   23
       sent on to him. Open all such letters except those marked   34
       'Private'. If you send on the letters themselves, take copies   47
       as a safeguard against loss in the post. When posting, make   59
       sure that the package or envelope is addressed to the place   71
       reached by your employer by the time it gets there. Mark the   82
       package clearly 'To await arrival'. State the address to   94
       which the package should be returned if it is not claimed   105
       within a certain time. You should also always keep a record   117
       of all correspondence you send, with the date of posting   128
       and the address to which it was sent. Some employers like   140
       to have a daily summary of all important letters. (SI 1.13)   150

       1 | 2 | 3 | 4 | 5 | 6 | 7 | 8 | 9 | 10 | 11 | 12 |

Record Your Progress—4½ minutes

OPEN PUNCTUATION

A number of organisations now use open punctuation in a variety of business documents. This means that the full stop is omitted from an abbreviated word (except at the end of a sentence) and is replaced by a space. Example: Mr (space) J (space) Smith, of W M Smith & Co Ltd, will discuss the terms of payment, etc, with Mrs U E St John-Browne.

Where an abbreviation consists of 2 or more letters with a full stop after each letter, the full stops are omitted and no space is left between the letters, but one space (or comma) after each group of letters. Example: Mrs G L Hunt, 21 South Road, will call at 7 pm today. She requires past examination papers from several bodies, eg, LCCI, RSA and UEI.

Grammatical punctuation must still be used.

PART ONE of this book is written in open punctuation, ie, no full stops are given in or after abbreviations.

IMPROVE YOUR TYPING TECHNIQUE

If a technique is faulty, check with the following list and carry out the remedial drill.

Faulty Technique		*Remedy*
MANUAL MACHINES		
Raised capitals caused by releasing shift key too soon.	I may go.	Drills 4–12 page 14; drills 4–12 page 15.
Uneven left margin, caused by faulty carriage return.	I may go.	Return carriage without looking up. Any 'Apply the keys you know'.
Heavy strokes, caused by not releasing keys quickly.	I may go.	Practise finger movement drills. Any 'Apply the keys you know'.
Light strokes, caused by not striking the keys hard enough.	I may go.	Practise finger movement drills. Any 'Apply the keys you know'.
MANUAL AND ELECTRIC MACHINES		
Omitting or inserting words (looked up from the copy).	may I go	Eyes on copy always. Page 23—Lines 1, 2 and 3 backwards.
Extra spaces, caused by your leaning on the space bar.	I may go.	Right thumb slightly above space bar. Drills 5–7 page 12.
Omitting spaces, caused by poor wrist position.	I maygo.	Say 'space' to yourself each time you tap space bar. Drills 5, 6 and 7 page 12, Drills 26, 27 and 28 page 18.
Fingers out of position	I ,au go.	Return fingers to home keys. Any 'Apply the keys you know'.
Turning letters around—eyes get ahead of fingers	I may og.	Eyes on copy always. Say each letter and space to yourself as you type. Any preceding drills.

ACCURACY/SPEED PRACTICE

Practice routine

1 Type a copy of the exercise.
2 Check and circle all errors.
3 Compare your errors with those shown above.
4 Practise the remedial drills.
5 Type as much of the exercise as you can in the time suggested.

6 If you made more than the stipulated number of errors, continue with the timed practice and aim for accuracy.
7 If your errors were below the tolerance given, type the exercise again (timed) and endeavour to type a little faster.

Set left margin at 25 Elite, 18 Pica

Accuracy/speed practice	19 wpm	One minute	Not more than one error

A/S 1 As those shoes are too small, you should take them   10
back and have them changed for the right size. (SI 1.00)   19

  1 | 2 | 3 | 4 | 5 | 6 | 7 | 8 | 9 | 10 |

Technique development

SEMI-BLOCKED LETTERS

The following points should be noted when typing semi-blocked letters

(a) DATE: This ends flush with the right margin. To find the starting point, backspace from right margin once for each character and space in the date.

(b) REFERENCE: Type at left margin on the same line as the date.

(c) BODY OF LETTER: The first word of each paragraph is indented 5 spaces from left margin. Tap in and set tab stop for paragraph indent.

(d) COMPLIMENTARY CLOSE: Start this approximately at the centre of the typing line.

(e) SIGNATURE: As in fully-blocked letters, turn up a minimum of 5 single spaces to leave room for signature. Type name of person signing, starting at the same scale point as the complimentary close.

(f) DESIGNATION: Begin to type official designation (if any) at the same scale point as complimentary close, ie, immediately below the name of person signing.

(g) PUNCTUATION: Semi-blocked letter may be typed with open or full punctuation.

Practise typing semi-blocked letters

1   Type the following semi-blocked letter using A5 portrait paper. Margins: Elite 15–60, Pica 10–55. Use open punctuation.

```
Our ref HWW/ACF                    20 June 1982

Messrs H Wilkins & Co
Cradock Road
SHEFFIELD
S2 2IX

Dear Sirs

        We are suppliers of metal strip suitable    Set tab stop
for the manufacture of tooth brushes and other      for paragraph
types of brush, and are in a position to quote      indents
you competitive prices and short delivery           Elite 20
periods.                                            Pica 15

        We can also supply wire in brass, nickel
silver and phosphor bronze, and if you are in
the market for such wire, we shall be pleased
to quote for your requirements.

        May we look forward to hearing from you
in the near future?

                    Yours faithfully




                    H W WALKER
                    Sales Manager
                    ↑
                    (Start approximately at the
                    centre of the line of typing.)
```

See **Practical Typing Exercises, Book One**, page 53, for further exercises on

In exercises A and B type each line or sentence 3 times. If time permits, complete your practice by typing each group of lines as it appears. Keep your eyes on the copy while you type and also when returning the carriage/carrier. Use single spacing with double between exercises. Set Left margin stop at 25 Elite, 18 Pica.

A   Review alphabet keys

1   It was emphasized that the very young juniors need
    extra food which cannot be quickly obtained.

Position of hyphen varies on different machines. Find it on your machine and practise drills

B   Practise ▆ (hyphen) key—; finger

2   ;-; ;-; p-; p-;-; blue-grey, one-fifth, part-time,

No space before or after hyphen

3   Over one-third are part-time day-release students.

4   Her father-in-law asked for all-wool yellow socks.

Accuracy/speed practice   20 wpm   One minute   Not more than one error

A/S 2   If you are good at figures, and are keen to have a   10
        job in our firm, we should like you to call on us.   20
                                            (SI 1.05)

A/S 3   I wish that you could have been with us on Tuesday   10
        to see the new office machines which were on view.   20
                                            (SI 1.15)

        1 | 2 | 3 | 4 | 5 | 6 | 7 | 8 | 9 | 10 |

Record your progress

Instructions for all RECORD YOUR PROGRESS exercises:

(a) Type ONCE as practice.

(b) Check for errors.

(c) With the assistance of your teacher, analyse your errors and carry out remedial work where necessary.

(d) Type as much of the passage as you can in the time allotted.

(e) Check and circle any errors.

(f) Record the number of words typed and the number of errors in the second typing. See SOLUTIONS MANUAL for Record Your Progress chart.

Record your progress   One minute

R 1   I know you will be pleased to hear that Mrs Thomas   10
      joined the firm on a part-time basis. He was told   20
      they would like to give her a short trial. (SI 1.11)   28

      1 | 2 | 3 | 4 | 5 | 6 | 7 | 8 | 9 | 10 |

Accuracy/Speed—One minute at 20 wpm
Record Your Progress—One minute

SKILL BUILDING

In exercises A and B, type each line or sentence 3 times. If time permits complete your practice by typing each group of lines as it appears. Keep your eyes on the copy while you type and also when returning the carriage/carrier.

A Review alphabet keys

Margins: Elite 22–82, Pica 12–72

1   After much coaxing, the queer-looking animal eventually
was persuaded to jump over the wire on to the trapeze bars.

B Increase speed on common word drill

2 arrive please Friday when send will last one you at by of in

3 I hope you will be able to meet us when we arrive next week.

4 Since our short visit last year, we have all been very busy.

Accuracy practice	30 wpm	4½ minutes	Not more than 4 errors

A 53   I am very pleased to see that a party from your school   11
visited the Moated Tudor Manor House last year, and I hope   23
that the tour was enjoyed by all. From the enclosed Annual   35
Report you will realise that the restoration work could not   47
have been carried out without your help: thank you very much   59
for your donation.   62

       Once again I appeal to you to organize a party from your   73
school. Light refreshments are on sale for the pupils, and   85
the Curator can provide a good "Schoolroom Tea" of tea, sand- 97
wiches, bread and butter, home-made jam, and home-made cakes   109
at 10p a head. If you require any further information,   120
please write direct to the Curator, Mr. E. McGuire, at the   132
above address. (SI 1.36)   135

1 | 2 | 3 | 4 | 5 | 6 | 7 | 8 | 9 | 10 | 11 | 12 |

Speed building	40 wpm	1½ minutes	Not more than 3 errors

S 9   It is a clear May evening. The shadows of the trees on   11
the fields become long as the sun sinks in the west, and the   23
sky is tinged with red, pink, and gold. We are told that   34
this type of sunset means a fine day tomorrow, and we hope   46
this is true. Now the sun has sunk, and the red glow remains 58
for a time. (SI 1.13)   60

S 10   We hear that you are planning to buy some new office   10
desks, and we enclose one of our books on this subject. We   22
feel sure that the points we raise about making good use of   34
the space you have will be of much interest to you. Choose   46
the desks and chairs you would like, and we will advise you   58
on a scheme. (SI 1.15)   60

1 | 2 | 3 | 4 | 5 | 6 | 7 | 8 | 9 | 10 | 11 | 12 |

Record your progress—page 158

Accuracy—4½ minutes at 30 wpm
Speed—1½ minutes at 40 wpm

UNIT 52   **Skill Building**   156

In exercises A, B and C type each line or sentence 3 times. If time permits, complete your practice by typing each group of lines as it appears. Keep your eyes on the copy while you type and also when returning the carriage/carrier. Use single spacing with double between exercises. Set left margin stop at 25 Elite, 18 Pica.

A   Review alphabet keys

1   A small quiet boy who lives next door to Jack came
out of the gate and went down the zigzag path.

Position of ? varies on different machines. Find it on your machine and practise drills

B   Practise [?] key—; finger

2   Now? When? Where? May she? Must we? Will you?

Two spaces after ? at end of a sentence

3   Who said so? What is the time? Is it late? Why?

Depress left shift key
One space after colon

C   Practise [:] (colon) key—; finger

4   ;;; ::: ;;; a:; l:; s:; k:; d:; j:; f:; hj:; gf:;a

5   Delivery Period: One month. Price: Nett ex Works.

Accuracy/speed practice   21 wpm   One minute   Not more than one error

A/S 4   We trust that the hints we gave for the removal of   10
stains will be found to be of great help to all of   20
you. (SI 1.09)   21

A/S 5   When are you coming to see us? We look forward to   10
hearing an up-to-date account about your trips out   20
East. (SI 1.24)   21

1 | 2 | 3 | 4 | 5 | 6 | 7 | 8 | 9 | 10 |

Record your progress   One minute

R 2   What time does your train get in? You should take   10
the following with you: spare pair of shoes, rain-   20
coat, sleeping bag, extra socks, and warm clothes.   30
(SI 1.17)

1 | 2 | 3 | 4 | 5 | 6 | 7 | 8 | 9 | 10 |

Accuracy/Speed—One minute at 21 wpm
Record Your Progress—One minute

UNIT 21   Question Mark and Colon   28

Type the following exercise on A4 paper.

HALF-SPACE CORRECTIONS

In making a correction (you have typed THE instead of THAT) how can you squeeze
in an extra letter? Erase the word wh you want to replace. You must now move
the word half a space to the left so th only half a space precedes and follows
it. To do this, you shd keep the carriage/carrier fr spacing normally. On
manual and electric machines you can, by means of the paper release lever, move
the paper so that the printing point is half a space to the left of the word
you have erased.

Depending on the make of machine, there are several other ways in wh you can
control the movement of the carriage/carrier.

1.   Electric Machines

     (a) Bring the carriage/carrier to the space before the first letter of the
          word you hv just erased.
     (b) Press the half-space key/bar and hold it down while you type the first
          letter of the word; then release the half-space key/bar.
     (c) Repeat (b) f the remaining letters.

2.   Manual Machines

     (a) On some typewriters the space bar can be held down to half-space the
          carriage. Follow same procedure as for electric machines above.
     (b) On other machines the backspace key may be used:
          i.   Bring the printing point to the space where the second letter of
                the erased word was typed.
          ii.   Hold down backspacer half a space, type first letter & then release
                backspacer.
          iii. Tap space bar once.
          iv.   Hold down backspacer half a space, type second letter, release
                backspacer & tap space bar once.

Job 56—Spot the errors   Proof-reading Target—2 minutes
                                                     Typing Target   —5 minutes

Read the following exercise very carefully. It contains one error in each line that may be line-
end division, punctuation, spelling, hyphenation, etc. When you have found and marked the
errors, type the corrected passage using margins of Elite 22–82, Pica 12–72. Do not type the
figures down the left-hand side.

Line number
1   Employee efficeincy is what every firm hopes and pays
2   for but can never be sure it gets, unless employee performa-
3   nce is measured or appraised, and many firms in distri-
4   bution have no system of performance appraisal.   Key on
                                                                     page 172
5   Informal appraisal is normally carried out on a day
6   to-day basis, but this often falls short of a firms need
7   for information to monitor its performance as a whole and
8   plan for it's future. Also, employees need to know how well
9   the are doing.

See **Practical Typing Exercises, Book One,** pages 67–69, for a further exercise on
                              Proof-Reading

In exercises A and B type each line or sentence 3 times. If time permits, complete your practice by typing each group of lines as it appears. Keep your eyes on the copy while you type and also when returning the carriage/carrier. Use single spacing with double between exercises. Set left margin stop at 25 Elite, 18 Pica.

A Review alphabet keys

1 In spite of the likely hazard, a decision was made
  to grant their request and give him the extra job.

Shift-lock key

When you need to type several capital letters one after the other, the shift lock must be used. When this is depressed, you will be able to type capitals without using the shift key.
  The following steps should be practised:
(a) Depress shift lock, using 'A' finger of left hand.
(b) Type capital letters.
(c) Depress left-hand shift key to release shift lock.

B Practise shift-lock key

2 BEFORE lunch please ring me in LUDLOW next MONDAY.

3 MEETINGS held in LONDON, LIVERPOOL and MANCHESTER.

4 Both LAURA and KATHLEEN were present at the party.

Accuracy/speed practice   22 wpm   One minute   Not more than one error

A/S 6 We fear that we shall be away for some months, but   10
      we shall keep in touch with you and will write you   20
      very soon. (SI 1.09)   22

A/S 7 We want a first-class employee: one who has a good   10
      knowledge of accounts. She must be able to manage   20
      a section. (SI 1.32)   22

      1 | 2 | 3 | 4 | 5 | 6 | 7 | 8 | 9 | 10 |

Record your progress   One minute

R 3 No extra charge will be made to them for a copy of   10
    the DAILY GAZETTE; but their accounts must be paid   20
    at the end of each month. Will this suit them? I   30
    would like a reply today. (SI 1.20)   35

      1 | 2 | 3 | 4 | 5 | 6 | 7 | 8 | 9 | 10 |

Accuracy/Speed—One minute at 22 wpm
Record Your Progress—One minute

Type the following memo on an A4 printed memo form. (a) Use suitable margins. (b) Use a suitable date. (c) Take one carbon copy.

FROM J. F. R. PENDLETON   c.c/

To   Miss F. Abingford A.

AGENDA FOR ADVISORY COMMITTEE MEETING

It has come to my notice tht there is an omission fr the Agenda f the Advisory Committee meeting wh is to be held on Tues 26 Oct. It was, I understand, prepared by one of the typists in the Secretarial Section. 30 copies hv bn duplicated but, unfortunately, the Agenda wl hv to be re-typed. [I give below the N.P. correct Agenda + shd be glad if y wod let me hv it by Mon. morning, 18 Oct, at the latest.

AGENDA
1. apologies for absence
2. correspondence
3. minutes
4. Matters arising fr Minutes
5. Motion: "That flex-time be introduced; the core-time to be 1000-1200, 1400-1600; the earliest start 0730, the latest finish 1930. Staff wl be required to work a 7½ hr day w one hr f lunch."
6. Report fr Mr. X. G. Ingram — "JOB TRAINING"
   I. F.

7. Outline of Programme for Annual Conference
8. Discussion about Press advertisements
9. Any other business
10. Date of next meeting

Type the following itinerary on A5 landscape paper.

ITINERARY

Aberdeen/London — 2nd July 1982

| Aberdeen Airport | Check-in at 1800 hours |
| | Take-off 1900 hours |

| London Airport | Arrive at 2030 hours |
| | Single room booked at the Chester Hotel, Highgate, for one night only. |

SKILL BUILDING

In exercises A and B type each line or sentence 3 times. If time permits, complete your practice by typing each group of lines as it appears. Keep your eyes on the copy while you type and also when returning the carriage/carrier. Use single spacing with double between exercises.

Left margin: Elite 25, Pica 18

A Review alphabet keys

1 The boy did just give a quick answer but could not
   find words to explain the amazing story.

B Practise ▉ (dash key)—; finger

2 ; - ; ; - ; Call today - no, tomorrow - after tea.

3 The book - it was his first - was a great success.

4 It is their choice — we are sure it will be yours.

— key
Practise ; to —
back to ;. Keep
first finger over
home key

ONE space *before*
and *after* dash

Upper and lower case characters

Characters requiring use of shift key are called UPPER CASE characters.
Characters not requiring use of shift key are called LOWER CASE characters.

Accuracy/speed practice   23 wpm   One minute   Not more than one error

A/S 8 If you feel some day that you would like a trip in   10
       the country, perhaps you could drive out to a farm   20
       to pick fruit. (SI 1.09)   23

A/S 9 Do you wish to take a holiday? Now is the time to   10
       take one of our out-of-season vacations. Send for   20
       our brochure. (SI 1.26)   23

       1 | 2 | 3 | 4 | 5 | 6 | 7 | 8 | 9 | 10 |

Record your progress   One minute

R 4 The goods which Miss Law saw last June are not now   10
     in stock, and we shall not be able to replace them   20
     for some weeks - perhaps a month - when we hope to   30
     receive a further supply. (SI 1.17)   35

     1 | 2 | 3 | 4 | 5 | 6 | 7 | 8 | 9 | 10 |

Accuracy/Speed—One minute at 23 wpm
Record Your Progress—One minute

DITTO MARKS

The double quotation marks may be used for the ditto sign. With indented style the ditto marks are centred under each word; with blocked style they are typed under the first letter of each word.

Type the following on a sheet of A4 paper, using suitable margins. Follow the layout EXACTLY.

P A P E R   S I Z E S

The 3 main sizes of typing paper are:

        A4 = $8\frac{1}{4}$" x $11\frac{3}{4}$" (210 x 297 mm)
        A5 (landscape) = $8\frac{1}{4}$" x $5\frac{7}{8}$" (210 x 148 mm)
        A5 (portrait) = $5\frac{7}{8}$" x $8\frac{1}{4}$" (148 x 210 mm)

HORIZONTAL SPACING

Elite

        A4 = 100 – centre point 50   ) 12 spaces
        A5 (landscape) = 100 – centre point 50) =
        A5 (portrait) = 70 – centre point 35   ) 1" (25 mm)

Pica

        A4 = 82 – centre point 41   ) 10 spaces
        A5 (landscape) = 82 – centre point 41) =
        A5 (portrait) = 59 – centre point 29) 1" (25 mm)

VERTICAL LINE SPACING

        A4 = 70 lines   ) 6 lines
        A5 (landscape) = 35 lines) =
        A5 (portrait) = 50 lines) 1"

        To leave $\frac{1}{2}$" clear, turn up 4 single-line spaces
         "   "   1"   "   "   " 7   "   "
         "   " $1\frac{1}{2}$"   "   "   " 10   "   "
         "   "   2"   "   "   " 13   "   "
         "   " $2\frac{1}{2}$"   "   "   " 16   "   "
         "   "   3"   "   "   " 19   "   "

Main headings are sometimes centred over the typing line. To find centre point of typing line, add together the points at which the margins are set and divide total by 2, e.g., margins 20 and 85 = 105 ÷ 2 = 52 (centre point).

STANDARD SIZES OF PAPER

In the office you will have to use different sizes of paper. The standard sizes are known as the 'A' series and are shown below. The most common of these sizes are: A4, A5 and A6.

Sizes

25 mm = 1"

A2 420 × 594 mm

A3 420 × 297 mm

A4 210 × 297 mm $8\frac{1}{4}'' × 11\frac{3}{4}''$ (approx)

A5 210 × 148 mm (landscape) $8\frac{1}{4}'' × 5\frac{7}{8}''$ (approx)

A5 148 × 210 mm (portrait) $5\frac{7}{8}'' × 8\frac{1}{4}''$ (approx)

A6 148 × 105 mm $5\frac{7}{8}'' × 4\frac{1}{8}''$ (approx)

VERTICAL LINE-SPACING

6 single vertical lines = 25 mm (1")

Number of single-spaced lines in the full length of A4 and A5:

70 single-spaced lines on A4 paper
35 single-spaced lines on A5 landscape paper
50 single-spaced lines on A5 portrait paper

HORIZONTAL SPACING

The 2 most usual type faces are

ELITE—12 characters = 25 mm (1")—known as 12 pitch
PICA —10 characters = 25 mm (1")—known as 10 pitch

Number of horizontal characters in full width of A4 and A5 paper:

	ELITE	PICA
A4	100 (centre point 50)	82 (centre point 41)
A5 (landscape)	100 (centre point 50)	82 (centre point 41)
A5 (portrait)	70 (centre point 35)	59 (centre point 29)

UNIT 24

**Sizes of Paper   Sizes of Type Faces
Vertical and Horizontal Spacing**

Type the following exercise on A5 landscape paper. Decide on suitable margins.

<u>MEASUREMENTS</u>

There will be a sale of stationery and office desks at 9 am on Thursday 30 November.

Bond paper for top copies, letterheads, etc. A4 — 8¼ in x 11¾ in (210 x 297 mm). Weight 60 gsm per 1,000.

Bank paper which is light weight and has many uses, eg, carbon copies. A5 portrait 5⅞ in x 8¼ in (143 x 210 mm). A5 landscape — 8¼ in x 5⅞ in (210 x 148 mm). Weight 45 gsm per 1,000.

Commercial manilla envelopes measuring 6⅜ in x 4½ in (162 x 114 mm). Window envelopes: 6 in x 3½ in (152 x 89 mm).

A variety of office desks measuring 5 ft x 1½ ft x 4½ ft (1.52 x 0.45 x 1.37 m).

Job 51   Production Target—9 minutes

In the HANDBOOK AND SOLUTIONS MANUAL there is a skeleton Stationery Requisition Form and copies may be duplicated.

(a) On a blank Stationery Requisition Form insert the following details

DEPT. Sales   Today's date
    4 reams   A4 Duplicating Paper (White)
    3 "   A4 Bank Typing Paper
    1 box   A4 Carbon Paper
    1 roll   Sellotape

(b) On another blank Stationery Requisition Form insert the following details

DEPT. Purchasing   Today's date

    6   HB Pencils
    3   Biro Pens (red)
    2 reams   A5 Bond Headed Paper
    3 boxes   Paper Clips
    3   Scrap Pads

LINE-SPACE SELECTOR

The line-space SELECTOR is a lever situated at the left- or right-hand end of the paper table. Most machines can be adjusted for single and double spacing and may also have the facility for 1½, 2½ and treble spacing. The selector controls the distance between the lines of typing. In previous exercises you have been typing in 'single' spacing—the line-space selector has been set on 'I'. You can also type in double (one clear space between each line of typing) or treble spacing (2 clear spaces between each line of typing).

	Single spacing (type on every line)	Double spacing (type on every second line)	Treble spacing (type on every third line)
6 single-line spaces equal 25 mm (1 inch) 25 mm	I am going to the market today	I am (*space*) going (*space*) to (*space*)	I am (*space*) (*space*) going (*space*) (*space*)

BLOCKED PARAGRAPHS

Paragraphs are used to break up the writing into short passages to facilitate reading and understanding. There are 3 different styles of paragraph but, for the time being, we will deal with the BLOCKED paragraph where all lines start at the left margin.

When typing BLOCKED paragraphs in SINGLE SPACING, turn up 2 SINGLE spaces between each paragraph, ie, leave one blank space between each paragraph.

Practise typing blocked paragraphs in single spacing

1   Type the following paragraphs on A5 landscape paper. (a) Margins: Elite 22–82, Pica 12–72. (b) Leave 25 mm (one inch) clear at the top of the page, ie, turn up 7 single spaces—for explanation of alignment guide, see page 2 No 8. (c) Single spacing.

We are sure you will already have noticed the effect of tax
on a large number of the goods you see in the shops.

We would like you to come and see the range of gifts on display at any one of our branches.

When typing BLOCKED paragraphs in DOUBLE SPACING, turn up 2 DOUBLE SPACES between each paragraph, ie, leave 3 blank spaces between each paragraph.

Practise typing blocked paragraphs in double spacing

2   Type the following paragraphs on A5 landscape paper. (a) Margins: Elite 22–82, Pica 12–72. (b) Leave 25 mm (one inch) clear at the top of the page, ie, turn up 7 single spaces. (c) Double spacing.

As you have already learnt, in blocked paragraphs all lines

start at the same scale-point.

When typing a blocked paragraph in double spacing, you must

turn up twice between paragraphs.

Type the following exercise on A4 paper. (a) Use double spacing. (b) The heading underscored in the body should be typed as a shoulder heading. (c) Use indented paragraphs, unless otherwise instructed. (d) Left margin 1½", right margin 1".

DUPLICATING METHODS

1. Stencilling *underscore*

A stencil consists of a sheet of tough, thin, fibrous paper base

wh is impregnated or coated with a wax-like composition.

N.P. [For convenience in handling it, the manufacturer fastens the stencil

sheet to a stiff backing sheet.   The stencil may be cut by typewriter, *in wh case the ribbon is disengaged,*

or it may be cut by hand w a special pen.

preparatory

○.Preparatory Steps.   There are certain s(teps to take before you start

to type a stencil.   These are as follows:-

1.   See th the type-faces are thoroughly clean.   Clean the type both

ers   after |and/before cutting the stencil.

3 ~~k~~.   Insert the stencil in the machine, making sure th the carbon &

as well as

backing sheet, ~~and~~ the stencil itself/ lie flat on the platen, as

otherwise creases or cracks can occur.

2 ~~k~~.   Place the ribbon-switch in the 'stencil' position.

TYPIST: Use single spacing for numbered paras. with double between ea. one.

Display the following notice on A5 portrait paper. (a) Centre the whole notice vertically. (b) Centre each line horizontally.

YE OLD MOAT HOUSE CLUB ← (Caps + u/s)   Single spacing

Gosport, Hants ← (Caps)

← Leave one clear space

Telephone: Gosport (code 070 17) 2140

← Leave 2 clear spaces

Luncheons and evening meals

← Leave one clear space

Late supper licence + dancing nightly

← Leave 2 clear spaces

Special Dance + Cabaret Show every Saturday

SKILL BUILDING

For all skill building exercises use A4 paper

In exercises A, B and C, type each line or sentence 3 times. If time permits, complete your practice by typing each group of lines as it appears. Keep your eyes on the copy while you type and also when returning the carriage/carrier. Use single spacing with double between exercises.

Left Margin: Elite 25, Pica 18

A Review alphabet keys

1 Agatha Dent wears the most beautiful and exquisite
   necklace of topaz and jade that Kay has ever seen.

B Build speed on fluency drills

2 the you she her did see new has had his him are an
3 they both your week that must time will days ours.
4 The man did not see the new tie she had given him.
5 Both boys said they knew that they must work hard.

C Build speed on phrase drills

6 we can, we may, we are, we will, we hope, we feel.
7 May we call to see you? We shall not be too long.
8 We hope we can go to the lake; it is not far away.
9 We feel we may be too late to enter for the races.

Accuracy/speed practice   24 wpm   One minute   Not more than one error

A/S 10 The account for May should now be paid, and I must   10

        ask you to let me have your cheque for the sum due   20

        as soon as you can. (SI 1.04)   24

A/S 11 When you leave the office at night you should make   10

        sure that your machine is covered up and that your   20

        desk is quite clear. (SI 1.12)   24

         1 | 2 | 3 | 4 | 5 | 6 | 7 | 8 | 9 | 10 |

Record your progress   One minute

R 5 Our parents are fond of telling us that, when they   10

     were young, they had to work very much harder than   20

     we do now - but we shall, no doubt, tell our chil-   30

     dren the same thing. (SI 1.15)   35

      1 | 2 | 3 | 4 | 5 | 6 | 7 | 8 | 9 | 10 |

Accuracy/Speed—One minute at 24 wpm
Record Your Progress—One minute

Consolidation

PRODUCTION TYPING

Job 46   Production Target—10 minutes

Type the following letter on A4 paper. (a) Use fully-blocked style and full punctuation. (b) Margins: Left 1½" (38 mm), right 1" (25 mm). (c) Type a C6 envelope. (d) Mark the letter and the envelope FOR THE ATTENTION OF MR. J. HILL.

Ref. IES/HW

Insert a suitable date

Messrs. Bradley & Sons, 5 Clarence Parade, Southsea, Hants. POS 3NN

Dear Sirs,

CLEANERS & POLISHERS

With ref to our rep's call on 14 Oct, when you enquired about prices for our new Cleaners & Polishers, we hv pleasure in quoting you as follows:

le/ Junior Model   £155.25   (TYPIST: Please leave
Junior de luxe model   £142.00   3 spaces between the
Extra super model   £153.75   2 columns)

NP/ The above prices do not include VAT. [We enclose a copy of our latest catalogue in wh. you wl. find illustrations of the
NP/ models in question. [If there is any further information you wld like to hv, please do not hesitate to communicate w. us.

Yours ffy

MIDLAND FURNITURE CO. LTD.   Sales Manager

Job 47   Production Target—8 minutes

Type the following exercise on A5 landscape paper. Use fully-blocked style.

THE CHRONICLE

ADVERTISING RATES

Classification	Per line	Semi-display	Full display
Church Announcements	£0.50	£2.00	£3.50
Property Exchanges Employment Wanted Private Messages	£0.60	£3.00	£4.75
Theatres and Cinemas	£0.75	£3.10	£4.90
Public Announcements Legal Notices Tenders and Contracts	£1.20	£6.30	£8.25
Charities	£0.40	£1.75	£3.00

Technique development

BACKSPACE KEY

Locate the backspace key on your machine. This is situated on either the top left or right of the keyboard. When the backspace key is depressed, the carriage/carrier will move back one space at a time. On most electric machines the carriage/carrier will continue to move for as long as the backspace key is depressed.

HORIZONTAL CENTRING—BLOCKED STYLE

When centring a piece of display in the full width of the paper, take the following steps:

(a) See that the left edge of the paper is at 0 on the carriage position scale.

(b) Move margin stops to extreme left and right.

(c) Divide by 2 the total number of spaces between 0 and the scale point reached by the right-hand edge of paper; this gives the centre point of paper.

(d) Bring carriage/carrier to the centre point.

(e) Locate the backspace key and backspace once for every 2 characters and spaces in the longest line. Ignore any odd letter left over.

(f) Set the left margin at the point reached.

(g) All lines in the exercise start at the left margin.

Practise horizontal centring

1 Type the following exercise on A5 landscape paper. (a) Leave 25 mm (one inch) at the top of the page. (b) Double spacing. (c) Centre the longest line. (d) Set left margin at point reached. (e) Start all the other lines at this point.

Shorthand-typist

required for

Sales Manager

Apply by letter to

Personnel Officer

Midland Motors Ltd

Worcester Street, Hereford ⟵—— This is the longest line

2 Type the following exercise on A5 landscape paper. (a) Leave 25 mm (one inch) clear at the top of the page. (b) Double spacing. (c) Centre the longest line. (d) Set left margin at point reached. (e) Start all the other lines at this point.

Winter Holidays

Spring Sale

Win a Television Recorder

Major Oil Find

Financial Planning

Market Research Co

8 Type the following letter on A5 portrait paper. (a) Take 2 carbon copies, one for Mrs. B. T. Mulvey and the other for File. (b) Fully-blocked style and full punctuation. (c) Margins: Elite 12–62, Pica 5–55. (d) Type a C6 envelope.

Our Ref. HGS/HOS

21st September 1982

N. J. Johnson & Co. Ltd.,
24 High Street,
BRADFORD,
West Yorkshire.
BD4 9HU

Dear Sirs,

In reply to your letter of 17th September, we are now arranging to deliver on Monday, 27th September, the 60 chairs which you recently ordered from us, and must apologise for the delay in despatch.

We now look forward to receiving the order for the tables and desks about which you consulted us.

Yours faithfully,
MIDLAND FURNITURE CO. LTD.

NOTE: If a date appears in the body of the letter it must be typed in the same form as the one before the address.

H. G. SIMMONS
Sales Department

c.c. Mrs. B. T. Mulvey
    File

9 Type the following letter on A5 portrait paper. (a) Take one carbon copy. (b) Margins: Left 1" (25 mm), Right ½" (13 mm). (c) Type a C6 envelope.

Our ref. BGJ/CH/0021

12 October 1982

Messrs. A. P. Fuller & Sons,
26 The Kingsway,
OXFORD. OX6 04BN

Dear Sirs,

Thank you for yr letter dated 7 October enquiring about the price of A4 paper. As you are interested in purchasing in quantities over 100 reams, we hv pleasure in quoting as follows:

1. White Paper
   (a) 101 to 200 reams   £2.07 per ream
   (b) 201 & over   £1.90 per ream

2. Coloured Paper
   (a) 101 to 200 reams   £2.24 per ream
   (b) 201 & over   £2.10 per ream

Yours faithfully, B. G. Jenkins Sales Manager

See **Practical Typing Exercises, Book One**, page 52, for a further exercise on

SKILL BUILDING

In exercises A, B and C, type each line or sentence 3 times. If time permits, complete your practice by typing each group of lines as it appears. Keep your eyes on the copy while you type and also when returning the carriage/carrier. Use single spacing with double between exercises.

Left margin: Elite 25, Pica 18

A   Review alphabet keys

1   The junior office clerks were then quite amazed at
    the extra reward given by their generous employer.

B   Practise 5 and £ key—F finger

2   fr5f fr5f f5rf f5rf 5 firs 5 fees 55 feet 55 files
3   We sold 5 pairs size 5 shoes to 5 men and 5 girls.
4   fr£f fr£f f£rf f£rf £5 £55 fr£f f£rf £55 £5 fr£ £5

Depress right
shift key for £

ONE space before £ but NO space after

5   Buy 5 at £5 and 5 at £55.   Take £555 to number 55.

C   Practise 6 and _ (underscore) key—J finger

6   jy6j jy6j j6yj j6yj 6 jars 6 jugs 66 jobs 66 jets.
7   Bring 6 bags, 6 toys, 6 rods, 66 pots and 66 jugs.
8   jy_j jy_j j_yj j_yj jy6j jy6j j6yj j6yj £565 £656.

Depress left shift
key/lock for
underscore

Before underscoring, back-space by depressing the back-space key. After underscoring, always tap space bar. Use shift lock when underscoring more than one character.

9   Send only 6.   See me today.   Ask for 56.   Take £5.

Accuracy/speed practice   25 wpm   One minute   Not more than one error

A/S 12   I have just moved to my new house and, when I have   10
         put it straight, I would be glad if you could then   20
         spend a few days with me.   (SI 1.00)   25

A/S 13   I am delighted to tell you that we have now joined   10
         the team.   We had hoped to do so last year, but we 20
         were then not old enough.   (SI 1.12)   25

    1 | 2 | 3 | 4 | 5 | 6 | 7 | 8 | 9 | 10 |

Record your progress   One minute

R 6   I am sorry to hear that my cheque - sent to you on   10
      Thursday - has not been received.   I think it must   20
      have gone astray in the post.   Shall I ask my bank   30
      to stop it?   I can then forward another. (SI 1.18) 38

    1 | 2 | 3 | 4 | 5 | 6 | 7 | 8 | 9 | 10 |

Accuracy/Speed—One minute at 25 wpm
Record Your Progress—One minute

UNIT 26   Skill Building   Figures 5 and 6   35

FULLY-BLOCKED LETTER WITH FULL PUNCTUATION

Letter display is exactly the same as given on pages 72 and 73 for Open Punctuation. However, when using Full Punctuation note the following points:

(a) Full stop after the abbreviation Ref. but no other punctuation in the reference.

(b) Note the punctuation and spacing in the 'For the attention of . . .' line, with no full stop at the end.

(c) The points for typing the name and address of the addressee are the same as those for typing envelopes given on page 146.

(d) Always type a comma after the salutation.

(e) Always type a comma after the complimentary close.

(f) Always type full stop after abbreviations Enc./Encs.

Practice typing a fully-blocked letter with full punctuation

7 Type the following letter in fully-blocked style using full punctuation. (a) A4 paper. (b) Single spacing. (c) Use suitable margins. (d) Type a C6 envelope.

```
Our Ref. BD/DAN

10 August 1982

FOR THE ATTENTION OF MR. J. T. FIRTH

Messrs. W. J. Southall & Sons,
St. Helen's Crescent,
CROYDON,
Surrey.
CR9 6BA

Dear Sirs,

TRIAL ORDER

Thank you for your letter dated 6 August and for your current
leaflet.

We shall be glad if you will forward immediately one each of
the 2 articles illustrated, viz.:

1 Child's Chair No. 7103 @ £15.75
1 Linen Basket No. 1428B @ £13.20

We enclose cheque for £28.95 in payment, and rely on you not
to fail to make prompt despatch, as both items are required
by 22 August.

Yours faithfully,



B. DANIELS
Sales Manager

Enc.
```

Technique development

VERTICAL CENTRING

To centre matter vertically on a sheet of paper take the following steps:

(a) Find the number of vertical single spaces on the paper.

(b) Count the number of lines and blank spaces between the lines in the exercise to be typed.

(c) Deduct (b) from (a).

(d) Divide answer in (c) by 2 to equalize top and bottom margins (ignore fractions).

(e) Insert paper with left edge at 0 on paper scale. See that the top edge of the paper is level with the alignment scale.

(f) Turn up the number of spaces arrived at in (d) PLUS ONE EXTRA SPACE.

Practise vertical and horizontal centring

1   Display the following notice on A5 landscape paper. (a) Centre the notice vertically. The vertical spacing at the side of the notice and the calculation below are given as a guide. (b) Centre the longest line horizontally. (c) Set the left margin and start all lines at this point.

			Turn up
1	Line 1	OUTSTANDING VALUE OFFERED IN	
2	Space		3 spaces
3	Space		
4	Line 2	Filing Folders	
5	Space		2 spaces
6	Line 3	Letter Racks	
7	Space		2 spaces
8	Line 4	Document Wallets	
9	Space		2 spaces
10	Line 5	Filing Cabinets	
11	Space		2 spaces
12	Line 6	Duplicating Paper	

The calculations for the vertical centring in the above exercise are as follows:

(a) Number of lines on A5 landscape paper = 35

(b) Number of lines and spaces in exercise = 12

(c) Deduct (b) from (a)   35 − 12 = 23

(d) Divide answer in (c) by 2 for top and bottom margins (ignore fractions) 23 ÷ 2 = 11

(e) Turn up 12 single spaces and type the first line of the notice. As you wish to leave 11 clear spaces, it is necessary to turn up the extra space as you will type on the 12th line, so leaving 11 clear spaces.

See **Practical Typing Exercises, Book One**, page 1, for further exercises on

STEPS IN TYPING A BUSINESS LETTER

(a) Insert paper into machine.
(b) Estimate approximate number of words in body of letter.
(c) Set appropriate spacing and margins.
(d) Type reference and date, and inside address and salutation. Check for errors.
(e) Type body of letter. Ensure even right margin. Check for errors.
(f) Type complimentary closing and signature. Check for errors.

NB Always final check your work before taking paper out of machine.

EXTRA POINTS TO NOTE WHEN TYPING LETTERS WITH EITHER FULL OR OPEN PUNCTUATION, BLOCKED OR SEMI-BLOCKED

(a) Whether using full or open punctuation 'st', 'nd', 'rd', 'th', may be used in dates. Similarly a comma may follow the month.
eg, 21st August, 1982
(b) If a date appears in the body of a letter then it must be in the same form as that used at the head of the letter.
(c) Whether using full or open punctuation the date may be typed on the same line as the reference and backspaced from the right margin.
(d) The words 'Our ref' may already appear in a printed letter heading. If this is the case, it is necessary to type the reference after it, irrespective of its position in the heading.
(e) The words 'Your ref' may also appear. This is the reference of the firm to whom you are writing, and if their reference is given then it must be inserted.

RIBBON CONTROL LEVER

This may be found on the left or right of your machine, but its position varies according to the make of typewriter. The lever may be set in 3 (more on certain models) positions:

(a) Black—to type on the top half of the ribbon.
(b) Red—to type on the bottom half of the ribbon.
(c) White or stencil—disconnects the ribbon for typing on stencils, etc.

Record your progress　　　Margins: Elite 22–82, Pica 12–72　　　4 minutes

R 25　　　We were very glad to learn from your letter of 16th July　11
that the prospects you spoke of when you called on us 3 weeks　23
ago are now materialising.　28

　　　You tell us that you have bought a new truck for busi-　39
ness and that you are able to save storage charges by hous-　51
ing it in your own factory building. We are sure that you　62
have calculated well and that the truck will cut down your　73
expenses.　75

　　　Have you had your insurance broker review your insur-　88
ance? We venture to suggest that you go over your policy　98
with your broker to ensure that there are no mistakes in it.　110
The fact that you have this truck in your works will change　122
the rates and may invalidate the policy. (SI 1.33)　130

1 | 2 | 3 | 4 | 5 | 6 | 7 | 8 | 9 | 10 | 11 | 12 |

Record Your Progress—4 minutes
Notes on Typing Business Letters
Ribbon Control Lever

EFFECTIVE DISPLAY

Important lines can be given prominence by using:

(a) Spaced capitals, ie, leave one space between letters and 3 spaces between words. To centre words that have to be typed in

S P A C E D ⌢ C A P I T A L S

say the letters and spaces in pairs, backspacing once for each complete pair, including the extra 2 spaces be-tween words; eg, Sspace Pspace Aspace Cspace Espace Dspace space-space Cspace Aspace, etc. DO NOT backspace for the last letter in the final word.

(b) Closed capitals—leave NO space between letters and ONE space between words.
(c) Capitals and small letters.
(d) Underscoring.

Practise making your display effective

Notice the use of spaced capitals, closed capitals and the underscore to stress important lines in the exercise below.

2 Display the following notice on A5 portrait paper. (a) Centre the whole notice vertically. (b) Centre the longest line horizontally.

S P E C I A L   O F F E R

Leave 2 clear spaces here ie, turn up 3 single spaces

Learn to be an appetizing cook

THE COMPLETE BOOK OF HOME COOKING

Compiled by

Audrey Baker

All your favourite recipes

3 Display the following notice on A5 portrait paper. (a) Centre the whole notice vertically. (b) Centre the longest line horizontally.

N O R T H   D E V O N   F A R M

offers

HOLIDAY ACCOMMODATION

Delightful situation

Good food, and good service

Ideal for children

2 clear spaces here

Write for Brochure to

J R Holmes
Home Farm
Barnstaple, North Devon

Type last 3 lines in single spacing

See **Practical Typing Exercises, Book One**, page 2, for further exercises on

The guide to the addressing of envelopes given on page 79 applies with the exception of inserting punctuation after abbreviations and at line-ends. It should be noted that Miss is not an abbreviation and, therefore, does not require a full stop.

eg Mr. M. Scott   Rev. C. S. Howe   Messrs. Payne & Sons   Miss V. P. Hammond

Miss E. A. McBrien,
Fearnan,
ABERFELDY,
Perthshire.
PH15 2AA

P. Williams, Esq., M.A., B.Sc.,
56 John Street,
MERTHYR TYDFIL,
M. Glam.
CF47 0AB

Points to note:

(a) Full stop after an initial followed by one clear space.
(b) Comma at the end of each line except for the last line before the postcode which is followed by a full stop.
(c) NO punctuation in postcode.
(d) Comma after surname followed by one space before Esq.
(e) Full stop and NO space between the letters of a degree, but a comma and space between each group of letters.
(f) Notice recognised abbreviation for Mid Glamorgan.

Practice typing names and addresses with full punctuation

5   Type each of the following lines twice in double spacing.

Margins: Elite 20–80, Pica 11–71

Mr. A. K. Smythe will call to see you next Tuesday at 3 p.m.

Address it to J. Ladd, Esq., M.D., B.A., at 69 Newtown Road.

Miss R. Y. Cruise will meet Mrs. Q. P. Carr at 9 a.m. today.

6   Address C6 size envelopes to the following. Use blocked style and full punctuation. Mark the envelope to Mr. Stone 'CONFIDENTIAL', and the envelope to the Victoria Casting Co. Ltd., 'FOR THE ATTENTION OF MR. F. W. NISBETT'. Do not copy the single quotation marks.

Mr. P. F. Stone, O.B.E., Wessex Close, BASINGSTOKE, Hants. RG21 3NP

Ms. J. Feeney, 14 Ennis Road, LIMERICK, Irish Republic.

Miss A. G. Watkins, 26 Lismore Place, CARLISLE, Cumbria. CA1 1LY

R. T. Williams, Esq., 14 Great Ormes, LLANDUDNO, Gwyned. LL30 2BW

Mrs. W. A. Phillips, 14 Moorway Lane, Littleover, DERBY. DE2 7FS

Sir Arthur W. Carmichael, 29 King Street, CRIEFF, Perthshire. PH7 3HB

Messrs. J. Barker & Sons, 8 Mill Lane, Cheshunt, WALTHAM CROSS, Herts. EN8 9JR

Rev. J. H. Haddington-Davis, 23 Daws Heath Road, LEWES, East Sussex. BN7 1AA

Smith & Brown Ltd., 124 Easemore Road, REDDITCH, Worcestershire. B98 8HB

The Victoria Casting Co. Ltd., 84 Ferry Road, BARROW-IN-FURNESS, Cumbria. LA14 2PR

See **Practical Typing Exercises, Book One**, page 52, for further exercises on
Forms of Address With Full Punctuation—

SKILL BUILDING

In exercises A, B and C, type each line or sentence 3 times. If time permits, complete your practice by typing each group of lines as it appears. Keep your eyes on the copy while you type and also when returning the carriage/carrier. Use single spacing with double between exercises.

Left margin: Elite 25, Pica 18

A Review alphabet keys

1 The taxi driver whizzed along the busy road and a small girl
  jumped quickly back to safety.

B Improve control of space bar

2 a s d f j k l a b c d e f g h i j k l m n o p q r s t u v w.
3 as is so or be in am if an me go my do he by us ask may you.
4 It is so. Ask me to go. You must be in time. I may do so.
5 Who is she? He can go home on 6 May. It is a 65-page book.

C Improve control of shift key

6 Frank Jones Denis Kelly Stock Louis Aston Roger Yates Epping
7 Frank Jones and Denis Kelly went to the West Indies in July.
8 Louis Stock and Nancy Ball visited Epping Forest on 6 April.
9 Roger Yates joined the Aston Villa Football Club on 5 March.

Accuracy/speed practice	25 wpm	1½ minutes	Not more than 2 errors

A/S 14 Just a year ago I said that you should be given a trial as a   12

clerk in sales and, as one of the staff will be leaving next   24

week, I would like you to take his place. Let me know if it   36

suits you. (SI 1.11)   38

A/S 15 There must be little imps who sleep until one begins to work   12

and then they come to our office and start to harass and try   24

us. We must all learn to keep our minds on the work that we   36

have to do. (SI 1.13)   38

  1 | 2 | 3 | 4 | 5 | 6 | 7 | 8 | 9 | 10 | 11 | 12 |

Record your progress   1½ minutes

R 7 Many thanks for your note about the desks we ordered. These   12

are not required right away but, if you can let us have them   24

by Thursday of next week, we will send you our remittance by   36

the end of the month. We prefer to pay by credit transfer.   48
                                                      (SI 1.23)

  1 | 2 | 3 | 4 | 5 | 6 | 7 | 8 | 9 | 10 | 11 | 12 |

Accuracy/Speed—1½ minutes at 25 wpm
Record Your Progress—1½ minutes

MEMORANDUM

From P T Anderson

To Mr S L Rogers

REF PTA/JR/WP2

DATE

WORD PROCESSORS

Following our discussion on Monday, I give below a no of points wh may help you to come to a decision lc/ abt the purchase of Word Processing Equipment.

the/ 1 Manufacturers of word processors claim th/ typist's output can be increased dramatically.

2 Benefits, such as higher efficiency & greater production, can only be gained y the office planning to introduce Word Processing is well organised in the first place.

3 Staff hv to be trained; working conditions hv to be considered; & changes in career structure may be necessary.

4 Some studies hv suggested th the display units
5 of Word Processors can cause eye strain, although there has bn very little hard medical evidence to back up the theory.

8 It is necessary to ensure th the new skills req'd
4 are given adequate rewards o th jobs are graded to fit this overall careers' structure for secretarial staff.

6 It shld be possible to increase the output & efficiency of the office by installing a word processor. Many of the repetitive tasks can be performed automatically by m/c, leaving the office personnel free to concentrate more on issues requiring human judgement & decision.

Technique development

TABULATION

A Arrangement of items in columns

You may be required to arrange items in column form in such a way that they are horizontally centred on the page, with equal spaces between the columns and with equal margins. This can easily be done by means of the backspacing method you have already used in display work.

B Tabulator key

All typewriters have 3 tabulator controls which you should locate on your machine as their positions vary on the different makes.

(a) A tab set key to fix the tab stops.
(b) A tab clear key to clear the tab stops.
(c) A tab bar or key to move the carriage/carrier to wherever a tab stop is set.

C Preliminary steps for arranging items in columns

(a) Move margin stops to extreme left and right.
(b) Clear all previous tab stops that may be already set. On most machines this can be done by pressing the clear key while returning the carriage/carrier. On other machines there are special devices for this purpose.
(c) Insert paper seeing that the left edge is at 0 on carriage position scale.
(d) Set the left margin and tab stops at the points given.
(e) Test your tab stop settings by returning the carriage/carrier and then depressing the tab bar or key.

D Typing the table

(a) Type the main heading at the left margin.
(b) Turn up 2 single (1 double) spaces.
(c) At left margin type first item in first column.
(d) Tabulate to second column and type first item; then tabulate to each of the remaining columns and type the first line.
(e) Continue in the same way with the rest of the table.

NOTE It is essential that you complete each horizontal line before starting the next line.

Practise typing column display

1 Carrying out the instructions given above, type the following table on A5 landscape paper. (a) Start the heading on the 14th single space from the top of the paper. (b) Set the left margin at the point given: the figures in brackets are for pica type. (c) Set the tab stops as shown. (d) Double spacing.

Left margin
30 (21)

1st tab 45 (36)
2nd tab 58 (49)

PERSONAL QUALITIES

Accuracy	Courtesy	Pleasantness
Alertness	Initiative	Punctuality
Ambition	Loyalty	Reliability
Common Sense	Neatness	Tact

2   Type the following memo on a printed A5 memo form. Insert today's date. Take 2 carbon copies.

M E M O R A N D U M

To Managing Director ....

From Office Manager .... Date ....

(Return carriage/carrier twice)

TELEPHONE CALLS

With the increased charges for telephone calls it has become necessary to limit, if at all possible, the time taken with each individual call.

Would you please, therefore, inform all staff that wherever possible calls must be limited to a maximum of 5 minutes. No long distance calls will be made except with the prior permission of the Heads of Departments.

Needless to say, no member of staff will be allowed private calls unless of a very urgent nature.

MTP/ACM

cc Sales Manager
   File

3   Type the following on a printed A5 memo form. Take 2 carbon copies. On the carbon copies type in the top left corner, 'Miss K Masterton – for information'. Do not type the single quotation marks.

From Mrs F W Waterhouse
To   Mr C B Barnsley   25 September 1982

u.c. As you know, we are hoping to order six typewriters for use in the office Services division. Approx £4000 has bn allocated for this purpose, + I shd be glad if you wd let me know if y hv any specific requirements as to make, & etc. & model,

N.P. I feel we shd hv at least one electronic typewriter, + th the others shd be electric machines w correction ribbons. [I am enclosing a leaflet wh gives details of one of the latest electronic typewriters. If you wd like to hv one for a trial period, perhaps you wd let me know + I will arrange it.

FWW/IK KR

2   Following the instructions given on page 39, type this table on A5 landscape paper.
    (a) Start the heading on the 14th single space from the top of the page. (b) Set the
    margin and tab stops at the points given: the figures in brackets are for pica type.
    (c) Double spacing.

Left margin
31 (22)

DIFFICULT SPELLING   1st tab 43 (34)
2nd tab 59 (50)

argument	accommodation	forfeit
omission	committed	rhythm
forcibly	occurred	separately
benefited	believe	definite

HORIZONTAL CENTRING—STEPS TO DETERMINE STARTING POINT FOR EACH COLUMN

(a) Backspace once for every 2 characters and spaces in the longest item of each column, saying them to yourself in pairs. If there is an odd letter left over in any column, carry this on to the next column.

(b) Add together the total number of spaces to be left between all the columns plus any odd character (if there is one) left from the last column and divide by 2—backspace this number (ignore fractions).

(c) Set left margin stop at the point thus reached.

(d) Starting from the left margin, tap space bar once for each character and space in the longest line of the first column and once for each blank space between first and second column. Set first tab stop at this point for the start of the second column and make a note of this figure.

(e) Starting from this first tab stop, again tap space bar once for each character and space in the longest item of the second column and for each blank space between second and third columns.

(f) Set second tab stop at this point for the start of the third column and make a note of this figure.

(g) Continue in the same way for any additional columns.

(h) Return carriage/carrier and test tab stop settings.

Practise horizontal centring

3   Carrying out the instructions given above, type the following table on A5 landscape
    paper. (a) Type the heading on the 13th single space from the top edge of the paper.
    (b) Leave 3 spaces between columns. (c) Double spacing.

PROPERTY FOR SALE

Coaching Inn	Arundel	West Sussex
Guest House	Eastbourne	East Sussex
Hotel	Christchurch	Dorset
Thatched Cottage	Clevedon	Avon
Family Business	Bridgend	Mid Glamorgan

EXTRA CARBON COPIES

Follow the rules given on page 81 for the typing of carbon copies. It is quite often necessary to type more than one carbon copy, any extra ones being for the information of others concerned. If this is the case the name(s) of these recipients are typed either (a) in the top right or left corner or (b) at the foot of the letter or memo. The names are usually typed one under the other (if more than one) and preceded by the words "Copy for . . .", "Distribute to . . .", or "cc . . .". When the completed letter is removed from the typewriter the individual names are ticked or underscored. A carbon copy should also be taken for the file.

eg	OPEN PUNCTUATION	*1st carbon* cc J Robinson ✓ Mrs M Rogers File	*2nd carbon* cc J Robinson Mrs M Rogers ✓ File	*3rd carbon* cc J Robinson Mrs M Rogers File ✓
	FULL PUNCTUATION	c.c. J. Robinson ✓ Mrs. M. Rogers File	c.c. J. Robinson Mrs. M. Rogers ✓ File	c.c J. Robinson Mrs. M. Rogers File ✓

MEMORANDA

Revise the points given on page 63 for the typing of memos. The layout of the printed forms used for memos varies considerably, but the same rules for typing them apply. Remember to leave 2 clear character spaces after the words in the printed headings before typing the insertions, and to use the variable line spacer to ensure their alignment. Never type a full stop after the last word of an insertion, unless it is abbreviated and full punctuation is being used.

NOTE: A memo with printed heading is given in the HANDBOOK AND SOLUTIONS MANUAL, and copies may be duplicated.

1 Type the following memo on a printed A5 memo form. (a) Indented paragraphs. (b) Take 2 carbon copies, one for the Salaries Branch and the other for the File. Mark the first carbon copy for the Salaries Branch and the second one for File. (c) Centre the subject heading. (d) Use full punctuation .

MEMORANDUM

From Personnel Officer   Ref. FRB/2

To Miss J. Plant   Date 22 October 1981
(Return carriage/carrier twice)
APPOINTMENT OF CLERICAL ASSISTANT — SALARIES BRANCH

Would you please let me know, as soon as possible, the time of Miss Croft's interview with me on Thursday next.

I understand that she could not attend at the time we originally stated in our letter to her, and that an alternative time has been arranged. I now have a meeting on Thursday at 9.30 a.m., so it is essential that Miss Croft's interview be arranged for the afternoon — preferably about 2.00 p.m.

c.c. Salaries Branch
     File

SKILL BUILDING

In exercises A, B and C type each line or sentence 3 times. If time permits, complete your practice by typing each group of lines as it appears. Keep your eyes on the copy while you type and also when returning the carriage/carrier. Use single spacing with double between exercises.

Left margin: Elite 25, Pica 18

A Review alphabet keys

1 The bold pilot was unable to land the jet owing to extremely
  thick fog which quite covered the whole zone.

B Build speed on fluency drills

2 Did for the key all dog why see you put car ask new her site
3 She did not see the new bus. Ask her for all the old shoes.
4 Tom has won the new car. Buy all the tea you can. See May.
5 Put out the cat and the dog now. You may see him for a day.

C Build speed on phrase drills

6 to me, to go, to ask, to see, to get, to the, to her, to him
7 I am to ask you to see if you can go to the game on Tuesday.
8 I will talk to him as soon as he is ready to go to the play.
9 In order to get to them, you must come to me for a road map.

Accuracy/speed practice   25 wpm   2 minutes   Not more than 2 errors

A/S 16 We were all happy to hear that you are now back at work, and   12
       we hope that the long rest by the sea will have restored you   24
       to good health. As soon as you can, please call and see us.   36
       You will notice that we have moved to a new house quite near   48
       the parks. (SI 1.06)   50

A/S 17 We have not yet been able to send the goods you ordered last   12
       week as they are not stock lines, but we shall do all we can   24
       to let you have some of the goods, if not all, by Tuesday of   36
       next week. We trust that you will excuse the delay in send-   48
       ing these. (SI 1.12)   50

       1 | 2 | 3 | 4 | 5 | 6 | 7 | 8 | 9 | 10 | 11 | 12 |

Record your progress   2 minutes

R 8 Have you ever thought of taking an out-of-season holiday? A   12
    winter break - in the New Year - may be just what you should   24
    take. In our brochure you will find a wide choice of places   36
    to which you can fly. Ask for details from: Sun Travellers,   48
    Great North Road, Nottingham. Write to us straight away for   60
    our new guide. (SI 1.22)   63

    1 | 2 | 3 | 4 | 5 | 6 | 7 | 8 | 9 | 10 | 11 | 12 |

Accuracy/Speed—2 minutes at 25 wpm
Record Your Progress—2 minutes

SKILL BUILDING

Type exercises A, B and C 3 times. Keep your eyes on the copy while you type and also when returning the carriage/carrier.

A   Review alphabet keys

Margins: Elite 22–82, Pica 12–72

1   I expected to make just sufficient space for the quaint old table with the green baize top by removing the armchair.

B   Build accuracy on letter-combinations

2   additional committee entitled definite credits remits visits

3   transport effort report inform story order work word for ore

4   Your committee are entitled to free transport for the visit.

5   Make a definite effort to prepare an additional credit note.

C   Improve accuracy on word-building drill

6   tend attend attends attended attending attendance attendants

7   be belie belief believe believes believed believing believer

8   We believe their attendance has tended to be poor this term.

9   The attendants believe that the attendance will now improve.

Accuracy practice   30 wpm   4 minutes   Not more than 4 errors

A 52   Please note that as from 22nd December there will be an   11
increase of 25 per cent in air fares because of higher land-   23
ing charges.   25

You are reminded that you must comply with police and   36
customs regulations at the points of departure and arrival,   48
and along the route. A journey may be broken at most stops   60
with no extra charge, on condition that you complete the   72
journey within the dates stated. As there are a number of   84
formalities to be complied with, the "check-in" time quoted   96
on your ticket is the time by which you must present your-   108
self with your luggage — if you are late, you will miss the   119
plane. (SI 1.33)   120

1 | 2 | 3 | 4 | 5 | 6 | 7 | 8 | 9 | 10 | 11 | 12 |

Speed building   40 wpm   One minute   Not more than 2 errors

S 7   Thank you for your note just to hand. We have received   11
the rest of our last order, and now enclose a cheque for the   23
full amount due. We shall be glad if you will keep in touch   35
with us from time to time. (SI 1.10)   40

S 8   The bright sunshine brought out more cars, thus causing   11
traffic in the narrow streets to be slowed down to a snail's   23
pace. To walk was the one sure way of getting from place to   35
place in the shortest time. (SI 1.15)   40

1 | 2 | 3 | 4 | 5 | 6 | 7 | 8 | 9 | 10 | 11 | 12 |

Record your progress—page 147

Accuracy—4 minutes at 30 wpm
Speed—One minute at 40 wpm

UNIT 50   Skill Building   142

Technique development

TABULATION—VERTICAL CENTRING

The proper vertical arrangement of columns will add greatly to the effectiveness of your display. Use the same method for vertical centring as explained on page 36.

Practise vertical and horizontal centring

1 Type the following table on A5 landscape paper. (a) Centre vertically and horizontally. (b) Leave 3 spaces between columns. (c) Double spacing.

EUROPEAN COUNTRIES AND THEIR CAPITALS

Austria	Vienna	Hungary	Budapest
Belgium	Brussels	Italy	Rome
Denmark	Copenhagen	Norway	Oslo
Greece	Athens	Sweden	Stockholm
Holland	Amsterdam	Switzerland	Berne

The calculations for the vertical centring in the above exercise are given below:

(a) Number of vertical line spaces on A5 landscape paper = 35
(b) Number of vertical lines and spaces in table = 11
(c) Difference to be divided between top and bottom margins 35 − 11 = 24
(d) Divide by 2 (ignore fraction) = 12
(e) Begin typing heading on 13th line so leaving 12 clear

2 Type the following table on A5 landscape paper. (a) Centre vertically and horizontally. (b) Leave 3 spaces between columns. (c) Double spacing.

WORDS AND THEIR OPPOSITES

agree	disagree	polite	impolite
important	unimportant	constant	inconstant
behave	misbehave	mobile	immobile
moderate	immoderate	complete	incomplete

3 Type the following table on A5 portrait paper. (a) Centre vertically and horizontally. (b) Leave 3 spaces between columns. (c) Double spacing.

DEPARTMENT MANAGERS

Assistant Buyer	Mr F Freeman
Sales Director	Mrs A Kennedy
Cashier	Ms M York
Chief Buyer	Miss G Perry
Works Engineer	Mr J Lycett

See **Practical Typing Exercises, Book One**, page 3, for further exercises on

TABULATION—LEADER DOTS

Quite often in the first column of a tab an item will extend to 2 lines. Where this is the case, as in the exercise below, the leader dots should be typed only after the last line of the item. The second and subsequent lines may be blocked or indented 2 spaces.

MULTIPLE-LINE COLUMN HEADINGS

Where column headings consist of more than one line or are of unequal depth, they are always typed in single spacing, and never underscored in RULED TABLES.
BLOCKED DISPLAY: all column headings start on the second single space after the first horizontal line—see exercise below. CENTRED DISPLAY: headings are centred on the longest line—see page 170. Blocked and centred display must NEVER BE MIXED.

16 Display the following table on A4 paper. Type in double spacing with the exception of the item which takes up 2 lines and these should be in single spacing. Insert leader dots and use blocked style. Type in order indicated by the figures down the left-hand side, but do not type figures

BUDGET FOR THE YEAR ENDED 31ST DECEMBER 1982

	Nett exclusive of VAT	VAT	Total inclusive of VAT
	£	£	£
uc/ 3 Meeting expenses	204.94	30.74	235.68
6 Telephone and Telex ...	139.63	20.94	160.57
5 Printing and Stationery	147.69	22.15	169.84
2 Insurance	5.50	Exempt	5.50
1 Annual Outing	246.00	37.05	284.05
4 Postages	194.14	Exempt	196.14
7 Travelling Expenses Train Fares	194.00	Zero Rated	194.00
	£1,132.90	£110.88	£1,243.78

NOTE: Column headings always typed in single spacing

£ sign typed at tab stop when blocked style is used

Transpose

Record your progress   Margins: Elite 22–82, Pica 12–72   3½ minutes

R 24   The number of guide cards used and their arrangement   10
depend on the filing system. The purpose of the guide cards   22
is, however, the same in all systems — to guide the eye when   34
finding and filing papers, and to support the folders. Guide   46
cards can be bought in all standard sizes, as well as for   58
special systems, such as fingerprint, hospital and insurance   70
files. Most guide cards have a tab along the top edge, and   81
this space contains a plain and clear reference to the folder   94
behind. It is important that this reference should be easy   105
to read, and it should give clear guidance to the order of   117
the folders. (SI 1.32)   120

1 | 2 | 3 | 4 | 5 | 6 | 7 | 8 | 9 | 10 | 11 | 12 |

Record Your Progress—3½ minutes
See **Practical Typing Exercises, Book One,** page 49, for further exercises on

TABULATION—TYPING COLUMN HEADINGS—BLOCKED STYLE

In addition to the main heading of a table, each column may have a heading. The length of the column heading must be taken into account when deciding which is the longest line in each column. When there are headings above columns, proceed as follows:

(a) Find longest line in each column. It could be the heading or a column item.

(b) Backspace as usual to find left margin, remembering to take into account the spacing between columns, and set left margin and tab stops. Column headings and column items start at the left margin and at the tab stops set for the longest line of each column/heading.

(c) Turn up 2 single (one double) after the main heading.

(d) Turn up 2 single (one double) after the column headings.

Practise typing column work with blocked headings

4 Following the above instructions, type this exercise on A5 landscape paper. (a) Centre the whole table vertically and horizontally. (b) Leave 3 spaces between columns. (c) Double spacing.

UNITS OF MEASUREMENT IN METRICATION

Turn up one double

Millimetres - mm	Centimetres - cm	Kilograms - kg
Baths	Blankets	Cement
Cookers	Clothing	Fertilizers
Roof tiles	Fabrics	Mortar
Sink Units	Pillow cases	Plaster

Turn up one double

5 Type the following exercise on A5 landscape paper. (a) Centre the table vertically and horizontally. (b) Leave 3 spaces between columns. (c) Double spacing.

EXAMINATION RESULTS

Name	Shorthand	Typing	Commerce
Alice Carter	Passed	Passed	Passed
John Brown	Distinction	Not passed	Passed
Edna Williams	Passed	Distinction	Not passed
Rose Davies	Not passed	Passed	Passed

6 Type the following exercise on A5 portrait paper. (a) Centre the table vertically and horizontally. (b) Leave 3 spaces between columns. (c) Double spacing.

GENERAL GUIDE TO OVEN TEMPERATURE

SLOW	MODERATELY HOT	HOT
Egg Dishes	Custard	Bread
Meringues	Biscuits	Baked Fish
Milk Puddings	Sponges	Sandwich Cakes

See **Practical Typing Exercises, Book One**, page 4, for further exercises on

TABULATION WITH LEADER DOTS

(a) Leader dots (full stops) are used to guide the eye from one column to another. There are 4 methods of grouping but, for the moment, we will use only continuous leader dots.

(b) Leader dots must be typed at the same time as you type the horizontal line to which they apply. DO NOT go back and type them in afterwards.

(c) There must always be one clear space between the last word and the first dot or the last dot and the vertical line, ie, leader dots must never be typed right up to the preceding or following word or line. No word or letter must be allowed to extend beyond the last leader dot, although leader dots may extend beyond the last word.

(d) Leader dots must always finish at the same point on every line, although the longest line may not have any leader dots—all dots on the other lines finish at the last letter of the longest line.

(e) In the exercise below the leader dots finish at the last letter of the longest line and, to ensure that you do not type them beyond this point, after typing the second horizontal line, move the typing point to tab stop 61 (52)—start of figure column—backspace 4 and type one full stop. When you have typed the details at the left margin, leave one clear space and continue to type the full stops until you reach the scale point where the dot has been typed.

Practise typing tables with leader dots

14 Type the following table on A5 landscape paper in double spacing. Leave 3 spaces between columns. Centre vertically and horizontally. Use blocked style and insert leader dots.

FINANCIAL SUMMARY IN £ STERLING

	1980	1981
Group Sales	48,168,000	42,506,400
Profit before tax	5,229,400	3,685,000
Profit after Tax to Ordinary Shareholders	1,947,300	1,203,400
Profit retained in business	497,300	380,000
Exports and Overseas Business	8,221,945	6,926,300

15 Type the following table on A5 portrait paper in double spacing. Centre vertically and horizontally. Use centred style and insert leader dots.

COMPARISON OF SALES FIGURES IN £000

Details	1982	1981
Home Sales	10,560	11,480
Exports	15,490	14,220
Subsidiaries	1,500	1,965
Total Sales	27,550	27,665
Trading Profit	2,072	3,414
Investment Income	240	220
Bank Interest	1,565	1,240

SKILL BUILDING

In exercises A, B and C, type each line or sentence 3 times. If time permits, complete your practice by typing each group of lines as it appears. Keep your eyes on the copy while you type and also when returning the carriage/carrier. Use single spacing with double between exercises.

Left margin: Elite 25, Pica 18

A   Review alphabet keys

1   Both the exhausted travellers, frozen by the cruel wind, and
dazed and weary from lack of rest, joined hands and squeezed
their way past the gaping chasm to safety.

B   Practise figure 1—L finger

Use small 'L' for figure 1

2   He requires 11 pairs size 11, also 11 dozen sizes 15 and 16.
3   Add up 1 plus 11 plus 15 plus 16 plus 51 plus 61 plus 1,516.
4   They have 15 pairs of size 6 socks for the 15 men and women.

If use of figure 1 key is preferred, use A finger

C   Practise figure 2 and " key—S finger

5   sw2s sw2s s2ws s2ws 2 seas 2 sons 2 sets 2 sips 2 sums 2ws2s
6   Send 2 red, 2 grey, 2 gold, 2 white, 2 black, also 22 green.
7   sw"s sw"s s"ws s"ws "2" "22" "12" "25" "26" "62" "The Times"

NO space after initial " and NO space before closing "

Depress right shift key for"

8   "Go for 12 days." "May I use your car?" "Call at 12 noon."

Accuracy/speed practice   26 wpm   One minute   Not more than one error

A/S 18   Tell your firm that they need not send us a cheque until the   12

tables are all sent. If it is their wish, then we will sell   24

on credit. (SI 1.12)   26

A/S 19   In spite of the rain all of us thought it had been an excel-   12

lent evening, but the guests could not travel till the storm   24

had passed. (SI 1.15)   26

1 | 2 | 3 | 4 | 5 | 6 | 7 | 8 | 9 | 10 | 11 | 12 |

Record your progress   One minute

R 9   Enclosed please find a copy of our latest price-list. After   12

you have studied its contents, please do not hesitate to let   24

us know if we can be of further help. May we ask our agents   36

to get in touch with you? (SI 1.25)   40

1 | 2 | 3 | 4 | 5 | 6 | 7 | 8 | 9 | 10 | 11 | 12 |

Accuracy/Speed—One minute at 26 wpm
Record Your Progress—One minute

12 Type the following table on A5 portrait paper. (a) Centre the table vertically and horizontally. (b) Use centred style and double spacing. (c) Leave 3 spaces between columns. (d) Rule horizontal lines by underscore and vertical lines in ink.

COMPARATIVE FIGURES IN MILLIONS

	1980	1979
	£	£
Turnover	742	611
Profit before tax	16	26
Net Assets employed	142	137
Order in hand at 30 June	1,810	1,688
Forward load at 30 June	1,073	1,006

13 Type the following table on A5 landscape paper and rule. Use double spacing and centred style. Leave 3 spaces between columns.

If there is a decimal point, the £ sign is typed over the unit of £s

C A R P E T   S A L E

Size	Content	Price/Medium Domestic
		£
2.74 m x 3.66 m	Wool	140.99
3.66 m x 3.66 m	Wool/Nylon	120.95
3.66 m x 4.57 m	Viscose/Nylon	110.75
3.66 m x 6.40 m	Wool	160.99
4.57 m x 6.40 m	Acrylic	190.10

See **Practical Typing Exercises, Book One**, page 48, for further exercises on

Technique development

TYPES OF DISPLAY HEADINGS

A   Main headings

The main heading, the title of a passage, is blocked at the left margin when using blocked paragraphs. Unless otherwise instructed, always turn up 7 single spaces 25 mm (one inch) from the top edge of the paper before starting the main heading. It may be typed in

(a) Closed capitals—leave one space between each word. The heading may or may not be underscored.

(b) Spaced capitals—leave one space between each letter and 3 spaces between each word. This heading may or may not be underscored.

(c) Lower case with initial capitals. This heading MUST be underscored.

(d) The underscore must not extend beyond the typing.

Practise typing an exercise with a main heading

1   Read through the exercise. (a) Type it on A5 landscape paper. b) Single spacing. (c) Margins: Elite 22–82, Pica 12–72. (d) Follow layout and instructions given in the exercise.

Turn up 7 single spaces

```
MAIN HEADING
```

Turn up 2 single spaces

```
Seven single spaces must be turned up from the top edge of
the paper before typing the main heading and, if the first
paragraph is in single spacing, the paragraph starts on the
second single-line space after the heading.
```

Turn up 2 single spaces

```
Notice that in this exercise the heading is in closed capi-
tals and is not underscored.
```

B   Subheadings

The main heading may be followed by a subheading which further clarifies the contents of the passage. Turn up 2 single spaces after typing the main heading and then type the subheading.

Practise typing an exercise with a subheading

2   Read through the following exercise. (a) Type it on A5 landscape paper. (b) Single spacing. (c) Margins: Elite 22–82, Pica 12–72. (d) Follow the layout and instructions given in the exercise.

Turn up 7 single spaces

```
MAIN HEADINGS
```

Turn up 2 single spaces

```
Subheadings
```

Turn up 2 single spaces

```
The subheading is also typed at the left margin when the
paragraphs are in blocked style.  It may be typed in CLOSED
CAPITALS or in lower case with initial capitals.  All head-
ings in lower case must be underscored.

Two single spaces should be turned up after the subheading,
when the text is in single spacing, before starting the
first paragraph.
```

See **Practical Typing Exercises, Book One**, page 5, for further exercises on

TABULATION—HORIZONTAL AND VERTICAL RULING

In addition to the horizontal lines, a boxed table has vertical lines and the left and right sides may or may not be closed in by vertical lines. The vertical lines between the columns must be ruled exactly in the middle of each blank space. It is therefore advisable to leave an odd number of spaces between the columns—one for the vertical ruling and an equal number on either side of the ruling. To rule the vertical lines, take the following steps:

(a) First set left margin for start of first column, tab stops for the remaining columns, and right margin as explained on page 136 (c).

(b) After typing main heading, return carriage to left margin and type first horizontal line as explained on page 136 (e). Then turn up 2 single spaces.

(c) Move to first tab stop and backspace 2; at this point make a pencil mark for the first vertical line.

(d) Move to next tab stop and backspace 2; at this point make a pencil mark for the second vertical line.

(e) Continue in the same way for any additional columns.

(f) When you have typed the horizontal line at the bottom of the table, mark in pencil the bottom of each of the vertical lines.

NOTE: When marking the top of the vertical lines, make a note of the scale point at which the vertical line has to be drawn so that when you have typed the bottom horizontal line you will know exactly where to make the pencil mark.

Vertical lines may be ruled by underscore or in ink. Horizontal lines may be ruled by underscore and the vertical lines in matching-colour ink. Do not allow the vertical lines to extend above or below the horizontal lines. They must meet precisely.

10   Type the following table on A5 landscape paper. (a) Centre the table vertically and horizontally on the paper. (b) Use BLOCKED style. (c) Double spacing. (d) Leave 3 spaces between columns. (e) Rule horizontal lines by underscore and vertical lines in ink.

BUSINESS TERMS

Insurance	Legal	Stock Exchange
Endowment	Affidavit	Jobber
Insurer	Attestation	Stockbroker
Insured	Endorsement	Gilt-edged
Proposal Form	Testator	Bulls

11   Type the following table on A5 landscape paper. (a) Centre the table vertically and horizontally on the paper. (b) Use CENTRED style. (c) Single spacing. (d) Leave 3 spaces between columns. (e) Rule horizontal lines by underscore and vertical lines in ink.

COMPARISON FIGURES

Details	April 1981	April 1982
	£	£
Home Sales	20,560	21,480
Exports	25,490	24,220
Tool Sales	37,550	37,665
Investment Income	1,240	3,330

£ sign is centred over longest line of figures if there is no decimal point

C Paragraph headings

Apart from the main heading and the subheading at the beginning of a passage, paragraph headings are used to indicate sub-divisions in the body of the text. In blocked style the paragraph heading starts at the left margin as in exercise 3 below.

Practise typing paragraph headings

3   Read through the following exercise. (a) Type it on A5 portrait paper. (b) Single spacing.
     (c) Margins: Elite 13–63, Pica 6–56. (d) Follow the layout and instructions given in the
     exercise. The small figure 2 after the word HEADINGS should not be typed. It indicates the
     number of character spaces to be left before the word These.

	Turn up 7 single spaces

G U I D E   T O   T Y P I S T S

Turn up 2 single spaces

Paragraph Headings

Turn up 2 single spaces

PARAGRAPH HEADINGS² These may be typed in capitals
with or without the underscore. Two spaces have
been left, in this paragraph, between the paragraph heading and the first word of the text which
follows.

Paragraph headings may run on without extra spaces
after the last word, as in this paragraph, and, if
typed in lower case, MUST be underscored.

D Blocked exercises typed in double spacing

(a) If the text is typed in double spacing, turn up 2 double spaces after the main heading before typing the first paragraph.

(b) If, in addition to the main heading, there is a subheading, turn up one double between the main and subheading and 2 doubles after the subheading before typing the first paragraph.

Practise typing a blocked exercise in double spacing

4   Read through the following exercise. (a) Type it on A5 portrait paper. (b) Double spacing.
     (c) Margins: Elite 13–63, Pica 6–56. (d) Follow the layout and instructions given.

Turn up 7 single spaces

TYPING EXERCISES IN DOUBLE SPACING

Turn up 1 double space

Blocked Style

Turn up 2 double spaces

Two double spaces are turned up after the main

heading or subheading — if there is one — before

typing the first paragraph in double spacing.

Turn up 2 double spaces

Two double spaces are turned up between blocked

paragraphs typed in double spacing.

See **Practical Typing Exercises, Book One**, pages 6 and 7, for further exercises on

UNIT 29   Paragraph Headings   Typing in Double Spacing   **46**

TABULATION WITH COLUMNS OF FIGURES

When columns in a table contain figures, care must be taken to see that units come under units, tens under tens, etc. Where there are 4 or more figures, these are grouped in threes starting from the unit figure, a space being left, or a comma inserted, between each group.

The above applies to column work only. When typing CONTINUOUS MATTER the commas MUST BE INSERTED.

Practise typing figures in columns

8   Type the following table on A5 landscape paper. (a) Centre the table vertically and horizontally on the paper. (b) Use BLOCKED style. (c) Double spacing. (d) Leave 3 spaces between columns. (e) Rule by underscore. (f) Turn up 2 single spaces before and after the £ sign.

COMPARATIVE DEPARTMENT TURNOVER

Department	1979	1980	1981
	£	£	£
Clothing	114 320	196 400	212 345
Furniture	1 100 450	2 368 500	2 432 546
Kitchen Utensils	800 000	909 120	345 625
Hardware	523 412	619 345	800 050
TOTAL	2 538 182	4 093 365	3 790 566

TYPIST: Check the totals

9   Type the following table on A5 landscape paper. (a) Centre the table vertically and horizontally on the paper. (b) Use CENTRED style. (c) Double spacing. (d) Leave 3 spaces between columns. (e) Rule by underscore.

WOMEN'S CLOTHING

Stock — December 1981

Item	Size (inches)	Colour	Number
Two-piece Cotton Suits	34"-38"	Mist Blue	120
Velvet Evening Skirts	34"-40"	Midnight Blue	60
Long-sleeved Blouses	32"-38"	Cream	96
Polyester Sun Dresses	34"-36"	Sunshine Yellow	120

See **Practical Typing Exercises, Book One,** page 47, for further exercises on

E Shoulder headings

When this form of heading is used, it is typed at the left margin and may be in closed capitals. If it is typed in lower case with initial capitals, it must be underscored. It is preceded and followed by one blank line as in the exercises below.

Practise typing shoulder headings

5 Type a copy of the following on A5 landscape paper. (a) Blocked paragraphs. (b) Single spacing. (c) Margins: Elite 22–82, Pica 12–72.

<u>GARDENING IN FEBRUARY</u>

Turn up 2 single spaces

PRUNING

Turn up 2 single spaces

Apple and pear trees can be pruned this month as long as it is not freezing. Frozen wood is brittle and tends to split.

Turn up 2 single spaces

SOWING UNDER GLASS

Lettuce, cabbage, cauliflowers, peas and hardy annual flowers can be sown under glass to plant out under cloches next month.

INDOOR PLANTS

Over-wintered plants of geranium and fuchsia can be moved to warmer, lighter positions and watered more freely to produce new growth.

6 Type a copy of the following on A5 portrait paper. (a) Blocked paragraphs. (b) Single spacing. (c) Margins: Elite 13–63, Pica 6–56.

<u>INCOMING AND OUTGOING MAIL</u>

<u>Daily Routine</u>

It is most important that the secretary acquires a routine for dealing with the mail each day.

<u>Incoming Mail</u>

Great care is needed when opening and sorting the incoming mail, and an efficient system should be devised.

<u>Outgoing Mail</u>

In smaller offices that do not have a Post Room, it may be the responsibility of the secretary to prepare letters and parcels for despatch. It is very important that all letters are dealt with in good time for posting.

See **Practical Typing Exercises, Book One**, page 8, for further exercises on

UNIT 29   **Shoulder Headings**   47

6 Type the following exercise on A5 landscape paper. (a) Use centred style of display. (b) Centre vertically and horizontally. (c) Double spacing. (d) Leave 3 spaces between columns.

BASIC SKILL TRAINING RECORD

<u>Filing</u>

<u>Topic</u>	<u>Date carried out</u>	<u>Trained by</u>
Marking-up	12 July 1982	A. Mann
Sorting	13 July 1982	A. Mann
Putting away	14 July 1982	M. Bain
Finding	15 July 1982	W. Martin
Recording out	16 July 1982	W. Martin

TABULATION—HORIZONTAL RULING

A neat and pleasing appearance may be given to column work by ruling in ink or by the use of the underscore. An 'open' table has no ruled lines. Its main use is for displayed columns of items in the body of a letter or report. A 'ruled' table has the column headings separated from the column items by horizontal lines above and below the headings, and below the last line in the table.

When typing a ruled table proceed as follows:

(a) Find vertical starting point by calculating number of typed lines and spaces—remember to count the horizontal lines.

(b) In the usual way backspace to find the left margin. Set margin and tab stops.

(c) From the last tab stop, tap space bar once for each character and space in the longest line of the last column PLUS 2 spaces, and set right margin at the point reached.

(d) Type main heading and sub-heading (if there is one) at left margin if blocked style is used, or centre for centred style. Turn up 2 single spaces and return carriage to left margin.

(e) Press margin release key and backspace 2. This gives you the starting point for the horizontal line which is typed by means of the underscore and finishes at the right margin.

NOTE: After the first horizontal line, remember to turn up TWICE after and ONCE before a horizontal line.

Practise typing a 'ruled' table

7 Type the following table on A5 landscape paper. (a) Use BLOCKED style and centre table vertically and horizontally on the paper. (b) Single spacing. (c) Leave 3 spaces between columns. (d) Rule by underscore.

1	Line 1	DISCOUNT WAREHOUSE		
2	Space			
3	Line 2	<u>Television Games</u>		NOTE: DO NOT underscore column headings in a ruled table
4	Space			
5	Line 3	_____		
6	Space			
7	Line 4	Catalogue Number	Game	Price
8	Line 5			
9	Space	_____		
10	Line 6	2345	Tennis	£27.50
11	Line 7	2409	Football	£26.75
12	Line 8	2411	Stunt Cycle	£25.25
13	Line 9	2412	Shooting	£23.40
14	Line 10	_____		

See **Practical Typing Exercises, Book One,** page 46, for further exercises on

Consolidation

PRODUCTION TYPING AND PROOF-READING

When we look at a typewritten document, we notice immediately if it is well or badly displayed. We do not know, and do not care about, the speed at which it was typed. When we read it, any errors in typing are immediately noticed. Therefore, good display and accuracy are of first importance. But your employer, unlike the reader, is concerned about the time you take to produce a document.

Inserting the paper, deciding line-spacing and margins, accurate division of words at line-ends, all are essential typing techniques that require constant practice to ensure speed and accuracy. A Production Target is the time you should take to complete each Production Typing job. At first, you will reach this target only after concentrated practice. Measure your progress by keeping each completed job in a Production Typing Folder. Make a note of the date and the Production Target at the top of each job.

Remember that proof-reading—checking for errors—is vitally important. In the Production Jobs, check your work carefully and circle any errors before removing the paper from the machine.

Job 1   Production Target—5 minutes

Type the following exercise on A5 landscape paper. (a) Leave 25 mm (one inch) clear at the top of the page. (b) Single spacing. (c) Margins: Elite 22–82, Pica 12–72.

BLANK CASSETTE TAPES

Special Offer

WHOLESALE PRICES The more you buy, the less you pay. If you buy 5 tapes - minimum purchase - these will cost you £6. An order for 55 tapes will cost only £65, less 5 per cent.

GUARANTEE All our C2 cassettes are of very high quality and carry a 5-year guarantee.

Job 2   Production Target—10 minutes

Type the following exercise on A4 paper. (a) Leave 25 mm (one inch) clear at the top of the page. (b) Single spacing. (c) Margins: Elite 20–85, Pica 10–75.

USE OF TELEPHONE

You must be certain that you know the correct number you wish to dial. Where you need to dial a code before the number you want, check this in the dialling instructions and make a note of the code and number before you dial.

DIAL

When you hear the dialling tone, place your finger in the correct number, turn the dial firmly round to the stop and let it return by itself. Do this for each figure that you need to dial.

ANSWERING CALLS

Answer your telephone without delay, giving your name, the name of your firm or your own number.

Check your work and circle any errors

3 Type the following exercise on A5 landscape paper. (a) Use centred style of display. (b) Centre the table vertically and horizontally. (c) Double spacing. (d) Leave 3 spaces between columns.

<pre>
                        ABBREVIATIONS

     Open Punctuation   Full Punctuation   Word in Full

          Ltd   Ltd.   Limited

          viz   viz.   videlicet

           g   g   gramme(s)

          ie   i.e.   id est
</pre>

If the column heading is shorter than the longest item in the column (as in exercise 4 below) the column heading is centred over the longest item:

(a) Set left margin and tab stops as usual.
(b) Find the centre point of the column by tapping space bar once for every 2 characters and spaces in the longest column item, beginning from the point set for the start of the column. This will bring the printing point to the centre of the column.

(c) From the point reached in (b), backspace once for every 2 characters and spaces in the column heading. Type the column heading at the point reached.
(d) The column items will start at the tab stop already set for each column.

4 Type the following exercise on A5 landscape paper. (a) Use centred style of display. (b) Centre the table vertically and horizontally. (c) Centre headings over the longest item in each column. (d) Double spacing. (e) Leave 3 spaces between columns.

<pre>
                        SPRING SALE

                        Sample Items

        Item   Description   Price

     Number 12   Stainless Steel Knife Set   £10.15

     Number 14   Leather Wallet   £15.20

     Number 15   Shopping Bag   £15.75

     Number 30   Aluminium Chip Pan   £17.14
</pre>

5 Type the following exercise on A5 portrait paper. (a) Use centred style of display. (b) Centre the table vertically and horizontally. (c) Double spacing. (d) Leave 3 spaces between columns.

<pre>
                   CURRENT PRICE LIST

               Valid Until 31 December 1982

        COLOUR TELEVISION   SCREEN SIZE   PRICE

          Prestel   21"   £375.80

          Touch Control   15"   £215.12

          Portable   12"   £184.60

          Remote Control   18"   £276.25
</pre>

See **Practical Typing Exercises, Book One**, page 45, for further exercises on

Job 3

Type the following exercise on A5 portrait paper. (a) Leave 25 mm (one inch) clear at the top of the page. (b) Double spacing. (c) Margins: Elite 13–63, Pica 6–56.

```
        T R E A T M E N T   I N   H O S P I T A L

        A SATISFIED PATIENT


        I recently saw some of the letters from relatives.

        One lady wrote that her mother had never had a           Check your work
                                                                  and circle any
        cross word to say about the treatment or staff.          errors


        From my research into this matter, it is obvious

        that the patient — who for a year went home at

        week-ends — had ample opportunity to complain at

        home had she wished to do so.
```

Job 4   Production Target—8 minutes

Type the following table on A5 landscape paper. (a) Centre vertically and horizontally. (b) Leave 3 spaces between columns. (c) Double spacing.

```
              EXAMINATION SUBJECTS

              TUESDAY        WEDNESDAY      THURSDAY

              Geography      German         French
              Geometry       History        Commerce
              Typewriting    Science        Botany
              Book-keeping   Algebra        English
```

Job 5–Spot the errors   Proof-reading Target—2 minutes
                                 Typing Target   —3 minutes

In the exercise below the sentences in COLUMN ONE have been repeated in COLUMN TWO. Those in COLUMN ONE are correct, but in each sentence in COLUMN TWO there is a typing error. Compare the sentences and see how quick you are at spotting the errors. Then type the sentences correctly, looking at COLUMN TWO and keeping COLUMN ONE covered while you do so.

COLUMN ONE	COLUMN TWO
1 The equipment has been moved.	1 The equippment has been moved.
2 Were you frightened?	2 Were you frightened ?
3 He was an independent man.	3 He was an independant man.
4 Let me have an up-to-date list.	4 Let me have an up-to date list.
5 John has gone to the race.	5 John hasgone to the race.
6 Ask for an acknowledgement.	6 Ask for an acknowledgement.
7 Joe — Joe Tait — has now left.	7 Joe — Joe Tait—has now left.
8 We have made our plans.	8 We have made our plans.
9 Therefore, you must tell me.	9 Therefore you must tell me.

See **Practical Typing Exercises, Book One**, pages 67–69, for further exercises on
Proof-Reading

Technique development

FULLY-CENTRED TABULATION

In previous exercises on tabulation all the tables were blocked. You must also become proficient in centring column work. The following points should be noted.

(a) Refer back to pages 40 and 42 for horizontal and vertical centring.

(b) The main heading and sub-heading (if there is one) are centred on the paper, ie, backspace once for every 2 characters and spaces from the centre of the paper.

(c) As in previous exercises on tabulation, backspace once for every 2 characters and spaces in the longest line in each column, plus half the number of spaces to be left between columns. Set your left margin at the point reached.

(d) Tap forward from left margin and set tab stops.

NOTE: Any one piece of tabulation must be BLOCKED or CENTRED—a combination of the 2 is unacceptable.

Practise typing fully-centred tabulation

1   Type the following exercise on A5 landscape paper. (a) Centre the exercise vertically and horizontally. (b) The main heading and sub-heading should be centred on the paper. (c) Double spacing. (d) Leave 3 spaces between columns.

SOME TOWNS NOT REQUIRING COUNTY IF POSTCODE IS USED

Further examples are given in Post Office Guide

Bath	Cardiff	Inverness	Shrewsbury
Belfast	Carlisle	Leeds	Sunderland
Bournemouth	Huddersfield	Newcastle-upon-Tyne	Wolverhampton
Bristol	Hull	Sheffield	York

TYPING COLUMN HEADINGS–CENTRED STYLE

If the column heading is the longest item in the column (as in exercise 2 below) the column items are CENTRED under the headings as follows:

(a) Type the column headings at the left margin and at the tab stops set.

(b) Find the centre of the heading by tapping the space bar once for every 2 characters and spaces in the heading, starting from the left margin or the tab stop set for the heading. This will bring the carriage/carrier to the centre point of the heading.

(c) From the point reached in (b), backspace once for every 2 characters and spaces in the longest line under the heading. This gives you the starting point for EACH ITEM in the column. Make a note of the point reached, then cancel the tab stop set for the heading and set another tab stop for the start of the column items.

2   Type the following exercise on A5 portrait paper. (a) Centre the exercise vertically and horizontally. (b) Centre the column items under the column headings. (c) Double spacing. (d) Leave 3 spaces between columns.

FOOD PRODUCTS

Vegetables	Meat and Poultry	Fresh Fruit
Beans	Lamb	Apples
Cabbage	Pork	Apricots
Celery	Veal	Bananas
Peas	Chicken	Pineapple

See **Practical Typing Exercises, Book One**, pages 44 and 45 for further exercises on

UNIT 49 Centred Tabulation—With or Without Column Headings 134

Display the following notice on a sheet of A5 portrait paper. (a) Centre the whole notice
vertically. (b) Centre the longest line horizontally and start all the other lines at the same
point. (c) Follow the use of spaced capitals, capitals, lower case letters and underscoring.

THE FIRST ELECTRONIC NEWSPAPER

P R E S T E L   T V   S E R V I C E

DAILY NEWS — 21211

BUSINESS NEWS — 21212

FINANCIAL NEWS — 21215

INTERNATIONAL NEWS — 21216

<u>Make a note of your Key Numbers</u>

Job 7   Production Target—9 minutes

Type the following exercise on A4 paper. (a) Leave 25 mm (one inch) clear at the top of the
page. (b) Double spacing. (c) Margins: Elite 20–85, Pica 11–76.

BOOKS OF REFERENCE

<u>Finding Information</u>

<u>The efficient typist</u> carries in her head only essential informa-
tion that she uses frequently. She knows immediately where to
check or find unusual or important information. She makes good
use of reference books.

<u>The preface</u> of a book will tell you about the purpose and content
of that book. Always read the preface to see what the author
has to say. One good example of this is an English Dictionary
where you will probably be unable to recognize the abbreviations,
accents, etc, used in the main part unless you have read the
preface.

Check your
work and
circle any
errors

<u>The index</u> is an alphabetical list of the contents of a book.

SKILL BUILDING

In exercises A, B and C, type each line or sentence 3 times. If time permits, complete your practice by typing each group of lines as it appears. Keep your eyes on the copy while you type and also when returning the carriage/carrier.

A   Review alphabet keys   Margins: Elite 22–82, Pica 12–72

1   In view of the money embezzled by a junior employee, we
must request you kindly to economise and avoid extravagance.

B   Improve control of shift key

2   Vale Kay Union Ruth Gwen Edna Lily Adam Nora Zena John Terry

3   York Coxon Olive Frank Henry Devon Innes Queen Wilson Barrie

4   Ask Miss Edna Terry to see Mr. P. St. John Coxon on Tuesday.

5   Adam, Olive, Frank, Lily and Ruth left Devon for York today.

C   Increase speed on common word drill

6   office where files have your were know are you did the as we

7   looked found there idea they left that not say had but no in

8   We know that the files were left in your office, but, as you
say they are not there now, we have no idea where they are.

Accuracy practice   30 wpm   3½ minutes   Not more than 3 errors

A 51   Throughout the ages leather has been used in countless   11
ways, and new methods of treating it have been found to make   23
it suitable for other uses. Primitive men used the skins   34
and hides of animals to provide themselves with warmth and   46
as protection against rocks and sharp thorns when they went   58
out to hunt for food. They also used them to keep themselves   70
warm at night.   72

      Today, although substitutes have been discovered, leather   84
is still much in demand, and for boots and shoes, for example,   96
it is also most durable and most reliable. (SI 1.35)   105

      1 | 2 | 3 | 4 | 5 | 6 | 7 | 8 | 9 | 10 | 11 | 12 |

Speed Building   35 wpm   2 minutes   Not more than 4 errors

S 5   On checking your invoice, which has just reached us, we   11
find you have charged us the full list-price for items 4, 5,   23
and 6. No doubt this is due to a mistake on the part of one   35
of the clerks in your office, because, in the past, you have   47
charged us the wholesale rates. Please check this with your   59
books, and then send us a new invoice or a credit note.   70
                                                    (SI 1.13)

S 6   When you walk through the woods you must look for a   11
very small plant that has green, glossy, oval-shaped leaves.   23
This plant does not grow very high. It has berries that are   35
a bright red colour and that stay there all the winter. The   47
name of this plant is the teaberry. Both berries and leaves   59
are quite pleasing to the taste, so we have been told.   70
                                                    (SI 1.17)

      1 | 2 | 3 | 4 | 5 | 6 | 7 | 8 | 9 | 10 | 11 | 12 |

Record your progress—page 141

Accuracy—3½ minutes at 30 wpm
Speed—2 minutes at 35 wpm

UNIT 49   **Skill Building**   133

Skill building

In exercises A, B and C, type each line or sentence 3 times. If time permits, complete your practice by typing each group of lines as it appears. Keep your eyes on the copy while you type and also when returning the carriage/carrier. Use single spacing with double between exercises.

Left margin: Elite 25, Pica 18

A   Review alphabet keys

1   Faith quickly jumped over the burning boxes, and walked away
    from the scene of the disaster with dazed feelings.

B   Practise 3 and / (oblique) key—D finger

2   de3d de3d d3ed d3ed 3 days 3 dogs 3 desks 33 dolls 33 drinks
3   Order 3 sets of 3 for 33 High Street.   There are 313 chairs.
4   de/d de/d d/ed d/ed 1/32 his/hers is/as yes/no am/pm 5/12/33

NO space before or after /

Depress right
shift key for /

5   "Call at 13/23 West Street."   "Ask him/her to call at 3 pm."

C   Practise 4 and @ key—F finger

Depress right
shift key for @

6   fr4f fr4f f4rf f4rf 4 fees 4 fans 4 figs 4 files 4 feet f4rf
7   There are 4 men, 4 women, 4 girls and 4 boys at 44 Eastside.
8   fr@f fr@f f@rf f@rf 4 @ 44 4 @ 45 4 @ 43 4 @ 46 1 @ 42 fr@rf
9   "Buy 4 @ £44 and 14 @ £64."   "Send 4 @ £4 to 44 North Road."

Accuracy/speed practice   26 wpm   1½ minutes   Not more than 2 errors

A/S 20 We feel we must write to say how sorry we were to learn that   12
        the women in your works have come out on strike over what is   24
        just a small dispute. We do hope that they will soon return   36
        to work again. (SI 1.15)   39

A/S 21 As a good typist you must be fast, accurate, and able to set   12
        out all kinds of documents. In your first post there may be   24
        some forms of layout that are not clear. If that is so, you   36
        may need help. (SI 1.18)   39

    1 | 2 | 3 | 4 | 5 | 6 | 7 | 8 | 9 | 10 | 11 | 12 |

Record your progress   1½ minutes

R 10 Some 6 months have passed since you left the Sales Office to   12
      study accounts, and we are certain it is now time to discuss   24
      the future. Over the past year we have been very happy with   36
      the high standard of your work and are certain you will want   48
      to do well. (SI 1.22)   50

    1 | 2 | 3 | 4 | 5 | 6 | 7 | 8 | 9 | 10 | 11 | 12 |

Accuracy/Speed—1½ minutes at 26 wpm
Record Your Progress—1½ minutes

SUPERSCRIPTS (SUPERIOR OR RAISED CHARACTERS)

A superscript is a character which is typed half a space above the line of typing. To type a superscript turn the paper down half a space and type the character to be raised. If your machine does not have half spacing, use the interliner. In the exercise below, notice the degree sign. On its own it is typed immediately after the figure, but when followed by C (Centigrade/Celsius) or F (Fahrenheit) there is a space between the figures and the degree sign but no space between the degree sign and letter C or F. Always use lower case o for the degree sign, eg, 10 °C. Superscripts are used for typing degrees and mathematical formulae. eg, $a^2 - b^2$.

SUBSCRIPTS (INFERIOR OR LOWERED CHARACTERS)

A subscript is a character which is typed half a space below the line of typing. To type a subscript turn the paper up half a space and type the character to be lowered. If your machine does not have half spacing, use the interliner, eg, H_2O $C_{12}H_{22}O_{11}$. Subscripts are used for typing chemical formulae.

Practise typing superscripts and subscripts

5   Type each of the following lines 3 times. (a) A5 landscape paper. (b) Double spacing. (c) Margins: Elite 22–82, Pica 12–72.

Subscripts are used in typing H_2SO_4, $CaCO_3$, N_2O and CO_2.

NOTE the use of the apostrophe for minutes and the double quotation marks for seconds.

Superscripts are used for typing degree sign – 4 $^{\circ}$C.

A right angle equals 90°; 1° equals 60', and 1' equals 60".

At 10 am the temperature was 4 $^{\circ}$C; at 2 pm it was 20 $^{\circ}$C.

$ax + b^2 = a^2 - bx$. $a^2 (a - x) + abx = b^2 (a - b)$. $x^2 - a^2$.

SLOPING FRACTIONS

When fractions are not provided on the typewriter, these should be typed by using ordinary figures with the oblique; eg, 2 fifteenths = 2/15; 3 sixteenths = 3/16. Where a whole number comes before a 'made up' fraction, leave a clear space between the whole number and the fraction. DO NOT put a full stop between the whole number and the fraction. Fractions already on the keyboard and sloping fractions may both be used in the same exercise.

Practise typing sloping fractions

6   Type the following exercise on A5 landscape paper. (a) Single spacing. (b) Margins: Elite 22–82, Pica 12–72.

$2\frac{1}{2}$, $3\frac{1}{4}$, 6 2/5, 2 5/16, 3 7/8, 4 8/9, 8 2/9, 7 3/7, 6 3/10, $5\frac{3}{4}$.
The following widths are in inches: $7\frac{1}{2}$, 4 3/8, $6\frac{3}{4}$, 7 1/10, $8\frac{1}{4}$.

Record your progress   Margins: Elite 22–82, Pica–12–72   3 minutes

R 23   We thank you for your request for a copy of our latest   11
          list, but have to state that we do not issue a general cata- 23
          logue, in view of the improvements which we make in our   34
          products from time to time, and we feel that any benefits   45
          should be passed on at once to our customers. We are send- 57
          ing you a few brochures which give full descriptions of some 69
          of our standard lines, and also details of our prices and   80
          terms of delivery. Our agent, Mr. F. A. Clarke, hopes to be 92
          in Inverness from 26th to 31st May, and would be pleased to 104
          call on you to help in any way he can. (SI 1.28)   112

      1 | 2 | 3 | 4 | 5 | 6 | 7 | 8 | 9 | 10 | 11 | 12 |

Record Your Progress—3 minutes
See **Practical Typing Exercises, Book One,** page 43, for further exercises on

Technique Development

TYPING FROM MANUSCRIPT COPY

You may have to type letters or documents from handwritten drafts. Take particular care to produce a correct copy. Before typing, first read the document through to see that you understand it. Some words or letters, not very clear in one part, may be repeated in another part more clearly. Check the completed exercise and circle any error before removing the paper from the typewriter.

Practise typing from manuscript copy

1 Type the following paragraph on A5 landscape paper. (a) Read the whole passage through before you start to type. (b) From the top edge of the paper turn up 7 single spaces. (c) Margins: Elite 22–82, Pica 12–72. (d) Double spacing. (e) Keep to the lines as in the copy.

CATALOGUE OF LOW-PRICED FURNITURE

We are very pleased to send you a copy of our new catalogue of low-priced furniture. As you will doubtless be aware, costs have been forced up, and we cannot, therefore, hold prices for very long. However, if you will forward your order before the end of the month, we will still execute it at the prices which we quote in the list.

2 Type the following paragraphs on A5 landscape paper. (a) Read the paragraphs through carefully before you start to type. (b) From the top edge of the paper turn up 7 single spaces. (c) Margins: Elite 22–82, Pica 12–72. (d) Double spacing. (e) Keep to the lines as in the copy.

FOLLOWING INSTRUCTIONS

It is important that you follow exactly every instruction given about an exercise. At the beginning of the exercise read the instructions and prepare for typing. Then read through the exercise and make sure that you understand it and that it makes sense. If you have a query, ask about it before you start to type.

Typing examiners do tell us that you can lose a great many marks if you do not carry out instructions. Any document typed for your employer must be typed according to his directions.

See **Practical Typing Exercises, Book One**, page 9, for further exercises on

Practise typing combination characters

2　Type each of the following lines 3 times on A5 landscape paper. (a) Single spacing.
　　(b) Margins: Elite 20–80, Pica 18–78.

```
From afar there came to our ears the call "Cuckoo!  Cuckoo!"
They had spent $300 on presents and came home with only 90¢.
The asterisk (*) is used for a reference mark in a footnote.
250 ÷ 5 + 50 ÷ 4 = 25; 25 x 5 - 15 ÷ 2 = 55; $125 ÷ 5 = $25.
```

The brace is used by printers for joining up 2 or more lines. To represent the brace in typing, use continuous brackets as shown in Exercises 3 and 4 below.

Practise typing brace

3　Type the following on A5 portrait paper. (a) Centre horizontally and vertically. (b) Double spacing except for bracketed items which should be in single spacing. (c) Leave 3 spaces between columns.

```
              CLASS LIST

                     Position   Marks

            H Jones     1         78

            A Adkins    2         76

            F Foster    3)        74)
            G Green     3)        74)

            H Hopkins   5)        70)
            L Jones     5)        70)
            L Lawson    5)        70)
```

HANDWRITTEN OR PRINTER'S BRACKET. This has to be replaced by the round brackets used in exercise 3 above. Where lines of unequal length are bracketed together, the brackets are typed immediately after the last characters in the longest line. All the brackets in any one group are typed at the same scale point.

4　Type the following on A5 landscape paper. (a) Use the same line spacing as in the exercise. (b) Margins: Elite 22–82, Pica 12–72. (c) Leave 5 spaces between the columns. (d) Replace the written bracket with the round brackets.

```
    SPACING BEFORE AND AFTER PUNCTUATION

    Full stop           Two spaces at end of sentence

    Comma      ⎫
    Semicolon  ⎬        No space before, one space after
    Colon      ⎭

    Dash                One space before and one space after

    Hyphen              No space before and no space after

    Exclamation sign)   No space before, 2 spaces after at end
    Question mark   )   of sentence
```

See **Practical Typing Exercises, Book One**, page 43, for further exercises on

SKILL BUILDING

In exercises A, B and C, type each line or sentence 3 times. If time permits, complete your practice by typing each group of lines as it appears. Keep your eyes on the copy while you type and also when returning the carriage/carrier. Use single spacing with double between exercises.

Left margin: Elite 25, Pica 18

A   Review alphabet keys

1   The liquid is just what was needed; but I must criticize the
    price asked and the most waxy finish which it now gives.

B   Practise 7 and & (ampersand) key—J finger

2   ju7j ju7j j7uj j7uj 7 jars 7 jets 7 jigs 77 jacks 77 jellies
3   These 7 boys and 7 girls sent 7 plates and 7 dishes to them.
4   ju&j ju&j j&uj j&uj 1 & 2, 3 & 4, 5 & 6, 6 & 7, 7 & 17 & 27.

Leave ONE space before and after &   Depress left
                                                                shift key for &

5   Let Jones & Co at 76 & 77 High Street have 77 jars of honey.

C   Practise 8 and ' key—K finger

6   ki8k ki8k k8ik k8ik 8 keys 8 pits 88 kids 88 kilts 88 kings.
7   About 8 men, 8 women, 8 girls and 8 boys were on the outing.

NO space before or after ' in middle of word   Depress left
                                                                shift key for

8   ki'k ki'k k'ik k'ik It's Joe's job.   Dad's car.   Mary's dog.
9   Bill's 8 vans are with John's 8 trucks at 87/88 King's Road.

Accuracy/speed practice   26 wpm   2 minutes   Not more than 2 errors

A/S 22 Last May we had a chance to buy a large stock of fine cotton   12
        sheets, and we are now selling these at a reduced price. If   24
        your own stock of sheets is low, now is the chance to obtain   36
        some of these goods at half price or less. Send an order by   48
        July at the latest. (SI 1.13)   52

A/S 23 I hope to come and see you soon, but I fear that it will not   12
        be until the end of July, as at the moment we are so busy at   24
        the office that I feel it would not be wise for me to leave.   36
        Next week I have to go away, but I feel sure it will be pos-   48
        sible to visit soon. (SI 1.17)   52

        1 | 2 | 3 | 4 | 5 | 6 | 7 | 8 | 9 | 10 | 11 | 12 |

Record your progress   2 minutes

R 11   On sheet one we set out the pay scales agreed to at the last   12
        meeting of the committee. You will see that salaries are to   24
        be increased by large amounts for all staff from the highest   36
        paid to the lowest. May we ask you to tell your staff about   48
        this award when you see them next Monday. The new rates are   60
        effective from March. (SI 1.23)   64

        1 | 2 | 3 | 4 | 5 | 6 | 7 | 8 | 9 | 10 | 11 | 12 |

Accuracy/Speed—2 minutes at 26 wpm
Record Your Progress—2 minutes

UNIT 32   Skill Building   Figures 7 and 8   53

Technique development

COMBINATION CHARACTERS

Some characters not provided on the keyboard can be typed by combining 2 characters, ie, by typing one character, backspacing and then typing the second character, or by typing one character and then the second immediately afterwards. In a few cases the interliner must be used to allow the characters to be raised/lowered.

Study the following examples and practise typing them:

Exclamation sign	!	Type apostrophe, backspace and type full stop. There are 2 spaces after an exclamation mark at the end of a sentence.
Division sign	÷	Type colon, backspace and type hyphen.
Dollar sign	$	Type capital S, backspace and type oblique.
Cent sign	¢	Type small c, backspace and type oblique.
Plus sign	+	Type hyphen, backspace and type apostrophe.
Equation sign	=	Use interliner. Turn platen roller slightly towards you and type hyphen. Then move platen roller slightly away from you, backspace and type second hyphen.
Asterisk	*	Type small x, backspace and type hyphen.
Brace (commonly called brackets)	( ) ( ) ( )	Continuous brackets typed one underneath the other. See exercise on next page.
Square brackets	[ ]	Oblique and underscore—see explanation below.

On modern typewriters many of the above characters are provided. On many machines it is difficult to type the division sign and plus sign as combined characters. Where this is the case, it would be wise to insert these in matching-colour ink.

When the ASTERISK has to be typed in the body of the text (exercise 2 on the next page), it is typed as a superscript (raised character). Before typing the combination asterisk, turn the platen roller one half space towards you, type small x, backspace and type hyphen; then turn back to normal writing line. Where the asterisk is already fitted, DO NOT lower the paper before typing as the sign on the type face is already raised.

To type a SQUARE BRACKET take the following steps:

Left bracket	Right bracket
(a) Type oblique sign	(a) Type oblique sign
(b) Backspace one and type underscore	(b) Backspace 2 and type underscore
(c) Turn platen back one full line space and type underscore	(c) Turn platen back one full line space and type underscore
(d) Turn platen up one single space, backspace once and continue with typing up to the right bracket	(d) Turn platen up one single space, tap space bar once, and continue with typing

Practise typing square brackets

1   Type each of the following lines 3 times. (a) Double spacing. (b) Margins: Elite 22–82, Pica 12–72.

[756 ÷ 12 = 63] [12 × 5 = 60] [200 ÷ 2 = 100] [10 + 15 = 25]

[20 + 6 ÷ 2 = 13] [200 × 2 ÷ 4 + 30 = 130] [40 + 6 ÷ 2 = 23]

See **Practical Typing Exercises, Book One**, page 43, for further exercises on

Technique development

TYPING MEASUREMENTS

When typing measurements note the following:

(a) The letter 'x' (lower case) is used for the word 'by', eg, 210 mm × 297 mm (space before and after the 'x')

(b) ONE space is left after the numbers and before the unit of measurement, eg, 210 (space) mm; 2 (space) ft 6 (space) in

(c) Groups of figures should not be separated at line ends

(d) Abbreviations do not take an 's' in the plural, eg, 6 in 2 yd; 6 lb; 2 mm; 4 kg

(e) When using OPEN PUNCTUATION there is no full stop after any abbreviation, unless at the end of a sentence

Practise typing measurements

1   Type each of the following lines 3 times on A5 landscape paper. (a) Margins: Elite 22–82, Pica 12–72. (b) Pay particular attention to spacing in measurements.

```
One rug measures 82 cm × 76 cm; and the other, 65 cm × 44 cm.

The carpets were all 6 ft 6 in × 5 ft 7 in or 16 ft × 15 ft.

Send me 5 lb of potatoes, 2 lb of sprouts, 3 lb of parsnips.
```

USE OF WORDS AND FIGURES

(a) Use words instead of figures for number one on its own and for numbers at the beginning of a sentence. But if number one is part of a list of figures it should be typed as a figure, eg, 'Follow the instructions 1, 2 and 3'.

(b) Use figures in all other cases.

Practise typing words and figures

2   Type the following exercise on A5 landscape paper. (a) Margins: Elite 22–82, Pica 12–72. (b) Turn up 7 single spaces from the top of the paper. (c) Double spacing. (d) Read the passage through before starting to type. (e) Follow line endings given in manuscript. (f) Note the use of words and figures.

TEST MATCH

Today Australia were sent spinning to a 7-wicket defeat by Pakistan with one day to spare in the First Test.

Two players claimed most of the glory, sharing 18 of the 22 Australian wickets during the match. One fast bowler had match figures of 11 for 118 and took his second innings' haul to 7 as Australia slid from 88 for 6 overnight to 144 all out.

See **Practical Typing Exercises, Book One,** page 10, for further exercises on
Typing Measurements

SKILL BUILDING

Type each exercise (A, B and C) 3 times. Keep your eyes on the copy while you type and also when returning the carriage/carrier.

Margins: Elite 22–82, Pica 12–72

A Review alphabet keys

1   These 2 travellers were sorely vexed and puzzled by the rapturous welcome they had just been given by the quiet, but kind, official.

B Build accuracy on one-hand words

2   dresses nylon extra jolly great knoll agree pylon gave on my

3   opinion trade union aware only safe upon area joy car him at

4   In our opinion, you were aware of the trade union wage rate.

5   I agree the extra trade in nylon dresses gave him great joy.

C Improve control of double-letter words

6   programmes possible running supply arrive proof agree added.

7   difficult football baggage accept excess rubber attend carry

8   Is it possible to supply a proof of the football programmes?

9   We agree that it was difficult to accept the excess baggage.

Accuracy practice	30 wpm	3 minutes	Not more than 3 errors

A 50   When you have regular payments to make each month or   10
each quarter, as, for instance, for rent, rates, car insur-   22
ance, there is no need for you to make out a cheque each   33
time. It will be quite simple for you to give a standing   44
order to your bank to pay such amounts on your behalf until   56
further notice, and these sums will be placed to the debit   68
of your account each month or quarter, as the case may be.   80
This method will save you a great deal of trouble. (SI 1.22) 90

    1 | 2 | 3 | 4 | 5 | 6 | 7 | 8 | 9 | 10 | 11 | 12 |

Speed building	35 wpm	1½ minutes	Not more than 3 errors

S 3   The repairs to your car have been put in hand, but they   11
will take 2 or 3 weeks. In spite of this, we shall be able   23
to have the car ready for you by the date required. We have   35
no doubt that you will be quite pleased with the quality and 47
standard of the work done. (SI 1.13)   52

S 4   Your name has now been put on our mailing list, and we   11
shall send you a copy of all our leaflets. We shall also be 23
pleased to let you have any details you like regarding the   35
work we do. Please get in touch with us if you think we can 47
be of help to you in any way. (SI 1.17)   52

    1 | 2 | 3 | 4 | 5 | 6 | 7 | 8 | 9 | 10 | 11 | 12 |

Record your progress—page 132

Accuracy—3 minutes at 30 wpm
Speed—1½ minutes at 35 wpm

UNIT 48   Skill Building   129

SKILL BUILDING

In exercises A, B and C type each line or sentence 3 times. If time permits, complete your practice by typing each group of lines as it appears. Keep your eyes on the copy while you type and also when returning the carriage/carrier. Use single spacing with double between exercises.

Margins: Elite 22–82, Pica 12–72

A   Review alphabet keys

1   Judy was thinking of increasing the size of her antique shop
    which, she said, would leave enough room for exhibits.

B   Practise 9 and ((parenthesis or bracket) key—L finger

Depress left
shift key for (

2   lo9l lo9l 19ol 19ol 9 laws 9 legs 99 lids 99 locks 99 lakes.
3   Send 9 cups and 9 saucers, 9 plates, 19 knives and 19 forks.

Leave ONE space before (but NO space after

4   lo(l lo(l l(ol l(ol (9 (8 (7 (6 (5 (4 (3 (2 (lad (log (loads

C   Practise 0 and) key—; finger

Depress left
shift key for)

5   ;p0; ;p0; ;0p; ;0p; 1900; 1930; 1940; 1950; 1960; 1970; 1980
6   ;p); ;p); ;)p; ;)p; 20); 30); 40); 50); 60); 70); 80); ;090)

Leave NO space before) but ONE space after

7   (a) 9 pots; (b) 2 pans; (c) 3 sets; (d) 7 cakes; (e) 10 dogs

Accuracy/Speed practice   27 wpm   One minute   Not more than one error

A/S 24   To give our legs a rest John and I sat down on a stone ledge   12
         near the edge of the cliff.   David thought he would look for   24
         empty sea shells.   (SI 1.04)   27

A/S 25   The day was sunny but cool.   After we had rested and had our   12
         snack, we packed our bags and set out for the distant cliffs   24
         some 2 miles off.   (SI 1.15)   27

A/S 26   We could hear the waves battering against the rocks below us   12
         and, as we travelled on, the clouds suddenly grew black, and   24
         the sun was gone.   (SI 1.26)   27

Record your progress   One minute

R 12   A thick haze covered the headland, and the wind, now at gale   12
       force, was very sharp and biting.   We walked slowly and in a   24
       long time we had covered only 3 miles.   We were then feeling   36
       very chilly and worried.   41

Accuracy/Speed—One minute at 27 wpm
Record Your Progress—One minute

Type the following exercise on a sheet of A4 paper. Use indented paragraphs and take a carbon copy.

TYPEWRITER RIBBONS

Fabric ribbons are made of silk nylon or cotton & may be monochrome (one colour — usually black) or bichrome (2 colours — the top half black and the bottom half red). Bichrome ribbons are not economical unless the red is used frequently. You can type on the bottom half of the ribbon by putting the ribbon-control on red.

<u>Fitting a new ribbon</u>   *caps and u/s*

The manufacturer always supplies a handbook w a new typewriter & complete instructions will be given on how to change the ribbon. Before removing the ribbon, look very carefully at how it is threaded.   Then

(a)   wind the ribbon on to one spool and detach the end, noting how it is hooked to the spool;

(b)   discard old spool & ribbon;

(c)   fasten end of the ribbon on to the empty spool;

(d)   depress shift lock: this makes it easier to thread the ribbon into the carrier;

(e)   place spools in their sockets;

(f)   thread ribbon ~~through~~ carrier.

Job 45—Spot the errors   Proof-reading Target—2 minutes
                                                     Typing Target   —5 minutes

Read the following passage carefully. Each line contains an error that may be spelling, spacing, hyphenation, omission of apostrophe, etc. When you have found and marked the errors, type the correct passage using margins of Elite 22–82, Pica 12–72. Use indented paragraphs. Do not type the figures down the left side.

Line
number

1   Word processing machines and many of todays typewriters use a   Key on
2   carbon or plastic film ribon which gives a very clear, even imprint. page 172
3   These ribbon can only be used once and are thus expensive.

4   A correction ribbon is used for correcting typing errors. This
5   correction ribbon may be completely seperate on additional spools
6   or it maybe the bottom half of the carbon ribbon. When you wish
7   to correct a typing error, switch to the correction ribbon, type
8   the same error-the correction ribbon will 'lift' the impression
9   from the paper. Swich to normal ribbon and type correct letter(s).

See **Practical Typing Exercises, Book One**, pages 67–69, for further exercises on
Proof-Reading

Technique development

FRACTIONS

Practise typing $\frac{1}{2}$ and % keys—; finger

1   Type each of the following lines 3 times

```
;;; ½½½ ;;; ½½½ ;½; ;½; 1½; 2½; 3½; 4½; 5½; 6½; 7½; 8½; 90½;
The prices are 2½p; 3½p; 4½p; 5½p; 6½p; 7½p; 8½p; 9½p; 10½p;
;;; %%% ;;; %%% ;%; ;%; ½%; 2%; 3%; 4%; 5%; 6%; 7%; 9%; 19%;
```

NOTE: In addition to the $\frac{1}{2}$, most typewriters have keys with other fractions. Examine your machine to find what fractions it has. These are all typed with the ; finger. Some will require the use of the shift key. Practise the reaching movement from the home key to the fraction key you wish to type. Remember: ALWAYS return your finger quickly to the home key.

DECIMALS

(a) Always use full stop for decimal point. This is usually typed in the normal position of the full stop.

(b) Leave NO space before or after decimal point.

(c) No punctuation required at the end of figures except at the end of a sentence.

(d) Always insert the number of decimal places required by using zero. Examples: 2 decimal places: type 86.40 NOT 86.4
3 decimal places: type 95.010 NOT 95.01.

Practise typing decimals

2   Type the following sentences 3 times

```
Add up 12.54, 13.02, 24.60, 6.75 and 0.20 and you get 57.11.
The sheet measures 1.200 × 5.810 × 2.540 m; the gross weight
is approximately 50.802 kg and the nett weight is 38.102 kg.
```

SUMS OF MONEY IN CONTEXT

(a) If the sum comprises only pounds, type as follows: £5, £10 OR £5.00, £10.00.

(b) If only pence, type: 10p, 97p.
NOTE: No space between figures and letter p, and no full stop after p (unless, of course, it ends a sentence).

(c) With mixed amounts, ie, sums comprising pounds and pence, the decimal point and the £ symbol should always be used, but NOT the abbreviation p. Example: £7.05.

(d) If the sum contains a decimal point but no whole pounds, a nought should be typed after the £ symbol and before the point. Example: £0.97.

(e) The halfpenny is expressed by a fraction. Example: 3½p OR £0.03½.

Practise typing sums of money in context

3   Type the following exercise in double spacing

```
We thank you for your cheque for £20.10, and we enclose our

credit note for £0.50, which, together with our previous

credit note for £1.90, makes up the total amount of our last

invoice for £22.50.  Our present discount for cash monthly

is 2½%.
```

See Practical Typing Exercises, Book One, page 11, for further exercises on

UNIT 33   Fractions   Decimals   Sums of Money in Context   **56**

Type the following on A4 paper. (a) Single spacing with double between each paragraph. (b) Set a tab stop at 18 Elite and 15 Pica for the start of the side headings. (c) Set the left margin for the start of the main body of the text and a right margin of one inch. (d) Use blocked display.

OFFSET LITHOGRAPHY

l.c. PREPARATION OF   You can type, write *or draw* on the Plate. Guide lines
       MASTER   may be drawn on the master w̄ a water-colour or non-
                             reproducing pencil.

stet MAKING   Pencil or typewritten ~~errors~~ *mistakes* can be corrected w a
        CORRECTIONS   soft eraser or correction fluid. W an eraser, care
                             shd be taken to avoid damaging the surface of the
                             plate.

       PHOTO-COPYING   An original may be photo-copied on to a master.
        PROCESS

       PROOF-READING   It is absolutely essential, as a great number of copies
                             is likely to be produced, that the master plate is
                             thoroughly checked before being run off. Proof-reading
                             is most effective when it is done:

                             (i)   by two persons — one reading to the other;
                             (ii) by someone other than the person who typed the
                                   original master.

Type the following on A4 paper. (a) Use double spacing and indented paragraphs. (b) Type the paragraph heading in upper case. (c) Use full punctuation. (d) Use suitable margins.

OFFICE SYSTEMS

THE ELECTRONIC OFFICE. It is forecast th in a few years' time

the office wl be completely electronic: an office in wh paper wl be

a thing of the past; files wl be stored in, & retrieved fr, a

computer's "memory"; communication wl be handled by a central electronic

system.

NEW TECHNOLOGY. The new office system wl use digital switching

& transmission technology f all communication services, & the first

step towards this wl be the computer-controlled automatic branch

exchange. Word processors, teleprinters, facsimile transmission machines,

etc., wl also be computer-controlled & wl form part of the central elec-

tronic system.

ENUMERATED ITEMS

Paragraphs and items are sometimes numbered or lettered as follows. The numbers or letters may stand on their own or be enclosed in brackets. Two spaces follow the last figure, letter or bracket,

eg	1 Surname	(1) Surname	A Surname	(a) Surname
	2 Christian name	(2) Christian name	B Christian name	(b) Christian name

Practise typing numbered items

4 Type the following on A5 landscape paper. (a) Use single spacing if an item goes on to more than one line but double spacing between each item. (b) Margins: Elite 22–82, Pica 12–72. (c) Leave 2 spaces after the item number.

CHARGES FOR CONFERENCE

12–15 July 1982

The payment of £125.00 covers the following inclusive of VAT:

1 All lectures

2 Accommodation

3 Morning coffee and all main meals from Tuesday morning until Saturday evening

4 Dinner/Dance on Wednesday evening

5 Visit to theatre (details to be given later).

NOTE; With OPEN PUNCTUATION there is no full stop after the figure or letter which numbers the item

5 Type the following on A5 portrait paper. (a) Use single spacing with double between each item. (b) Margins: Elite 13–63, Pica 6–56. (c) Leave 2 clear spaces after the bracketed letters.

WORD PROCESSING TERMS

The WORK STATION is the place where the operator works and usually consists of

(a) Typewriter keyboard plus function keys.

(b) Visual Display Unit (VDU) which displays any typed text.

NOTE; In continuous matter, only one space is left after the closing bracket.

(c) One or 2 disk drives for recording and processing text typed on the disks.

There are 2 kinds of disks

(a) The programme disk which controls all system operations.

(b) Text disks which are used for recording and storing the typed text.

See **Practical Typing Exercises, Book One,** page 12, for further exercises on
Enumerated Items

Job 40   Production Target—5 minutes

Display the following menu on A5 portrait paper. (a) Centre all lines. (b) Use full punctuation as shown. (c) Use double spacing except where otherwise indicated.

J. HEATH & CO. LTD.
ANNUAL DINNER } Spaced caps
M E N U
Salmon Mousse in Aspic
Mushroom Soup
Roast Saddle of Lamb
Redcurrant Jelly   } Single
Roast Potatoes   spacing
Cauliflower with Cheese Sauce
Cold Lemon Meringue
Coffee

Job 41   Production Target—3 minutes

There is a skeleton of the form shown below in the HANDBOOK AND SOLUTIONS MANUAL, 4/E, and copies may be duplicated. Insert the form into your typewriter and then type the words written in manuscript.

PRINCIPAL   Sandersfield Technical College
S M PLANT BSc CEng MIMechE   Drayton Street, BIRMINGHAM B5 7DB

VICE PRINCIPAL   Telephone 021 330 1234
S W Blain MA MInstP

                                   DEPARTMENT OF BUSINESS ADMINISTRATION
Course Tutor   Head of Department
J W Barton DMA FSCT   G S Andrews BCom MBIM

The following students were absent from

Course SHAZEB

on Wednesday 22 March 1982

Names	Time	
	From	To
Gillian Banks	0900	1700
Fiona Cartwright	0900	1215
Phillip Edwards	0900	1700

Employer Fullers & Co Ltd

Address Burlington House, Smith Street, Birmingham, B2 3RE

SKILL BUILDING

Type exercises A, B and C 3 times. Keep your eyes on the copy while you type and also when returning the carriage/carrier.

Margins: Elite 22–82, Pica 12–72

A Review alphabet keys

1 A falling off in zinc supplies in July will have been noted, and prices may be expected to sink very quickly.

B Review hyphen key

2 p-p; p-p; 2-9, 3-8, 4-7, 5-6, con- com- mis- pre- for- dis-.
3 full-time, up-to-date, blue-grey, 48-page, re-cover, co-opt.
4 Full-time students wore pin-striped blue-grey ties. He considered that the up-to-date 248-page document was now ready.

C Build accuracy on punctuation review

5 "Is John — John Mann, not John Green — here, please?" "No."
6 We discussed many things: the staff; an up-to-date building; annual holidays. "What happened then?" "We did not agree."
7 I think (in fact I'm sure) that Mrs Laing will arrive today.

Accuracy/speed practice	27 wpm	1½ minutes	Not more than 2 errors

A/S 27 Did you know that you might have to go to court and be fined | 12
for driving too close to the car in front of you? It is not | 24
easy for us to tell how far we are from the car, but we must | 36
try hard at all times. (SI 1.05) | 40

A/S 28 At the moment, there is no guide to help us to judge how far | 12
we are from the roadside or from the car in front of us. We | 24
know that a device is being made that will help us gauge how | 36
far away we may be. (SI 1.22) | 40

A/S 29 Until this device is fitted to cars, you must learn to drive | 12
with care and leave plenty of space between you and the car | 24
in front, so that you can stop and not cause damage to other | 36
vehicles on the road. (SI 1.22) | 40

1 | 2 | 3 | 4 | 5 | 6 | 7 | 8 | 9 | 10 | 11 | 12 |

Record your progress   1½ minutes

R 13 Have you ever been to a large airport just to watch the end- | 12
less movement of people and planes? You can see hundreds of | 24
folk getting on and off the large new jets, and it makes you | 36
wonder how these aeroplanes ever get into the air or land so | 48
very gracefully. (SI 1.25) | 51

1 | 2 | 3 | 4 | 5 | 6 | 7 | 8 | 9 | 10 | 11 | 12 |

Accuracy/Speed—1½ minutes at 27 wpm
Record Your Progress—1½ minutes

Job 38

Type the following table on A5 landscape paper. (a) Use double spacing. (b) Centre the table horizontally and vertically. (c) Leave 3 spaces between columns.

A G E N T S

Port	Names	Telegraphic Address
Durban	J. S. Union & Co.	Union, Durban
Boston	Wm. J. George Inc.	Sans, Boston
Melbourne	Lyndon & Co. Ltd.	Luxury, Melbourne
Vancouver	L. G. Davis Inc.	Anchor, Vancouver

Job 39

Type the following letter on A4 paper. (a) Margins: Elite 22–82, Pica 12–72. (b) Take one carbon copy. (c) Leave 3 spaces between the columns.

Our Ref HMS/TUR

12 February 1982

Miss D J Hughes

5 Bakewell Road

MATLOCK

Derbyshire

DE4 3AP

Dear Miss Hughes

SAILINGS TO AUSTRALIA

stet The following passenger lines wl ~~depart from~~ leave
Southampton on the dates given below:

Glen More	6 August
Glen Nevis	10 September
Glen Isla	15 Oct

N.P. [May we point out the return tickets (wh are cheaper than the single fares) are valid for 18 months fr the date of departure to the date of embarkation on the final stage of the return journey. The full fare for both outward & return journeys must be pd for before the start of the initial

N.P. journey. [We enclose a booklet giving booking information. Please do not hesitate to contact us if there are any points on wh you are not clear.

Yours sincerely   H. W Sylvester Manager

Enc

Technique development

SECURING A SATISFACTORY RIGHT MARGIN

Up to this stage in the book you have always returned the carriage/carrier at the same point as in the exercise from which you have been copying. This is not usually possible, of course, and in a great many exercises you will have to decide your own line-endings to secure a satisfactory right margin. To warn you that you are nearing the right margin a bell will ring.

MARGIN BELL

Before you can practise making your own right margin, it is necessary to become accustomed to listening for the margin bell. On your own typewriter find out how many spaces there are after the margin bell has rung before reaching the set right margin. On electronic machines a signalling device will warn you that you are nearing the line end.

Practise listening for the margin bell

1   Type the following on A5 landscape paper, and note the instructions. (a) Use single spacing. (b) Margins: Elite 22–82, Pica 12–72. (c) Listen for the margin bell BUT follow the copy line for line.

```
MARGIN BELL

Five to 10 spaces from the right margin a bell on your type-
writer will ring to warn you that you are almost at the end
of the writing line.  It is necessary to train yourself to
listen for this warning bell, and to react as follows:

(a)  if the bell rings at the beginning of a new word of
more than 5-10 letters, divide the word at the first
available point;

(b)  if the bell rings at the end of a word, do not type a
new word on that line unless it is a word of less than
5-10 letters (or 2 words such as 'for it' or 'I am',
etc) or unless the new word can be divided at an appro-
priate point.

The object of dividing a word at the end of a line is to
avoid an uneven right margin.
```

MARGIN RELEASE

If you have to complete a word which cannot be divided, the margin can be unlocked by pressing the margin release key (usually found at the top right- or left-hand side of the keyboard). The word can then be completed. Use the margin release key only when absolutely necessary—a good typist rarely uses it. The margin release key will release the left margin as well as the right.

Practise using the margin release

2   Type each of the following sentences exactly as they appear, using the margin release key where necessary. (a) Use A5 landscape paper. (b) Double spacing. (c) Margins: Elite 22–82, Pica 12–72.

```
A roaring gale had been raging for some days almost incessantly.

She found it extremely difficult to do the job to her satisfaction.

Typewriting errors should always be neatly erased and corrected.
```

PRODUCTION TYPING

Job 36

Type the following exercise on suitable memo paper. (a) Take a carbon copy. (b) Use suitable margins and full punctuation.

FROM   R. T. Hallett
To   Mr. P. Harris
DATE   16.4.82.
SALES STATISTICS

In the Sales Statistics for the last 3 months you give the following comparative figures:

	1981	1982
January	£20,295	£23,176
February	£19,456	£17,982
March	£25,789	£24,765

uc/ At the Sales Mtg on 7 April you said th the 1982 figs for Feb & March were up on the previous yr's figs. Please check the figs quoted above & let me know if they are correct.

Job 37

Type the following exercise on A4 paper. (a) Single spacing with double between each paragraph and between each of the numbered items. (b) Centre the main heading and use indented paragraphs. (c) The numbered paragraphs are to be in hanging paragraph form. (d) Open punctuation.

ELECTRONIC TELEPHONES

Electronic telephone exchanges use electronics as a route-finding method instead of the electro-mechanical system wh has bn in use f many years. The electronic switching system is reliable & faster. The telephone gives access to a wide range of features:

1   Within the instruments are facilities for calling people by using a single key instead of dialling all the numbers.

2   A light denoting th a call is waiting to be connected while you are speaking.

3   Several different ways of holding & transferring calls — & getting them back again.

4   There is a priority facility whereby a user can interrupt an engaged telephone in order to speak to a particular person.

5   There is automatic re-call feature wh connects a waiting caller as soon as an engaged line becomes free.

Facilities are also built into the system for telex, facsimile data transmission, centralised dictation, answering machines, radio paging, public address systems, etc.

GUIDE FOR DIVIDING WORDS AT LINE-ENDS

It may be necessary to divide some words in order to keep the right margin as even as possible. Always type the hyphen at the end of the line before typing the remaining part of the word on the next line.

Divide words—

(a) According to syllables
    per-fect, under-stand

(b) After a prefix, or before a suffix
    com-bine, wait-ing

(c) When a consonant is doubled divide between the 2 consonants
    excel-lent, neces-sary

(d) Compound words and words already hyphenated must be divided at the hyphen
    pre-eminent, self-taught

(e) The pronunciation of a word should not be changed
    prop-erty, not pro-perty

Do not divide—

(a) Words of one syllable or their plurals
    niece, nieces, case, cases

(b) At a point which would bring 2 letters only to the second line
    waited not wait-ed

(c) After an initial one letter syllable
    again not a-gain

(d) Proper names
    Johnson, Cambridge

(e) Numbers or courtesy titles from the words to which they refer
    10 years, Mr Jones

(f) On more than 2 consecutive lines

(g) The last word of a paragraph or page

(h) Sums of money or figures

Practise line-end division of words

3 Copy each of the following lines once for practice and then once for accuracy. (a) Use A5 landscape paper. (b) Margins: Elite 22–82, Pica 12–72. (c) Single spacing. (d) Note where the word is divided and where division is not possible.

```
sten-cil, pad-lock, mur-mur, pen-cil, prac-tise, elec-trical
com-ply, con-sent, dis-agree, sec-tion, trust-ing, pay-ments
cab-bage, stut-ter, neces-sity, suf-fix, sup-pose, sup-plied
self-support, re-entrance, dinner-time, chil-dren, prob-lems
case, cases, box, boxes, dose, doses; quickly, wrecked, into
unit, await, adore, eject, ideal, obey; Adams, London, Paris
```

4 Type the following paragraph, making correct line-end division where necessary. (a) Use A5 landscape paper. (b) Margins: Elite 22–82, Pica 12–72. (c) Double spacing.

NOTE: The words to be divided are: subsequent, improvement, offset

```
This year there was a much reduced profit from fire and subsequent

fall in dividends.  Motor insurance rates are still too fine, but

it is possible there may be a slight improvement due to the effects

of the energy crisis.  Increases in the rates of insurance will be

necessary so that we may offset erosion by inflation.
```

5   Type the following letter on A4 paper. Use suitable margins and take one carbon copy.

Our Ref NY/PAS/Sales/22

4 January 1982

FOR THE ATTENTION OF MR O R NICOLSON

L Ellison & Sons Ltd
22 Dublin Road
LARNE
Northern Ireland

Dear Sirs

recent/ Further to our/telephone conversation, we hv pleasure in
enclosing price details covering a full range of our Photo-
NP/ copying machines. The four most popular models are:

1   RG 059   Maximum copy area $8\frac{1}{4}'' \times 11\frac{3}{4}''$ £110.20
2   RG 175   Maximum copy area $8\frac{1}{4}'' \times 13\frac{1}{2}''$ £120.17
3   RG 156   Maximum copy area $8\frac{1}{2}'' \times 14''$ £170.33
4   RG 280   Maximum copy area $9\frac{1}{2}'' \times 15\frac{1}{2}''$ £288.75

extremely/ I wd like to emphasize the/protracted delivery schedules
at present in existence — we are quoting some 5 to 6 months
for delivery of equipment — &, as you are anxious f the
equipment to be installed by 1 March 1982, it would
stet/ be wise for you to place yr order as ~~quickly~~ as possible.
soon

enclosed We hope th the/information wl be of help to you.

Yours faithfully

N YEARSLEY
SYSTEMS SPECIALIST

ENC

Record your progress   2½ minutes

R 22   Added to the return which the owner of a business gets   11
        for the use of his office, his work, and the cash he has put   23
        into it, he hopes to gain a profit. Profit is the amount   34
        that is left when all costs, even those which have been   45
        supplied by the owner, have been paid for. Pure profits are   57
        the reward he hopes to get for all the risks he has to take   69
        by gambling on the success, or failure, of his venture.   80
                                                            (SI 1.23)

    1 | 2 | 3 | 4 | 5 | 6 | 7 | 8 | 9 | 10 | 11 | 12 |

SECURING A SATISFACTORY RIGHT MARGIN

Practise making your own line-endings

5 Type the following exercise on A5 portrait paper. (a) Make your own line-endings.
(b) Margins: Elite 12–60, Pica 6–54. (c) Double spacing.

Normally, house prices average 3.3 times average annual

earnings. About the middle of 1980 this ratio was 3.7

and has been falling back since to the current level of

3.5.

The high cost of money is partly to blame as a great many

people cannot possibly afford expensive mortgages, and a

very grave fear of redundancy also holds them back. Even

if the Bank of England's minimum lending rate were to fall

soon, it would need to drop back by at least 2 per cent

before the building societies would consider cutting their

rates.

6 Type the following exercise on A5 landscape paper. (a) Make your own line-endings.
(b) Margins: Elite 20–85, Pica 11–76. (c) Single spacing.

Many manufacturers of electronic office equipment are giving us advice on
how voice, text and data should be linked together.

In New York today a manufacturer demonstrated an example of integrated
office systems. The various pieces of equipment at present in use in the
office (typewriter, data store, printer, word processor, computer) are
connected together by coaxial cable along which data travels at an absurd
rate of 2.5 million bits of information a second. It was said that it
would be possible to transfer the entire text of The Bible from one office
to another in 20 seconds.

7 Type the following exercise on A5 landscape paper. (a) Make your own line-endings.
(b) Margins: Elite 22–82, Pica 12–72. (c) Single spacing.

It is proper that the Government should now close loopholes in the tax
laws which allow certain persons to avoid paying large sums of money
to the Inland Revenue.

The Government must soon look at the question of discrimination against
ratepayers and amend the law so that all electors who benefit from local
government services contribute directly towards them.

In our town there are roughly 18,000 ratepayers, and over 37,000 electors.
Some of them may make a contribution, but it is equally certain that many
get their services paid for by others.

See **Practical Typing Exercises, Book One,** page 13, for further exercises on

3 Type the following exercise on A4 paper in double spacing. Use suitable margins and blocked paragraphs.

MICROFILM FILING

Instead of filing documents in the usual way, the documents are photographed at a reduced scale & the film is filed, &, where an organisation uses 4 or more 4-drawer filing cabinets, it is said to be more economical to change to microfilm filing.

The benefits to be gained are: /N.P.

1. Space Saving

Ninety-seven per cent of usual filing space is saved.

2. Copies

Copies of the microfilm images can be obtained at the push of a button.

3. Retrieval

A particular document can be found in seconds; therefore, queries can be answered immediately & a great deal of time saved.

4. Misfiling

Microfilmed documents never get out of sequence. N.P. Manufacturers are now offering a fully-automated microfiche production line w. its own mini-computer.

4 Type the following on A5 portrait paper in single spacing. Use margins of Elite 11–60, Pica 6–55.

TRAVEL INSTRUCTIONS

Please read carefully the following notes:

1. Passports: travellers must hold valid pass-
    ports, and a visa is necessary for certain
    countries.

2. Departure times: we reserve the right to
    alter departure times. Check with your
    local office 24 hours before departure.

3. All timings are based on the 24-hour clock
    and in local time.

Example of 24-hour system

12.30 a.m.	0030
3.15 a.m.	0315
Noon	1200
2.10 p.m.	1410
9.20 p.m.	2120

See **Practical Typing Exercises, Book One**, pages 41 and 42, for further exercises on

SKILL BUILDING

In exercises A, B and C, type each line or sentence 3 times. If time permits, complete your practice by typing each group of lines as it appears. Keep your eyes on the copy while you type and also when returning the carriage/carrier. Use single spacing with double between exercises.

Margins: Elite 22–82, Pica 12–72

A Review alphabet keys

1 After all the questions had been answered, an exclamation of joy broke out from the vast audience who had gathered around to listen to the popular quiz.

B Build speed on word-family drill

2 day hay gay lay say pay way may did kid hid lid rid bid mid.
3 dine nine fine line mine pine wine lane sane wane vane pane.
4 The boy may have hid in the hay. Did he say she went today?
5 They may want wine when we dine at Pine Lodge in North Lane.

C Improve control of word division

6 able, mail-able, read-able, suit-able, sens-ible, flex-ible.
7 so-cial, par-tial, ini-tial, finan-cial, spe-cial, pala-tial
8 pro-mote, pro-vided, per-mit, per-fume, pur-suit, pur-suant.
9 dis-may, dis-miss, dis-patch, dis-place, dis-grace, des-pair

Accuracy/speed practice	27 wpm	2 minutes	Not more than 2 errors

A/S 30 You must not feel that your friends should sit down to write   12
to you if you do not write to them. This does not mean that   24
you must send long letters — a note will do. Would not most   36
of you rather have a note than no reply? Like us, you would   48
want to hear from your friends. (SI 1.06)   54

A/S 31 He said that if you want a garden then you will have to do a   12
great deal of work, but in these days you can buy many tools   24
which will be helpful for the heavy work, and thus save time   36
and effort. You would not need to employ hired help, and so   48
you could then save some money. (SI 1.13)   54

    1 | 2 | 3 | 4 | 5 | 6 | 7 | 8 | 9 | 10 | 11 | 12 |

Record your progress

2 minutes

R 14 There is still a very real risk of fire from many oil stoves   12
and lamps. A portable oil stove must have a firm base (with   24
a guard around it) and it should always be placed out of the   36
children's reach. Also, clothes left too near an oil stove,   48
or a gas fire that has no guard, might be set alight easily.   60
(SI 1.18)

    1 | 2 | 3 | 4 | 5 | 6 | 7 | 8 | 9 | 10 | 11 | 12 |

Accuracy/Speed—2 minutes at 27 wpm
Record Your Progress—2 minutes

Technique development

ENUMERATED ITEMS

See guide on pages 57 and 97. As well as being blocked to the left, Roman numerals may be blocked to the right with or without full stops. Full stops are never used with brackets. There are 2 spaces after the full stop, the bracket and after the figure without a full stop.

Example:

I (2	i. (2	(1) (2	1. (2	A. (2	(a) (2	NOTE: No full
II spaces)	ii. spaces)	(2) spaces)	2. spaces)	B. spaces)	(b) spaces)	stops with open
IIi	iii.	(3)	3.	C.	(c)	punctuation

Practise typing enumerated items

1 Type the following exercise on A5 landscape paper. (a) Single spacing with double between each numbered item. (b) Margins: Elite 22-82, Pica 12-72. (c) Blocked headings.

A. G. ROBINSON PUBLIC LIMITED COMPANY

<u>Annual General Meeting</u>

SECTION IV - RESOLUTIONS

1.   (a)   Adoption of Accounts and Reports of the Directors.
      (b)   Declaration of Final Dividends.

2.   Re-election of John Bryden DFC as a Director.

3.   (a)   Appointment of Auditors.
      (b)   Authorisation of Directors to fix the Auditors'
            remuneration.

2 Type the following exercise on A4 paper. (a) Single spacing with double between each numbered item. (b) Centre the main heading. (c) Use suitable margins. (d) Indent the first paragraph but use hanging paragraphs for those numbered with small Roman numerals. (e) Block Roman numerals to the right. NOTE: When blocking Roman numerals to the right always leave 2 spaces after the last number, full stop or bracket before the start of the text. This means that extra spaces are needed before the shorter numbers.

                         RECORDED DELIVERY

              This service provides a record of posting and delivery and
        limited compensation in the event of loss or damage in the post.

Indent one space
from margin ──────────────→ I   METHOD OF POSTING

Indent 2 spaces from 'M'
in METHOD ────────────────→ i   A recorded delivery fee must be paid in addition to the
                                  normal postage.

                            ii   The address of the packet must be written on a special
                                  recorded delivery receipt.

                            iii The receipt form and the packet must be handed to an
                                  official of the Post Office.

Type at left margin ──────→ II DELIVERY

Indent 2 spaces from 'D'
in DELIVERY ──────────────→ i   A receipt is obtained on delivery at the address on
                                  the packet.

Technique development

VARIABLE LINE SPACER

The variable line spacer is found on the left or right platen knob. By pressing this in, the platen roller can be moved to any position desired. Its purpose is to ensure that you have proper alignment of the details to be typed on dotted lines, ruled lines, or when inserting details in a form letter or a memo.

INTER-OFFICE MEMORANDA

A message from one person to another in the same firm, or from the Head Office to a Branch Office, or to an agent, is often in the form of a memorandum—usually referred to as a 'memo'. Inter-office memoranda may be typed on any of the usual sizes of paper. The layout of headings may vary from organisation to organisation.

Important points to remember when typing memos on headed forms:

(a) Margins: Elite 13–90, Pica 11–75. These margins may vary depending on the size of the form and the length of the message to be typed.

(b) After the words in the printed headings leave 2 clear character spaces before typing the insertions, and use the variable line spacer to ensure their alignment.

(c) Date: correct order—day, month, year. The month should never be typed in figures.

(d) Some memos have a subject heading which gives the reader information about the contents of the memo. The heading is typed 2 single spaces below the last line of the printed headings, ie, turn up 2 single spaces.

(e) If there is no subject heading, start the body of the memo 2 single spaces after the last line of the printed headings.

(f) The body of the memo is usually typed in single spacing with double between paragraphs.

(g) After the last line of the body, turn up 2 single spaces and type the reference. This is usually the dictator's and typist's initials which identify the department or person dictating the memo.

(h) If an enclosure is mentioned in the body of the memo, this must be indicated by typing Enc (or Encs if more than one enclosure) at the left margin. After the reference turn up at least 2 single spaces before typing Enc or Encs.

Practise typing memos

NOTE: A memo with printed heading is given in the HANDBOOK AND SOLUTIONS MANUAL and may be copied and duplicated.

1   Type the following memo on a printed A5 memo form or prepare your own form. Follow the instructions given above, using margins of Elite 13–90, Pica 11–7.5. Make your own line-endings.

MEMORANDUM

From   General Manager

To   Head of Training School

Date   20 January 1982

Turn up 2 single spaces

STYLE OF LETTERS

Turn up 2 single spaces

It has now been decided that all departments should use the blocked style of letters. Please, therefore, give instructions to all office trainees to adopt this style in future. For their guidance, the enclosed specimen should be attached to the notice board.

Turn up 2 single spaces

AD/PM

Turn up 2 single spaces

Enc

SKILL BUILDING

In exercises A, B and C, type each line or sentence 3 times. If time permits, complete your practice by typing each group of lines as it appears. Keep your eyes on the copy while you type and also when returning the carriage/carrier.

A   Review alphabet keys

Margins: Elite 22–82, Pica 12–72

1   The Principals soon realized that extra milk would have to be requisitioned each morning for the lively young pupils in the junior school.

B   Build speed on word family drill

2   look took hook book nook cook best pest rest jest west nest.

3   call hall fall pall wall tall will pill bill hill fill mill.

4   He took a look at the book and said that he would call soon.

5   The birds will nest in a nook of the west wall of that mill.

C   Build speed on fluency drill

6   right both they land wish held firm hand sign paid when form

7   busy lane fork pays dial make rich maps with half fuel road.

8   They wish both firms to sign the forms and pay for the land.

9   It is a busy lane to the right of a fork road by the chapel.

Accuracy/speed practice

Speed can be built up more easily on short, simple exercises, and, as we have now reached 2½ minutes at 30 wpm, and will continue at 30 wpm with increased length of timing, in this and subsequent Skill Building Units we are separating the accuracy and the speed. You may wish to practise the accuracy or the speed, or perhaps both. As a guide, we would suggest that, if you have more than one error for each minute typed, then you should continue with the Accuracy Practice. If you have less than one error for each minute typed, you may wish to build your speed by using this Speed Building material.

Accuracy practice   30 wpm   2½ minutes   Not more than 2 errors

A 49   The Chairman of the Board has written to me to say that   11
Mr. T. Young has been badly hurt in an accident, and that he   23
will not be at work for at least 18 months. You are aware,   35
no doubt, of the fact that he has a large number of speaking   47
engagements in many different cities, and these will have to   59
be cancelled at once unless we are able to engage someone to   71
take over from him. (SI 1.24)   75

    1 | 2 | 3 | 4 | 5 | 6 | 7 | 8 | 9 | 10 | 11 | 12 |

Speed building   35 wpm   One minute   Not more than 2 errors

S 1   In the spring we always go to a farm, where we are made   11
most welcome. We are allowed to do more or less as we like,   23
and we have a fine time. We often wish we could live there.   35
                                                    (SI 1.11)

S 2   Once a month most firms send to each of their customers   11
a statement which shows how much they owe to the firm at the   23
end of the month. It also shows the trade during the month.   35
                                                    (SI 1.14)

    1 | 2 | 3 | 4 | 5 | 6 | 7 | 8 | 9 | 10 | 11 | 12 |

Record your progress—page 123

Accuracy—2½ minutes at 30 wpm
Speed—One minute at 35 wpm

2 Type the following memo on a printed A5 memo form or on your own prepared form. Follow the instructions given on page 63, using margins of Elite 13–90, Pica 11–75. Make your own line-endings.

M E M O R A N D U M

From General Manager

To Personnel Officer

Date 22 January 1982

STAFF MEETING

A meeting will be held in the Conference Room on Monday at 1700 hours. Will you please advise all members of the clerical staff that they are expected to attend the meeting.

RCB/JC

3 Type the following memo on a printed A5 memo form or on your own prepared form. Follow the instructions given on page 63, using margins of Elite 13–80, Pica 11–75. Make your own line-endings.

M E M O R A N D U M

From V Campbell

To Mr J Gascoyne

Date 3 March 1982

CONFERENCE AND ANNUAL DINNER

As you requested in your letter dated 26 February, I have booked accommodation for you and Mrs Gascoyne at the Grosvenor Hotel, Tidy Street, Brighton, for the nights of Monday and Tuesday, 15 and 16 March.

As the journey from Edinburgh may prove difficult by car at this time of year, our Managing Director suggests that you travel by night train.

The conference meetings will be held at the Bedford Hotel, and full information is given in the enclosed programme.

VC/HOS

Enc

4 Type the following memo on a printed A5 memo form or on your own prepared form. Follow the instructions given on page 63, using margins of Elite 13–90, Pica 11–75. Make your own line-endings.

MEMORANDUM
FROM Managing Director
TO Sales Manager   DATE 21 January 1982
COMPLAINTS
It has come to my notice that orders received from customers are not being acknowledged promptly. Please look into this and report to me immediately.
TN/POS

See **Practical Typing Exercises, Book One**, page 14, for further exercises on

SIDE HEADINGS

These headings are typed to the left of the set left margin. Side headings are usually typed in closed capitals with or without the underscore, but lower case with the underscore may also be used.

The following steps should be taken:

(a) First decide on left and right margins.
(b) Set right margin.
(c) Set a tab stop at the point where you intended to set the left margin.
(d) From the tab stop set in (c) tap in once for each character and space in the longest line of the side headings, plus 3 extra spaces.
(e) Set the left margin at this point.
(f) To type the side headings, use the margin release and bring typing point to tab stop set in (c).

Practise typing side headings

6 Type the following on A4 paper. (a) Double spacing. (b) Set a tab stop at Elite 18, Pica 15 for the side headings. (c) Margins: Elite 36–88, Pica 33–72. (d) Centre the main and sub-heading over the typing line, ie, centre point Elite 53, Pica 43.

LEASING OF MACHINERY

1st January 1982

LONG TERM   At the end of the period you may continue to lease

the machine and the monthly leasing payment becomes

the annual leasing payment.

PAYMENT   All leases are normally paid by Banker's Order or by

Post Office Giro or by cheque.

VALUE ADDED TAX[3] Value Added Tax is chargeable on all charges for

machines leased.

7 Type the following on A5 landscape paper. (a) Single spacing with double between each paragraph. (b) Centre the main heading over the typing line. (c) Set a tab stop at Elite 18, Pica 15, for the side headings. (d) Margins: Elite 33–88, Pica 30–72.

EXTRACT FROM MINUTES OF BOARD MEETING
HELD ON 27 AUGUST 1982

OVERTIME   It was unanimously agreed th overtime payment shd be made in accordance w instructions given in the Union Circular No. 28.

LONG SERVICE Agreed th a cheque for £500 shd be given to ea of the 4 employees who had bn in the co's employment for 40 yrs.

See **Practical Typing Exercises, Book One,** page 40, for further exercises on

PROOF-READING

The most competent typist makes an error occasionally, but that error does not appear in the letter or document placed on the employer's desk for signature. Why? Because the typist has carefully proof-read the work before it has been taken from the machine; the error has been detected and it has been corrected.

While proof-reading has always been an integral part of the typist's training, it is now doubly important because if you wish to operate a word processing machine, your ability to check quickly and correct errors in typing, spelling, grammar, etc, is even more meaningful. Documents prepared on a word processing machine are often used over and over again and you can well imagine the disastrous results if you typed the wrong figures, were careless in checking your finished work, and your original error is then repeated hundreds of times.

5　Type the following memo on a printed A5 memo form or on your own prepared form. Use margins of Elite 13–90, Pica 11–75. Make your own line-endings. Before removing from the machine check carefully and circle any errors.

MEMORANDUM

From　Typing Pool Supervisor

To　All Typists

Date　17 March 1982

It is imperative that you check your typing and if there is an error, correct it while the paper is still in the machine.　You will find it much more difficult to make a neat correction if you have to put the paper back into the machine to make the correction.

When proof-reading, bear in mind the following types of errors:

1　Spelling, punctuation and grammar.
2　Wrong, or inconsistent, spacing.
3　Typographical errors — you struck the wrong key.
4　Word substitution — FROM for FORM, YOU for YOUR, IS for IT, etc.
5　Figures not typed in correct sequence — check with original.
6　Inconsistencies: in use of capitals; in spelling.

One way to prevent errors is to read through the work to be copied and make any amendments in pencil before you start to type.

CAS/ANN

6　Spot the errors

In the exercise below, the sentences in COLUMN ONE have been repeated in COLUMN TWO. Those in COLUMN ONE are correct, but in each sentence in COLUMN TWO there is a typing error. Compare the sentences and see how quickly you can spot the errors. Then type the sentences correctly, looking at COLUMN TWO and keeping COLUMN ONE covered while you do so.

COLUMN ONE	COLUMN TWO
1　Thank you for your letter.	1　Thank you for your letter.
2　Please book the accommodation.	2　Please book the accomodation.
3　Our cheque for £221.00 is here.	3　Our cheque for £212.00 is here.
4　Ask to see that painting.	4　Ask to see the painting.
5　The book is on your desk.	5　The book is on your Desk.
6　His name is Mr B Edwardes.	6　His name is Mr B Edwards.
7　Call in to see me on 12 May.	7　Call in to see me on 12 May
8　He took 3 years to write the book.	8　He took three years to write the book.
9　Send me £20.00.	9　Send me £20.00p.

See **Practical Typing Exercises, Book One,** pages 67–69, for further exercises on

INDENTED PARAGRAPH HEADINGS

See guide given on page 46 for paragraph headings. The paragraphs may also be indented and the headings typed in either of the forms given on page 46. A full stop may also be typed after the paragraph heading, 2 spaces being left after the full stop.

Practise typing paragraph headings with indented paragraphs

4   Type the following on A5 landscape paper. (a) Single spacing with double between paragraphs. (b) Indented paragraphs. (c) Underscore the paragraph headings and type a full stop after each one, as shown. (d) Margins: Elite 13–94, Pica 11–77. (e) Make your own line-endings. (f) Centre the main heading.

TELEX SERVICE

<u>Teleprinters.</u>[2] The Post Office Telex Service provides a fast means of printed communication — the sender and the receiver each have a typed copy of a message sent by teleprinter. A teleprinter has a keyboard similar to that of a typewriter, and to send a message to a particular organisation, dial the telex number of the organisation. If the 'line' is free you will be connected. The sender then types the message on the teleprinter and it is typed automatically, at the same time, on the receiver's teleprinter.

<u>Telex Directories.</u>[2] Subscribers are supplied with a free copy of the United Kingdom Telex Directory.

<u>Extra Equipment.</u>[2] Details of automatic transmitters, receivers, and perforators are available from the Post Office.

SHOULDER HEADINGS

See guide given on page 47 for shoulder headings. The paragraphs that follow the shoulder headings may be indented.

Practise typing indented paragraphs with shoulder headings

5   Type the following exercise on A4 paper. (a) Double spacing. (b) Indented paragraphs. (c) Suitable margins. (d) Centre the main heading. (e) Type the shoulder headings at the left margin in capitals and underscored.

<u>COUNTY BOUNDARY CHANGES</u>

<u>LOCAL GOVERNMENT ACT 1972</u>

trs/   The Local Government Act of 1972 changed the names & boundaries of a no. of counties in Scotland <u>England</u>, & Wales, &, as county names normally form part of the postal address, the Post Office hv asked customers to use the new counties. To avoid confusion, the PO hv said th the counties of <u>Greater Manchester</u> & <u>Hereford & Worcester</u> shld not be used. Towns in these new counties shld be addressed in

NP/   the same way as previously. [It shld be noted th only the county names hv changed, & tth the Post Towns (i.e., towns to wh mail is routed for delivery) & Postcodes hv not bn altered.

<u>POST TOWNS</u>

    Post Towns are an important part of the postal system & on envelopes, & on the letter, shld always be typed on a fresh line in caps. If you do not know the correct Post

uc/   Town for a particular address, check in the Post Office <u>guide</u>.

See **Practical Typing Exercises, Book One**, pages 39 and 40, for further exercises on

CORRECTION OF ERRORS

From now on, if you make an error in your Production Work it must be corrected. Correct the error as soon as you know you have made a mistake and read through the whole exercise when you have finished typing it and while the paper is still in the machine, in case there is an error you had not noticed before.

There are various methods which may be used to correct errors:

(a) Rubber

(i) Turn up the paper so that the error is on top of the platen or paper table.

(ii) Press the paper tightly against the platen or paper table to prevent slipping.

(iii) Erase the error by rubbing gently up and down, blowing away rubber dust as you do so. (Too much pressure may cause a hole.)

(iv) If you are using a new or heavily inked ribbon, erase first with a soft rubber and then with a typewriter eraser.

(v) Turn paper back to writing line and insert correct letter or letters.

(vi) Always use a clean rubber.

NOTE: If the typewriter has a carriage, move it to the extreme right or left to prevent rubber dust from falling into the mechanism of the machine.

(b) Correction Paper

This specially-coated strip of paper is placed in front of the printing point over the error, and the incorrect letter is typed again through the correction paper. The letter will then be covered with a film of powder and the correct letter may be typed on top.

(c) Correction Fluid

This correction fluid is produced in various shades to match the typing paper and is applied with a small brush. The incorrect letter is obliterated and when the fluid is dry, the correct letter may be typed over the top. The liquid may be spirit- or water-based. If the spirit-based liquid is used, it is necessary to add thinner to the bottle as, after a time, the original liquid tends to thicken. Spirit-based liquid dries more quickly than water-based.

7 Type the following exercise on A4 paper. (a) Margins: Elite 22–82, Pica 12–72. (b) Double spacing. (c) Check carefully and correct any typing errors.

BUSINESS EXHIBITION

The business exhibition will have 2 venues this year. The first will be in London from 8-11 June, and then later on in the year it will be held in Manchester. One aim of the exhibition is to provide the smaller businessman with the opportunity to compete on equal terms with his larger counterpart.

One aspect of this is that a maximum of 6 stands can be booked by any one company thus preventing the larger companies swamping the smaller.

Over 500 stands have already been booked for the exhibition.

HEADINGS CENTRED IN THE TYPING LINE

To centre headings in the typing line, find the centre point of the line by adding the 2 margins together and dividing by 2. Then backspace from this point, one space for every 2 characters and spaces in the heading.

Examples: Margins set at Elite 22 & 82   22+82 = 104 ÷ 2 = 52 (centre point)
                              Pica 12 & 72   12+72 = 84 ÷ 2 = 42 (centre point)
                             Elite 18 & 88   18+88 = 106 ÷ 2 = 53 (centre point)

A   Main headings centred

See guide given on page 45 for main headings. Centred headings are generally used with indented paragraphs. The heading is centred in the typing line.

B   Sub-headings centred

See guide given on page 45 for sub-headings. If the main heading is centred it is usual to centre the sub-heading in the typing line.

Practise centring main and sub-headings

3   Type the following exercise on A4 paper in double spacing throughout, ie do NOT turn up extra spaces between paragraphs. (a) Centre the headings in the typing line. (b) Indented paragraphs. (c) Margins: Elite 18–88, Pica 15–72. (d) Make your own line-endings.

DRIVER'S LICENCE

"L" Tests

Before you are allowed to drive a motor vehicle, you must pass a driving test which has to satisfy an examiner that you can handle your vehicle with safety, whatever the traffic conditions.

The "L" tests were started on 9 June 1935. In that year 83 per cent of candidates passed. In 1975 the pass rate was 45 per cent. Forty million tests have been carried out and the demand has risen from 246,000 in 1935 to 1,621,000 in 1974. The peak year for tests was 1967 with a total of 2,010,000.

In 1934 there were 2,400,000 licensed vehicles; in 1974 there were 17,300,000.

NOTE: No extra spaces when using double spacing and indented paragraphs

See **Practical Typing Exercises, Book One,** page 39, for further exercises on

Consolidation

PRODUCTION TYPING

NOTE: In the consolidation exercises you must carry out any instructions given. Where there are no instructions, you should follow the layout indicated and apply the theory points covered in previous units. What is important is that the final typing will look good and that there are no typing errors—you will have corrected them before taking the paper from the machine.

Margins: If the exact margins are not given use the following as a guide:

	Left margin Elite Pica	Right margin Elite Pica
A4	19 16 (1½"—38 mm)	88 72 (1"—25 mm)
A5 landscape	19 16 (1½"—38 mm)	88 72 (1"—25 mm)
A5 portrait	13 11 (1"—25 mm)	64 53 (½"—13 mm)

NB   Left and right margins may be equal but the right margin is NEVER wider than the left.

Job 8   Production Target—6 minutes

Centre the following exercise vertically and horizontally on A5 portrait paper.

2 December 1982

£8.50 plus 15% VAT

PALACE HOTEL, BLACKPOOL

Leave 2 clear spaces

M E N U

Leave 2 clear spaces

DINNER

Tomato Soup
Chilled Melon

Roast Beef and Yorkshire Pudding
Creamed Potatoes
Carrots/Beans/Cabbage
Horseradish Sauce

Chocolate Slice
Apple Pie and Fresh Cream

Coffee

Check your work and correct any errors before removing the paper from the machine

---

Job 9   Production Target—6 minutes

Type the following exercise on A5 landscape paper. (a) Margins: Left 1½" (38 mm), Right 1" (25 mm). (b) Single spacing with double between paragraphs.

SPECIAL CONDITIONS OF PURCHASE

QUOTATIONS   These should be submitted in triplicate and on the contractors' printed headings. Prices should be in the currency of the country of origin.

DELIVERY   The delivery period of the equipment forming the subject of the order should be indicated, and this should be firm for 30 days.

PAYMENT   Our conditions of payment are: 80% against shipping documents and 20% on the starting up of the installation and after the approval of the engineers has been obtained.

Technique development

HORIZONTAL CENTRING—ALL LINES CENTRED

Follow the points given for horizontal centring on page 34, but do not set a left margin, and centre every line, not just the longest one. For this purpose set a tab stop at the centre point of the paper, and backspace one space for every 2 characters and spaces as before.

VERTICAL CENTRING

To centre the matter vertically on a sheet of paper follow the points (a) to (f) as given on page 36.

Practise horizontal and vertical centring

1   Type the following notice on A5 portrait paper. Set a tab stop at the centre point, ie, Elite 35, Pica 29, and centre each line horizontally and the whole notice vertically.

ANNUAL GENERAL MEETING

↓

of the   2 clear spaces

S O C I A L   C L U B

will be held on

FRIDAY 14 JULY

at 12 noon

in the Main Hall
↓   2 clear spaces
All members are requested to attend

2   Type the following notice on A5 landscape paper. Set a tab stop at the centre point, ie, Elite 50, Pica 41 and centre each line horizontally and the whole notice vertically.

A N N U A L   D I N N E R

will be held

on 31 January 1982

at the

GRAND HOTEL

Reception 7 p.m.

Tickets obtainable from the

SOCIAL CLUB SECRETARY

See **Practical Typing Exercises, Book One,** pages 37 and 38, for further exercises on
**Horizontal Centring—All Lines Centred
Vertical Centring**

Centre the following table vertically and horizontally on suitable paper.

SOME POST TOWNS WITH NEW AND OLD COUNTIES

POST TOWN	NEW COUNTY	OLD COUNTY
Aberystwyth	Dyfed	Cardiganshire
Barmouth	Gwynedd	Merioneth
Bilston	West Midlands	Staffordshire
Birkenhead	Merseyside	Cheshire
Bradford	West Yorkshire	Yorkshire
Dudley	West Midlands	Worcestershire

Job 11   Production Target—9 minutes

Type the following exercise on A4 paper. (a) Double spacing. (b) Margins: Elite 20–85, pica 12–77.

INTERCHANGE SYSTEMS LTD

The Ultimate in Word Processing

Our products enable you to obtain the benefit of low and high cost systems — £3,000 to £950,000.

Other benefits:

1 Once trained the operator can operate any of our word processing systems — no need for retraining.

2 Choice of daisy wheel printers

(a) Standard — 15 inch paper capacity

(b) Wide — 20.5 inch paper capacity

(c) Ten and 12 pitch.

Check your work and correct any errors before removing the paper from the machine

SKILL BUILDING

Type each exercise (A, B and C) 3 times. Keep your eyes on the copy while you type and also when returning the carriage/carrier.

Margins: Elite 22–82, Pica 12–72

A Review alphabet keys

1   If she makes a determined and real effort, we are quite sure she will very quickly be enjoying a high place with the experts, and may win a valuable prize.

B Improve control of figure keys

2 wee 233 our 974 try 546 ere 343 wit 285 ire 843 too 599 678.

3 330 339 338 337 336 992 993 994 995 123 456 789 101 293 234.

4 Final 7%, payable 3rd August, making 12½%. Profit £456,890.

5 Flight 417 leaves at 1350, while Flight 1482 leaves at 1619.

C Build accuracy on common suffix drill

6 using ending asking making turning morning replying advising

7 comment shipment equipment settlement adjustment arrangement

8 We will not comment about the shipments of equipment to you.

9 In the morning we shall be asking him what car he is taking.

Accuracy/speed practice   30 wpm   2 minutes   Not more than 2 errors

Note: Use indented paragraphs

A/S 47   Some large offices have a pool of typists who share the | 11
work to be done, but we do not know whether or not this is a | 23
good plan. This is a matter which must be left to each firm | 35
to decide, based on the amount of work which has to be done, | 47
and on the staff employed. You may like working in a typing | 59
pool. (SI 1.17) | 60

A/S 48   With the keen competition which we have to face both at | 11
home and abroad, we must do our best to bring up to date all | 23
our equipment. It is only by doing so that we shall be able | 35
to increase our output, and so reduce our costs. In my view | 47
it is essential to decide here and now on the best course to | 59
take. (SI 1.25) | 60

1 | 2 | 3 | 4 | 5 | 6 | 7 | 8 | 9 | 10 | 11 | 12 |

Record your progress   2 minutes

R 21   Since the beginning of the year we have employed about | 11
275 more men than ever before, and 340 more than last year. | 23
Under our new profit scheme we should like to pay 5% to the | 34
workmen and 5% to the staff, and we shall require at least | 46
£10,000 extra to enable us to do so. Your Board proposes to | 58
add another £15,000 to the reserve fund, bringing it up to | 69
£275,000. (SI 1.27) | 71

1 | 2 | 3 | 4 | 5 | 6 | 7 | 8 | 9 | 10 | 11 | 12 |

Accuracy/speed—2 minutes at 30 wpm
Record Your Progress—2 minutes

Type the following exercise on A4 paper. Left margin: 1½″ (38 mm), right margin: 1″ (25 mm)

BATHROOM FITTINGS

BATHS

The standard size for baths is 1700 mm × 700 mm, but lots of other sizes are available. They can be made from cast iron, pressed steel or an acrylic material.

BASINS

The material most commonly used for basins is vitreous china, but they can be made from metal or marble. The most common shape of basin is the pedestal type with a central 'stem' to support the basin bowl. Standard sizes are 635 mm × 455 mm and 560 mm × 405 mm.

SHOWERS

Five or 6 showers can usually be taken with the water that would be used for one hot bath. To install a shower separately from a bath, you would need a floor area of about 91 cm (3 ft) square. It is important to remember when you are installing a shower that you must have a good 'head of water', at least 1 m (39 in) between the bottom of the cold water tank and the shower rose.

Job 13　　　　　　　　　　　　　　Production Target—9 minutes

Display the following table on A5 landscape paper. (a) Double spacing. (b) Leave 3 spaces between the columns. (c) Centre the table vertically and horizontally.

METRIC UNITS FOR CERTAIN COMMODITIES

METRES	CENTIMETRES	MILLIMETRES	KILOGRAMS
Fabric length	Clothing	Lawn mowers	Butter
Carpet width	Fabric width	Kitchen units	Tea
Carpet length	Blankets	Shoes	Sugar
Timber length	Sheets	Hardware	Chocolates

6 Type the following on A5 landscape paper. (a) Margins: Left 1½″ (38 mm), Right 1″ (25 mm). (b) Single spacing. (c) Hanging paragraphs.

Open punctuation takes less time and space than full punctuation and it is therefore wise to adopt this method from the beginning of your typewriting training.

If a name and address appear in a heading or in one line in the text, and open punctuation is being used, it should be typed with commas between each item, eg, Mr J Appleton, 12 Grange Drive, Bury, BL8 2BG.

7 Type the following exercise on A5 landscape paper. (a) Margins: Elite 22–82, Pica 12–72. (b) Single spacing with double between each paragraph. (c) Make your own right margin. (d) Open punctuation. (e) Note the use of abbreviations. (f) Indented paragraphs.

When typing measurements always use the small 'x' for the multiply sign, and leave one space either side of the 'x', eg, 20 (space) ft (space) × (space) 10 (space) ft = 20 ft × 10 ft. The same spacing is necessary when using metric measurements, eg, 1 m = 100 cm; 1 m = 1000 mm; 1 m × 1000 = 1 km.

NOTE use of apostrophe for feet and double quotation marks for inches

You can also use the sign for feet and inches, eg, 20 ft 10 in × 15 ft 9 in = 20' 10" × 15' 9". You will see that, when using the sign, there is no space between the figures and the sign, but there is one space after the sign.

Do not add 's' to the plural of ft, in, lb, m, kg, etc. In imperial measurements a full stop is used after an abbreviation when using full punctuation, but in metric measurements full stops are never used after symbols even with full punctuation, except at the end of a sentence, eg, 210 mm × 297 mm.

8 Type the following exercise on A4 paper. (a) Margins: Elite 22–82, Pica 12–72. (b) Single spacing with double between each paragraph. (c) Full punctuation. (d) Blocked paragraphs.

As a typist in business, or in a typewriting examination, you wl be expected to remember and apply certain points of theory.

When writing to individuals, a courtesy title is essential. If you do not know whether a lady is Mrs. or Miss, type Ms. A man shd be addressed as Mr. or Esq., never both. If you use the courtesy title Dr. or Rev., do not use Mr. or Esq. [The word "Messrs." is used as a courtesy NP title for partnerships, e.g., Messrs. Barnes & Sons, Messrs. Rodney & Smith.

It is usual to hv the left margin slightly wider than the right margin — except in display and tabulation work. When using A4 paper for business letters do not hv a left margin of less than 1" (25 mm) and the right margin shd not be less than half an inch (13 mm).

See **Practical Typing Exercises**, Book One, page 36, for further exercises on

Type the following memo on a printed form, or on your own prepared memo form.

FROM Mrs B K Tomkinson
To   Mr P Llewellyn
DATE 20 October 1982
CALENDARS — 1983/1984

I have just received from the printers, the calendars for 1983/1984. I am enclosing a copy for you to see. It is a pity that the days of the week have not been printed in a bolder type, but otherwise I feel it is quite effective, and should prove to be a good advertising venture.
We are distributing them to over 150 of our customers.
BKT/JC
Enc

Job 15—Spot the errors

Read the following passage carefully. Each line contains an error that may be spelling, spacing, line-end division, hyphenation, etc. When you have found and noted the errors, type the corrected passage using margins of Elite 22–82, Pica 12–72. Do not type the numbers.

Line
number

1	Their are 2 basic systems for keying data into a computer	
2	system: one is on-line and one is off-line. An on-line	
3	input device is connected directly to the storage or proc-	Key on
4	essing unit of a computor system; when a key is struck, the	page
5	data is instantaneously recorded and stored. Off line devices	172
6	are independent of the computer in operation, and they tem-	
7	porarily store the data on punched cards, tapes, diskettes	
8	and so on.	

Type the following exercise on A5 portrait paper. (a) Double spacing and insert extra spaces where appropriate. (b) Margins: Elite 13–63, Pica 6–56.

OFFICE STATIONERY

Many firms have the rule that stationery supplies must be requisitioned on definite days or at certain times.
Arrange your own supplies neatly in the drawers of your desk or cupboard.
If at any time you notice that you need fresh supplies of a particular item, enter full details at once in your desk diary under the next requisition date.
The good secretary always has the necessary tools to do her job properly.

See **Practical Typing Exercises, Book One**, pages 67–69 for further exercises on
Proof-Reading

PARAGRAPHING

Paragraphs are used to separate the different subjects or sections. This breaks the writing into short passages to facilitate reading and understanding. There are 3 different forms of paragraphing, viz, blocked, indented and hanging.

A Blocked paragraphs

Practise typing blocked paragraphs

3   Type the following on A5 landscape paper. (a) Margins: Left 2″ (51 mm), Right 1½″ (38 mm). (b) Single spacing with double between each paragraph. (c) Blocked paragraphs.

As you have already learnt, in blocked paragraphs all lines start at the same scale-point.

When single spacing is used, as in this exercise, you turn up 2 single spaces between the paragraphs.

However, when double spacing is used you should turn up 2 double between each paragraph.

B Indented paragraphs

When using indented paragraphs the first line of each paragraph is indented 5 spaces from the left margin. This indentation is made by setting a tab stop 5 spaces from the point fixed for the left margin. When using indented paragraphs, 2 single spaces only should be turned up between paragraphs, whether typing in single or double spacing.

Practise typing indented paragraphs

4   Type the following on A5 landscape paper. (a) Margins: Elite 22–82, Pica 12–72. (b) Single spacing with double between each paragraph. (c) Set a tab stop at 27(17) for the paragraph indentation.

Insert the paper so that the top edge is flush with the top edge of the alignment scale. Then turn up 7 single spaces.

Return carriage twice on single

⟶

You should then have a clear 25 mm margin above the first line of typing. It is incorrect to have a top margin of less than 25 mm.

C Hanging Paragraphs

Practise typing hanging paragraphs

5   After reading through the exercise type it on A5 landscape paper. (a) Margins: Elite 22–82, Pica 12–72. (b) Single spacing with double between each paragraph. (c) Hanging paragraphs as shown.

A third type of paragraph is known as a hanging paragraph. This means that the first line of the paragraph starts 2 spaces to the left of the second and subsequent lines as in this exercise.

Hanging paragraphs are sometimes used in display work to draw attention to particular points.

SKILL BUILDING

Type exercises A, B and C 3 times. Keep your eyes on the copy while you type and also when returning the carriage/carrier.

Margins: Elite 22–82, Pica 12–72

A Review alphabet keys

1 The big cyclist, known as Jack, seemed quite relaxed when he received first prize at the end of the arduous rides through the snow and ice of the mountains.

B Improve control of figure keys

2 ewe 323 woe 293 our 974 rye 463 you 697 tour 5974 writ 2485.
3 Type 1 and 2 and 3 and 4 and 15 and 16 and 17 and 80 and 90.
4 Drill: 10, 29, 38, 47, 56, 234, 567, 890, 010, 343, 678, 86.
5 Accounts: 00-11-2345, 00-12-6789, 00-13-5858, 00-14-2679-80.

C Improve control of shift key

6 Dear Sir, Yours truly, Mr J Brown, New York, Hong Kong, Miss
7 Dear Mr Brown, Dear Mrs Green, Yours faithfully, Miss R Grey
8 Hamburg-America Line, 109 Jermyn Street, New York, 10040 NY.
9 We do not want every Tom, Dick and Harry to apply in August.

Accuracy/speed practice   28 wpm   One minute   Not more than one error

A/S 32 Each year there are some new typewriters for you to use, and   12
you must know about them so that you are up to date when you   24
wish to change jobs. (SI 1.11)   28

A/S 33 A computer is now being made that will store voice patterns.   12
It will know your voice when you speak to it, and it will be   24
able to reply to you. (SI 1.21)   28

A/S 34 Will this computer mean that you will not be needed any more   12
in your job of work? It is not likely, as it will take many   24
years to produce it. (SI 1.25)   28

    1 | 2 | 3 | 4 | 5 | 6 | 7 | 8 | 9 | 10 | 11 | 12 |

Record your progress   One minute

R 15 For a great number of years we have been specialists in many   12
kinds of fitted carpets — all of our selling and our fitting   24
staff having spent their whole lives in this trade. All our   36
work is done by experts. (SI 1.24)   41

    1 | 2 | 3 | 4 | 5 | 6 | 7 | 8 | 9 | 10 | 11 | 12 |

Accuracy/speed—One minute at 28 wpm
Record Your Progress—One minute

(iii) Abbreviations always used

Open punctuation	Full punctuation	
eg	e.g.	exempli gratia—for example
etc	etc.	et cetera—and others
ie	i.e.	id est—that is
NB	N.B.	Nota Bene—note well
viz	viz.	videlicet—namely
Esq	Esq.	Esquire
Messrs	Messrs.	Messieurs—Gentlemen
Mr	Mr.	
Mrs	Mrs.	
Ms	Ms.	

NOTES:
There is no space in the middle of an abbreviation.

Miss is not an abbreviation and does not require a full stop.

Practise typing abbreviations with open punctuation

1 Type the following sentences on A5 landscape paper. (a) Note the use of abbreviations. (b) Margins: Elite 22–82, Pica 12–72. (c) Blocked paragraphs. (d) Single spacing with double between each group of sentences. (e) Open punctuation.

Use the abbreviation Ltd in the name of a limited company (or PLC in a public limited company) if that is how it appears in the printed letterhead.

The book is printed in 3 volumes. Vol 2 has 600 pages, but Vol 3 is not so bulky, as it has only 400 pages.

The room measured 26 ft 4 in × 14 ft 2 in.

Mr & Mrs J F Browne arrived at 2 pm, ie, 10 minutes early.

Mr S V Gordon has addressed the parcel to Messrs Trent Bros instead of to Johnson & Co Ltd.

A top margin of at least 25 mm should be used when typing on plain paper.

Practise typing abbreviations with full punctuation

2 Type the following sentences on A5 landscape paper. (a) Margins: Elite 22–82, Pica 12–72. (b) Blocked paragraphs. (c) Single spacing with double between each group of sentences. (d) Full punctuation. (e) On completion compare with the previous exercise. NOTE: One space after a full stop at the end of an abbreviation. No space after a medial full stop within an abbreviation.

Use the abbreviation Ltd. in the name of a limited company (or P.L.C. in a public limited company) if that is how it appears in the printed letterhead.

The book is printed in 3 volumes. Vol. 2 has 600 pages, but Vol. 3 is not so bulky, as it has only 400 pages.

The room measured 26 ft. 4 in. × 14 ft. 2 in.

Mr. & Mrs. J. F. Browne arrived at 2 p.m., i.e., 10 minutes early.

Mr. S. V. Gordon has addressed the parcel to Messrs. Trent Bros. instead of to Johnson & Co. Ltd.

A top margin of at least 25 mm should be used when typing on plain paper.

See **Practical Typing Exercises, Book One**, page 35, for further exercises on

Technique development

BUSINESS LETTERS—OPEN PUNCTUATION—FULLY BLOCKED

Letters are ambassadors and advertisements for the firm who sends them. You must therefore ensure that your letters are well-displayed and faultlessly typed. Each firm has its own method of display but the examples which follow are in fully-blocked style (sometimes known as blocked) where every line begins at the left margin.

<table>
<tr><td>Telephone
0274 3669</td><td style="text-align:center">N J JOHNSON PLC
Registered Office
24 High Street · BRADFORD
West Yorkshire · BD4 9HU</td><td>Registered Number
53287 England</td></tr>
</table>

Turn up 2 single spaces

1	Reference	Our Ref JH/MB	

Turn up 2 single spaces

2	Date	9 March 1982

Turn up 2 single spaces

3	Attention of	FOR THE ATTENTION OF THE BUYER

Turn up 2 single spaces

4	Addressee	A Wilkes & Sons Ltd Hartfield Road NORTHAMPTON Northants NN1 2HX

Turn up 2 single spaces

5	Salutation	Dear Sirs

Turn up 2 single spaces

6	Subject heading	ENQUIRY FOR QUOTATION

Turn up 2 single spaces

7	Body	We have pleasure in referring to our Mr Richmond's call on Wednesday of last week, and, as requested, we attach our estimate for the woven material about which you enquired. You will no doubt recall that the quality of the material previously purchased by you is a special weave, and, as prices have risen considerably since our last supply, we are taking the opportunity of quoting you for an alternative.

Turn up 2 single spaces

8	Complimentary close	Yours faithfully

Turn up 1 single space

9	Name of firm	N J JOHNSON PLC

Turn up 5 single spaces

10	Name of signatory	MISS JOAN HARPER
11	Designation	SALES ASSISTANT

Turn up minimum of 2 single spaces

12	Enclosure	Enc

OPEN PUNCTUATION

1 You will see from the business letter set out above that no punctuation is inserted in the reference, date, name and address of addressee, and salutation.
2 In the body of the letter, the points mentioned on page 26 apply.
3 There is no punctuation in the complimentary close or in any of the wording which follows it.

PRINTED LETTERHEAD—when using paper with a printed heading, turn up 2 single spaces before typing the reference.

OPEN PUNCTUATION

Up to this point in the book all the exercises have been displayed with open punctuation. This means that full stops have not been inserted after abbreviations, and letters have been typed with the omission of commas after each line of the address, and after the salutation and complimentary close. The modern trend is to omit punctuation in those cases as it simplifies and speeds up the work of the typist. However, punctuation is always inserted in sentences, so that the grammatical sense is clear.

FULL PUNCTUATION

It is also acceptable to insert punctuation after abbreviations and after each line of an address as well as after the salutation and complimentary close. Grammatical punctuation is always inserted. Open and full punctuation must NEVER be mixed: a document must be typed in either open or full punctuation.

ABBREVIATIONS

In typewritten work abbreviations should not, as a rule, be used. There are, however, a few standard abbreviations which are never typed in full, and others which may be used in certain circumstances. Study the following lists, so that you will know when not to use abbreviations and when it is permissible to use them. You must always be consistent in their use.

(i) Used in the cases indicated

Open punctuation	Full punctuation	
Ltd	Ltd.	Limited. Used only in names of private limited companies. It must be typed in full if that is how it appears in the printed letterhead.
PLC or plc	P.L.C. or p.l.c.	Public Limited Company. Used in names of public limited companies. It may be typed in full or abbreviated.
Co	Co.	Company. Used only in names of companies. It must be typed in full if that is how it appears in the printed letterhead.
OHMS	O.H.M.S.	On Her Majesty's Service. Usually abbreviated but occasionally typed in full.
PS	PS.	Postscript. Used only at the foot of a letter.
v	v.	Versus. May be abbreviated or typed in full. It is usual to follow the copy.
&	&	And, known as the 'ampersand'. Used in names of firms, such as Smith & Brown, and in numbers such as Nos 34 & 35 (Nos. 34 & 35).
@	@	At. Used only in invoices, quotations and similar documents.
%	%	Per centum. May be abbreviated or typed in full. It is usual to follow the copy.
Bros	Bros.	Brothers. Used only in the names of companies.

(ii) Used with figures only

am	a.m.	ante meridiem—before noon	
pm	p.m.	post meridiem—after noon	
in	in.	inch(es)	
ft	ft.	foot (feet)	
g	g	gramme(s)	Punctuation is
kg	kg	kilogram(s)	NEVER used in metric
mm	mm	millimetre(s)	abbreviations
m	m	metre(s)	
km	km	kilometre(s)	

1 Reference—Our Ref, Your Ref
    (a) Type at the left margin or in the space provided on the headed paper.
    (b) In their simplest forms they consist of the dictator's and typist's initials, eg, AMD/ACM.

2 Date
    (a) Correct order is day, month, year, eg, 3 May 1982. Never type the month in figures.
    (b) Turn up 2 single spaces after reference and type date at left margin. (c) No punctuation.

3 For the attention of
    (a) Some companies adopt the rule that all correspondence should be addressed to the company and not to individual persons by name. The sender of a letter may wish it to reach or be dealt with by a particular person or department. This is indicated by typing the words FOR THE ATTENTION OF . . . at the left margin and 2 single spaces below the date. (b) No punctuation.
    (c) The modern tendency is to type in capitals without the underscore.

4 Addressee (Inside address)
    (a) Turn up 2 single spaces after FOR THE ATTENTION OF and type name and address of addressee at left margin. (If there is no FOR THE ATTENTION OF line, then turn up 2 single spaces after the date before typing the name of the addressee.)
    (b) No punctuation. (c) Single spacing. (d) Each item on a separate line.
    (e) Name of post town in capitals.

5 Salutation
    (a) Turn up 2 single spaces after the last line of the address and type the salutation at left margin. (b) No punctuation.

6 Subject heading
    (a) Turn up 2 single spaces after the salutation and type at the left margin.
    (b) Usually typed in capitals when it need not be underscored. (c) No punctuation.

7 Body of letter
    (a) Turn up 2 single spaces after salutation and type the paragraphs—each line starts at the left margin.
    (b) Type in single spacing with double between paragraphs.
    (c) Short letters may be typed in double spacing.

8 Complimentary close
    (a) Turn up 2 single spaces after the last line of last paragraph and type at left margin.
    (b) No punctuation.

9 Name of firm sending the letter
    (a) Some companies type the name of their firm immediately after the complimentary close.
    (b) Turn up one single space after complimentary close and type name of firm.
    (c) Type at left margin. (d) No punctuation.

10 Name of signatory
    (a) Turn up 5 single spaces after the complimentary close (or name of firm if there is one) before typing the name of the person who will sign the letter.
    (b) Type at left margin. (c) No punctuation. (d) A lady may wish to insert a title (Mrs/Miss/Ms) either before her name or in brackets after her name.

11 Designation
    (a) After the name of the person signing the letter, turn up one single space and type the designation (official position of the person signing the letter).
    (b) Type at left margin. (c) No punctuation.

12 Enclosure
    (a) The inclusion of papers or documents in a letter is indicated by typing the abbreviation Enc (or Encs if more than one) at the left margin.
    (b) Turn up a minimum of 2 single spaces after the designation. (c) No punctuation.

SKILL BUILDING

In exercises A, B and C, type each line or sentence 3 times. If time permits, complete your practice by typing each group of lines as it appears. Keep your eyes on the copy while you type and also when returning the carriage/carrier.

Margins: Elite 22–82, Pica 12–72

A Review alphabet keys

1 As the young musician, who wore a jacket of vivid colouring, strolled slowly round the piazza, the quaint sounds from his guitar and his relaxed manner reflected the evening calm.

B Speed up control of shift key

2 Ben More, Great Yarmouth, New Haven, Victoria Road, Cheddar.

3 Weston-super-Mare, Port Talbot, Jedburgh, Upton, Iver, Stow.

4 Great Yarmouth is in the county of Norfolk; Cheddar in Avon.

5 New Haven, Conn, USA. Upton-upon-Severn, Worcs, Gt Britain.

C Speed up control of space bar

6 For the fit old men, the new day will be one of fun and joy.

7 We will go to the park in time to see the start of the game.

8 One of the best ways to gain speed is to type easy material.

9 He is on the way. I am to go to the boat in that bay. Yes.

Accuracy/speed practice   30 wpm   1½ minutes   Not more than one error

A/S 45 You will be pleased to learn that we have made more machines   12
this year than we did last year, and that we are also making   24
all vital spare parts. Over the next 12 months we shall not   36
need orders as we are to produce new models. (SI 1.18)   45

A/S 46 There is nothing that annoys a businessman more than clerks   12
who forget to do jobs given to them. A very good idea is to   24
have a pad on your desk, so that you can write down straight   36
away anything that you may be required to do. (SI 1.27)   45

1 | 2 | 3 | 4 | 5 | 6 | 7 | 8 | 9 | 10 | 11 | 12 |

Record your progress   1½ minutes

R 20 We have had your name and address on our list since January,   12
but although we have, from time to time, sent you details of   24
properties, we have not heard from you. If you still desire   36
to buy a country residence, please complete and return to us   48
the attached form, so that we may know what the position is.   60
(SI 1.28)

1 | 2 | 3 | 4 | 5 | 6 | 7 | 8 | 9 | 10 | 11 | 12 |

Accuracy/speed—1½ minutes at 30 wpm
Record Your Progress—1½ minutes

NOTE: A suitable printed heading for this and other letters is given in the HANDBOOK AND SOLUTIONS MANUAL. PLC stands for Public Limited Company: for an explanation see page 84.

Practise typing fully-blocked letter with open punctuation.

1 Type the following letter on A5 portrait paper. (a) If you are not using headed paper, turn up 7 single spaces before typing Our ref. (b) Margins: Elite 13–63, Pica 6–56. (c) Keep to the spacing and layout indicated.

Telephone 0283 0246   Telex 848756

Midland Furniture Co. Ltd.

Registered Office : BROAD STREET
BURTON-ON-TRENT
STAFFORDSHIRE
DE14 1RF

Registered No. 740051 England

1 Reference	Our ref HGS/HOS	Turn up 2 single spaces
2 Date	7 October 1982	Turn up 2 single spaces
4 Name and address of addressee	N J Johnson PLC 24 High Street BRADFORD West Yorkshire BD4 9HU	Turn up·2 single spaces
5 Salutation	Dear Sirs	Turn up 2 single spaces Turn up 2 single spaces
7 Body of letter	Our representative, Mr J Smith, will be in your district next week, and will take the opportunity of calling on you on Wednesday next, 13 October, at 10 am.	Turn up 2 single spaces
	If this date is not suitable, please let me know when it will be convenient for you to see Mr Smith.	Turn up 2 single spaces
8 Complimentary close	Yours faithfully	Turn up 5 single spaces
10 Signatory 11 Designation	H G SIMMONS SALES MANAGER	Turn up one single space

2 Type the following letter on a sheet of A5 portrait paper. (a) If you are not using headed paper, turn up 7 single spaces before typing Our ref. (b) Margins: Elite 13–63, Pica 6–56. (c) The details as far as the salutation are exactly as those in the letter above. (d) After typing the salutation, turn up 2 single spaces and then type the following paragraphs.

Thank you for telephoning me this afternoon. As I explained to you, a letter is already in the post about Mr Smith's proposed visit.

I now confirm that Mr Smith will be pleased to call on you on Thursday, 14 October, at 2 pm.

(e) The complimentary close, etc, is the same as in the letter above.

See **Practical Typing Exercises, Book One**, page 16, for further exercises on

Part Two

This part covers open and full punctuation, blocked and semi-blocked letters, blocked and centred display, and blocked and centred tabulation.

CONTENTS

Practise typing a letter with ATTENTION line and enclosure

3 Type the following letter on A4 paper. (a) If you are not using headed paper, turn up 7 single spaces before typing Our Ref. (b) Use margins of Elite 25–80, Pica 15–70. (c) Keep to the spacing and layout indicated.

Telephone
0274 3669

N. J. JOHNSON PLC

Registered Number
53287 England

Registered Office

24 HIGH STREET · BRADFORD
WEST YORKSHIRE · BD4 9HU

Turn up 2 single spaces

Our Ref ABC/DEF

Turn up 2 single spaces

19 February 1982

Turn up 2 single spaces

3 Attention of FOR THE ATTENTION OF MR J WHITE

Turn up 2 single spaces

Midland Furniture Co Ltd
Broad Street
BURTON-ON-TRENT
Staffordshire
DE14 1RF

Turn up 2 single spaces

Dear Sirs

Turn up 2 single spaces

We enclose a cheque for £4,680 in settlement of the attached statement. You will notice that we have deducted the sum of £120, representing $2\frac{1}{2}\%$ discount, as in your letter of 21 January 1982 you agreed to allow us this discount for prompt payment.

Will you please confirm that you will continue to allow us this cash discount.

Yours faithfully

A B COOKE
Secretary

Turn up minimum of
2 single spaces

12 Enclosure   Enc

4 Type the following letter on a sheet of A4 paper. (a) Margins: Elite 25–80, Pica 15–70. (b) The details as far as the salutation are the same as the letter above except for the date which is 27 February 1982. (c) After typing the salutation, turn up 2 spaces and then type the following paragraphs.

Further to our letter of 19 February, we have received another 3 invoices from you and the $2\frac{1}{2}\%$ discount has not been deducted.

As we are anxious to clarify the position, would you please ask your Mr Smith to call and see us on Thursday or Friday afternoon of next week.

The 3 invoices referred to above are enclosed.

(d) The complimentary close, etc, is the same as the letter above but, as there are 3 enclosures, the notation Encs must be used.

See **Practical Typing Exercises, Book One,** page 17, for further exercises on

UNIT 37   Business Letters—Attention Line and Enclosures   75

Type the following exercise on a sheet of A4 paper.

BACKING SHEETS

To prevent damage to the cylinder of the typewriter, always use a backing sheet. Other uses of the backing sheet are:

I　Typing on cards and memoranda

when typing on cards and memoranda, you may hv, of necessity, to type near the bottom. To ensure th yr typewriter grips the card (paper) & thus prevents the bottom line(s) fr "running off" the paper, always use a backing sheet. In fact, whenever you hv to type within one inch of

c.c.　the bottom, always use a Backing Sheet wh extends below the bottom of the page.

II　Aid to centring　　　　　　　vertical

On your backing sheet rule a / line down the centre & also a heavy horizontal line across the centre. This wl help you when centring material on a page.

III　Top and bottom margins

top/h　with the underscore type a line on the seventh single space fr the / edge of the paper. This wl remind you th you always turn up 7 single spaces before you start to type. Likewise, one inch fr the bottom of the backing sheet draw a dark horizontal line to remind you th you are nearing the bottom of the page.

Job 35—Spot the errors　　　　　　Proof-reading Target—2 minutes
　　　　　　　　　　　　　　　　　　Typing Target　　　　—5 minutes

Read the following passage carefully. Each line contains an error that may be spelling, spacing, line-end division, hyphenation, etc. When you have found and marked the errors, type the corrected passage using margins of Elite 22–82, Pica 12–72. Do not type the figures on the left-hand side.

Line
number

1	Typists who are going to use word proceing equipment must
2	be trained in setting up reports and table for all types of
3	documents and correspondence. They must have excellent editt-
4	ing skills and , in the first instance, be proficient in
5	operating the typewriter at speed & with a high standard of
6	acuracy. The skilled word processor operator will have been
7	trained to high degree of proficiency in the use of the
8	type writer.

Key on
page 172

See **Practical Typing Exercises, Book One**, pages 67–69, for further exercises on
Proof-Reading

5   Type the following letter on A4 paper. (a) Margins: Elite 22–82, Pica 12–72.

Ref JH/MB

9 March 1982

FOR THE ATTENTION OF THE BUYER

A Wilkes & Sons Ltd
Hartfield Road
NORTHAMPTON
Northants
NN1 2HX

Dear Sirs   Turn up 2 single spaces

6 Subject   ENQUIRY FOR QUOTATION   Turn up 2 single spaces
Heading

We have pleasure in referring to our Mr Richmond's call on
Wednesday of last week, and, as requested, we enclose our
estimate for the woven material about which you enquired.

You will no doubt recall that the quality of the material
previously purchased by you is a special weave, and, as
prices have risen considerably since our last supply, we are
taking the opportunity of quoting you for an alternative.

We hope that we can be of assistance to you in this respect
and await your further advice.

Yours faithfully
9 Name of   N J JOHNSON PLC
company

MISS JOAN HARPER
SALES ASSISTANT

ENC

NOTE: This exercise contains all the
parts of a business letter. Keep your
copy and refer to it when necessary.

There is a skeleton of the form shown below in the HANDBOOK AND SOLUTIONS MANUAL, and copies may be duplicated. Insert the form into your typewriter, and then type the information given below in the appropriate place on the form. Check work before removing paper from machine and correct any errors.

MESSAGE FOR

M...

While You Were Out

M...

TELEPHONE NO ....

TELEPHONED		PLEASE RING	
CALLED TO SEE YOU		WILL CALL AGAIN	

MESSAGE ....

....

....

....

SIGNATURE ....

DATE .... TIME ....

Message for Mrs Joan Robinson. Mr Peter Fellows, telephone number 021 440 2345 telephoned (please tick, in ink, the appropriate box). He will be telephoning again at 1400 hours tomorrow, and would be glad if you could let him have the Sales figures for this month. Sign the form in ink, and type today's date and the time that you are typing this document.

6 Type the following letter on A5 portrait paper using margins of Elite 13–63, Pica 6–56. It will be necessary for you to listen for the margin bell and make your own right margin in the body of the letter.

```
Our Ref HS/LE                          NOTE: After "Our Ref" turn up 2 single
                                       spaces and type "Your Ref TM/PN", then
Your Ref TM/PN                         turn up 2 single spaces and type date.

6 April 1982

FOR THE ATTENTION OF MR M HAYNES

H A Ashworth & Co Ltd
28—30 Habberley Road
KIDDERMINSTER
Worcestershire
DY11 5PG

Dear Sirs

ORDER NUMBER 165/6

We refer to your order of 1 April and enclose our confirmation.

We regret that we shall be unable to despatch the goods before the
end of next month because for the last 3 weeks our warehouse staff
have been on strike.  Please accept our sincere apologies for the delay.


Yours faithfully
```

NOTE: As there is no name and designation, turn up 8 single spaces before typing Enc so that there is sufficient space for signature

```
Enc
```

7 Type the following letter on A4 paper using margins of Elite 25–80, Pica 15–70. It will be necessary for you to display the letter according to the instructions given on page 73 and to make your own line-endings.

Our Ref HS/TOM

14 April 1982

FOR THE ATTENTION OF MR D CASEY

Imperial Products Ltd   29 Jiggins Lane   BIRMINGHAM   B32 3EL

Dear Sirs

ENQUIRY REF J/456

As requested in your letter dated 9 April, we have pleasure in enclosing our latest illustrated catalogue which contains details of our present prices and conditions of sale. We allow a cash discount of 5% for payment within 7 days and 2½% for monthly settlement.

Yours faithfully   H SMITH   SALES MANAGER   Enc

See **Practical Typing Exercises, Book One**, page 19, for further exercises on

See **Practical Typing Exercises, Book One**, page 19, for further exercises on

UNIT 37   **Business Letters**   77

Type the following exercise on A4 paper and use double spacing.

A changing world ← Caps and underscore

The advent of electricity ← Caps

In the world of the 1900's electricity was in its experimental stages (only).

Run on/ There were not even any electric bell-pushes, bells being /slet operated by a strong spring. [Trams were conveyed to the city by 2 horses w a cabby to drive them.

NP/

star/ In districts/areas where a steep hill was encountered on the tram route, a third horse was hitched on to ease the burden.

NP/ [Life was comparatively simple in those days — nothing but horse trams and horse cabs on the road. One could take a quiet walk and enjoy the scenery without distraction.

NP/ [All the electrical facilities th are now taken for granted — light bulbs, fires, cookers, vacuum cleaners hair driers, and the rest were things of the unknown future.

Type the following exercise on A4 paper. (a) Take a carbon copy. (b) Leave a margin of $1\frac{1}{2}$" (38 mm) on the left and 1" (25 mm) on the right. (c) Single spacing with double between paragraphs. (d) Leave 2 spaces after the right bracket in the longest numbered item, ie, (iii).

METRIC MEASUREMENTS

When typing metric measurements, pay particular attention to the following:

(i)   Never add an 's' to the symbol to form the plural — symbols are the same in the plural as they are in the singular, eg, 20 metres — 20 m.

(ii)   Never put a full stop after a symbol unless it occurs at the end of a sentence.

Check work before removing paper from machine and correct any errors

(iii)   Always leave a space between the figure(s) and the symbol, eg, 20 (space) m.

(iv)   Most symbols are small letters, but there are a few in upper case, such as C and M which stand for Celsius and Mega. Certain keyboards (teleprinters for example) have upper case letters only, and when using such machines the unit should be typed in full, eg, 15 MILLIMETRES.

(v)   At line ends never separate the figure(s) from the symbol.

(vi)   The symbol l (small L) should not be used for litre — type the word in full or insert a handwritten, looped ℓ .

SKILL BUILDING

In exercises A, B and C, type each line or sentence 3 times. If time permits, complete your practice by typing each group of lines as it appears. Keep your eyes on the copy while you type and also when returning the carriage/carrier. Use single spacing with double between exercises.

Margins: Elite 22–82, Pica 12–72

A   Review alphabet keys

1   Then the expert cricketer, who judged the flight precisely, hit the ball with zest, and very quickly made a good score.

B   Improve skill on fluency drill

2   she her his him are not has had any our who did but was see.
3   they that week know time will days this here your food when.
4   They know that this food must have been left here some days.
5   Your team hope that they will have much more time this week.

C   Build speed on phrases

6   to me, to go, to do, if it, if he, if we, do we, do it, out.
7   and the, for the, may the, can the, you are, you can, it is.
8   If you are late, you can get the last train to go from town.
9   If he calls, do we want him to do the work for the firm now?

Accuracy/speed practice   28 wpm   2 minutes   Not more than 2 errors

A/S 35   I wish you could try out our new car. It is as swift and as   12
smooth as a cloud. I am sure you will like it and will want   24
to drive it when we go on holiday to Rye. I think we should   36
leave here early and then we will be on the main road before   48
the city rush hour. Yes, we will do so. **(SI 1.09)**   56

A/S 36   When you eat your Brazil nuts at Christmas do you ever think   12
of the men who pick them and of the risks they run to do so?   24
One of the risks is the falling of nuts from the trees which   36
grow to a very great height. What we usually call nuts are,   48
in fact, really the seeds from the tree. **(SI 1.20)**   56

    1 | 2 | 3 | 4 | 5 | 6 | 7 | 8 | 9 | 10 | 11 | 12 |

Record your progress   2 minutes

R 16   Different kinds of wild plants do not grow in the same place   12
because they need the soil and conditions to suit them, just   24
as we have our likes and dislikes. A plant which flourishes   36
in a warm, dry place will die if we move it to a place which   48
is cold and damp. It may be possible to alter its habits if   60
we do it slowly over long periods of time. **(SI 1.20)**   68

    1 | 2 | 3 | 4 | 5 | 6 | 7 | 8 | 9 | 10 | 11 | 12 |

Accuracy/speed—2 minutes at 28 wpm
Record Your Progress—2 minutes

UNIT 38   **Skill Building**   78

Type the following table on A5 landscape paper. (a) Leave 3 spaces between the columns.
(b) Use double spacing. (c) Centre the table horizontally and vertically.

NETT TURNOVER FOR 6 MONTHS ENDED 30 JUNE

MONTH	CLOTHING	FOOTWEAR	TOTAL
	£	£	£
January	940.45	646.00	2,553.45
February	1,532.75	1,020.70	1,642.65
March	827.30	814.35	2,337.10
April	1,215.50	1,121.60	1,718.55
May	964.25	754.30	1,754.80
June	745.60	1,009.20	1,586.45
TOTAL	6,225.90	5,367.15	11,593.05

Type the following exercise on suitable memo paper. (a) Take one carbon copy. (b) Two
spaces above printed heading at left margin type the word CONFIDENTIAL in capitals and
underscore. (c) Address an envelope to Mr Peter Thacker.

From Carmel Barnes
To Mr Peter Thacker
Date 4 Nov 1982
Salary Settlement ← Caps

l.c Certain difficulties hv arisen in the translation
of the recent award to Secretarial grades. As it
is yr wish th the 2 months' back pay shld be pd
lc at the end of this Month, I confirm our tel.
conversation when it was agreed th we hv a
uc meeting with Miss M H Gill on monday next
stet to discuss the points raised on the ~~attached~~ sheet.
~~enclosed~~
CB/WO

Check work before
removing paper from
machine and correct any
errors

ENVELOPES

There are numerous sizes of envelopes, but the size will be used that best fits the letter and enclosures. The 3 most commonly used sizes are:

C5—229 × 162 mm (9″ × 6⅜″) takes A5 paper unfolded and A4 folded once
C6—162 × 114 mm (6⅜″ × 4½″) takes A4 folded twice and A5 folded once
DL—220 × 110 mm (8⅝″ × 4¼″) takes A4 equally folded into 3 and A5 folded once

1 Type the following exercise on A4 paper. (a) Leave 25 mm (one inch) clear at the top of the page. (b) Margins: Elite 20–85, Pica 11–76. (c) Single spacing with double between each numbered item.

```
GUIDE FOR TYPING ENVELOPES

1  Always type the envelope for each letter immediately after
typing the letter.

2  The name and address should always be parallel to the longer
side of the envelope.

3  On most envelopes the address should be started about one-
third in from the left edge.

4  The first line must be approximately half-way down the
envelope.

5  Each line of the address must occupy a separate line.

6  Single spacing is preferable on smaller envelopes — double
spacing on larger envelopes.

7  The post town must be typed in CLOSED CAPITALS.

8  The postcode is the last line in the address and should have
a line to itself.  The code is always typed in BLOCK CAPITALS.
Do not use full stops or any punctuation marks between or after
the characters in the code.  Leave one clear space between the
2 halves of the code.

9  Special instructions such as PERSONAL, CONFIDENTIAL, PRIVATE
or FOR THE ATTENTION OF should be typed 2 spaces above the
name of the addressee.
```

FORMS OF ADDRESS—OPEN PUNCTUATION

A Degrees and qualifications—no punctuation. No spaces between the letters representing a degree or qualification, but one clear space between each group of letters.

eg Mr (space) F (space) Eastwood (space) MA (space) BSc   Mr F Eastwood MA BSc

B Courtesy Titles

(a) Must always be used with a person's name
eg Miss M K Green   J Bishop Esq   Mr W P Stevens   Mrs G Hill   Ms S G Matthews
(b) Use either Mr or Esq when addressing a man, never both
(c) Rev replaces Mr or Esq   eg Rev R S Smith
(d) Partnerships—the word Messrs is used before the name of a partnership
eg Messrs Martin & Sons   Messrs Johnson & Co   Messrs Bowron & Jones
(e) Courtesy titles are not used in the following cases
(i) Before the name of a limited company
eg P Yates & Co Ltd   W Robertson & Sons Ltd   Carter & Bailey PLC
(ii) With impersonal names   eg The British Non-ferrous Metal Co
(iii) When a title is included in a name
eg Sir John Brown & Co   Sir Arthur Hamilton-Grey

Consolidation

PRODUCTION TYPING

Job 27   Production Target—15 minutes

Type the following letter on A4 paper. (a) Take one carbon copy. (b) Type a C6 envelope.
(c) Margins: Elite 22–82, Pica 12–72. (d) Insert subject heading ENQUIRY NO 817/7/82.

Our ref FJA/ME

8 July 1982

FOR THE ATTENTION OF MR GEORGE T HAMILTON

Messrs J Barker & Sons
74 Thomas Street
LIVERPOOL
L6 5BJ

Dear Sirs

We obtain yr address from the enclosed advertisement
which appeared in Office Supplies. Wd you please quote
us for the following Unit Furniture:

UF 477   Sliding Door Unit   500 x 700 x 400 mm
UF 833   4-drawer Unit   500 x 500 x 400 mm
UF 983   Open Storage Unit   500 x 500 x 245 mm

In the first instance we wd place an order for 3 of each
item, but, shd this type of furniture prove popular, we
wd then order in larger quantities. Please let us know
your Trade and Discount Terms.

Yours faithfully

F J ADAMS
Purchasing Officer

Enc

Check work before
removing paper from
machine and correct any
errors

Job 28   Production Target—6 minutes

Type the following addresses on paper cut to C6 envelopes. Mark the first envelope
PERSONAL.

Paul J Byrne Esq 17 Kerry Road Cork Irish Republic

Messrs Wm Lloyd & Co 8 Court Road Reading Berks RG7 4PW

Mrs J J Connaught Park View Rd 26 Hyde Road Harborne Birmingham B32 2JZ

ADDRESSING ENVELOPES

Approximately one-third in from left edge
↓

First line half way down ──────────────→ Mr F Eastwood MA BSc
12 The Grove

Each item on
Post town in capitals ────────────────→ OTTERY ST MARY   a separate
Devon   line

One space between 2 halves of code ────→ EX11 1AD

C6 envelope—162 × 114 mm (6³⁄₈″ × 4¹⁄₂″)

FOR THE ATTENTION OF MS S G MATTHEWS

P Yates & Co Ltd
17 New Street
DUDLEY
West Midlands
DYA FG6

Practise typing envelopes

2   Type the following addresses on paper cut to represent C6 envelopes. Mark the first
envelope PRIVATE, and the second FOR THE ATTENTION OF MR J KENNEDY.

W R Wiseman Esq   20 Northbrook Road   BRIGHTON   BN1 1NP
Messrs W Kennedy & Co   32 Main Street   BALLINAMORE   Co Leitrim   Irish Republic
F L Booth & Co Ltd   High Street   CARDIGAN   Dyfed   SA43 1JH
Mr W Willis   16 West Street   BILLINGHAM   Cleveland   TS23 2LR
Mr J Scott   4 North Road   LERWICK   Shetland   ZE1 0AA
Messrs Smith & Sons   40 Clapgate Road   WARRINGTON   WA5 5AF
REV H A Field   4 Hunt Road   LIVERPOOL   L3 9EG
The Cresswell Engineering Co   Bridge Road   LUTON   Bedfordshire   LU1 0RW

See **Practical Typing Exercises, Book One**, page 20, for further exercises on

CREDIT NOTES

Practise typing credit notes

7 Type the following credit note on a suitable form. Please see HANDBOOK AND SOLUTIONS MANUAL, for a printed form.

CREDIT NOTE   No C 782

THE UNIVERSAL SUPPLY CO LTD
84–114 High Street
ABERDEEN   AB2 3HE

VAT Reg No 992 3872 78   24 February 1982

Messrs J H Bowkett & Co
25 Crescent Road
MACDUFF
Banffshire
AB4 1YA

Reason for credit	Quantity and description	Total credit excluding VAT	VAT credited	
			Rate	Amount
		£	%	£
Returned goods (damaged)	1 Single Lens Camera	80.00	15	12.00
	Total credit	80.00		
	Total VAT	12.00		
		£92.00		

Original tax invoice No 1654
dated 2 February 1982

E & OE

See **Practical Typing Exercises, Book One**, page 34, for further exercises on

CARBON COPIES

All business firms keep an exact copy of letters, invoices, and other documents they send out. For this purpose the typist uses *carbon paper*. To take a carbon copy—

(a) Place face downwards on flat surface the sheet on which typing is to be done.

(b) On top of this, with coated (shiny) surface *upwards*, place a sheet of carbon paper.

(c) Place on top of these the sheet of paper on which carbon copy is to be made. If additional copies are required, repeat steps (b) and (c).

(d) Pick up all sheets together and insert into machine with coated surface of carbon paper facing platen.

(e) Make sure that feed rolls grip all sheets at the same time.

Carbon paper has a dull side and a glossy side. The glossy side does the work.

Glossy side of carbon is put against the paper on which the copy is to be made.

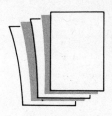

You always have one more sheet of typing paper than of carbon paper.

Straighten sides and top of pack carefully before inserting it in your machine.

Hold pack with left hand; turn cylinder smoothly with right hand.

Erasing errors on carbon copies

(a) Correction paper

Before inserting the correction paper in front of the printing point for the top copy, insert the special correction paper prepared for carbon copies between the shiny side of your carbon paper and the carbon copy. Then place the correction paper for the top copy in front of the printing point and type the incorrect letter through all sheets. Remove the strips of paper and type the correct letter(s).

(b) Correction fluid

Apply the appropriate fluid to the error on the carbon copy and the appropriate fluid to the error on the top copy. It is imperative that the fluid should be quite dry before any attempt is made to type in the correction.

(c) Rubber

Before erasing, insert a strip of thickish paper between the shiny side of your carbon paper and the carbon copy. Then erase on the top copy. Remove the strip of paper and erase on the carbon copy. If you are taking more than one carbon copy, insert strips of paper behind the shiny surface of each sheet of carbon paper. Erase on top and all carbon copies. Remove the strips and then return the carriage/carrier to the typing point and type the correct letter(s).

INVOICES—VALUE ADDED TAX (VAT)

A trader registered for VAT who supplies taxable goods to another taxable person must issue a VAT invoice giving the VAT registration number, tax point, type of supply, etc. (For details of VAT regulations as applied to invoices, please see PRACTICAL TYPING EXERCISES, BOOK ONE, Page 65).

Practise typing a VAT invoice

6 Type the following invoice on a suitable form. Please see HANDBOOK AND SOLUTIONS MANUAL, for printed form.

INVOICE   No 1654

THE UNIVERSAL SUPPLY CO LTD
84–114 High Street
ABERDEEN   ABS   3HE

VAT Registration No 992 3872 78   Date: 2 February 1982

Messrs J H Bowkett & Co
25 Crescent Road
MACDUFF
Banffshire
AB4 1YA

Your Order No PUR 972/82   Terms: Nett 30 days

Tax Point	Type of Supply	Description	Price	VAT Rate	VAT Amount
			£	%	£
2 2 82	Sale	5 Single Lens Reflex Cameras @ £80 ea	400.00	15	60.00
2 2 82	Sale	2 Cine Cameras — 9-30 mm Zoom @ £125 ea	250.00	15	37.50
		Total Goods	650.00		97.50
		Total VAT (Nett)	97.50		
			£747.50		
		E & OE			

See **Practical Typing Exercises, Book One**, page 33, for further exercises on

Practise typing letters with carbon copy

3 Type the following letter on A4 paper. (a) Margins: Elite 27–77, Pica 18–68. (b) Take a carbon copy. (c) Type a C6 envelope. (d) On completion read through carefully and correct any errors.

```
Ref JAH/LMN

5 May 1982

R Lewis & Co Ltd
North Street
CONWY
Gwynedd
LL31 9DB

Dear Sirs

We are advised by our Cardiff Branch Manager that our
Central Heating System has been installed in your
office, and we now have pleasure in enclosing our
account for the amount due.

We feel sure you will find this system to be most help-
ful both in relation to comfort and utility.

Yours faithfully


J A HARRIS
Secretary

Enc
```

4 Type the following letter on A4 paper. (a) Margins: Elite 22–82, Pica 12–72. (b) Take a carbon copy. (c) Make your own line-endings. (d) Type a C6 envelope. (e) On completion read through carefully and correct any errors.

Ref ARM/JAY

19 May 1982

Messrs H J Manson & Sons
Woodland Road
LEOMINSTER
Herefordshire
HR6 8JJ

Dear Sirs

NON-DELIVERY OF GOODS

We have received your letter of 17 May concerning the non-delivery by British Rail of the goods sent to you 2 weeks ago.

We have made enquiries in our Despatch Department and find that these goods were handed to the railway company's carriers, who signed for the receipt of the goods which were securely packed and correctly labelled.

We have taken the matter up with British Rail and enclose a copy of our letter.

Yours faithfully   A R Miller   Manager   Enc

See **Practical Typing Exercises, Book One**, page 20, for further exercises on

INVOICE NO   1543

THE BLACKBURN SUPPLY CO
West Addison Street
BLACKBURN
BB2 6AT

24 May 1982

Mrs B Granger
42 Witton Street
BLACKBURN
BB1 6JN

Note: After the second horizontal line, turn up 2 spaces and type the £ sign in the appropriate columns. Then turn up another 2 spaces before starting the items.

FIGURES—units must always be typed under units, tens under tens, etc. Follow the text carefully when typing the TOTAL column, and, if necessary, refer to page 99.
Where possible, leave 2 clear spaces after the vertical lines before typing the items with the exception of the money columns where the decimal points must fall underneath one another.

QUANTITY	DESCRIPTION	PRICE	TOTAL
		£	£
1	Lounge Unit	34.95	34.95
2	Shelf Units	49.95	99.90
1	500 mm Chest Unit	29.95	29.95
			164.80
	Delivery charge		12.50
			£177.30
	Prices include VAT		
	E & OE		

INVOICES

An invoice is the document sent by the seller to the purchaser and shows full details of the goods sold. The layout of invoices varies from firm to firm according to the information to be given. Invoices are always printed with the seller's name, address and other useful information.

Practise typing invoices

4   There is a skeleton invoice form in the HANDBOOK AND SOLUTIONS MANUAL, and copies of this may be duplicated. If you do not have a suitable invoice form, place a sheet of A4 paper over the exercise above and lightly trace with a pencil the printed ruling. Insert the paper into your typewriter and set margin and tab stops for the beginning of each column. Then type the information exactly as it appears.

5   On another invoice form display the following:

Invoice No 1723   Supplier: the same as above   Date: 14 June 1982
Purchaser: P W BURNETT & CO   11 Brownhill Road   BLACKBURN   BB1 9BA

100	1 kg Bags Superfine Sugar	0.30	30.00
50	tins (large) Garden Peas	0.21	10.50
60	tins Best Quality Salmon	0.98	58.80
40	tins (medium) Tomato Soup	0.25	10.00
			109.30
	Container (returnable)		10.00
			£119.30

SIMPLE DISPLAY IN FULLY-BLOCKED LETTERS

Emphasis may be given to important facts in a letter by displaying these so that they catch the eye of the reader. Such displayed matter starts at the left margin, one clear space being left above and below, as in the specimen that follows.

Practise typing fully-blocked letter with displayed matter

5   Type the following letter on A4 paper. (a) Margins: Elite 22–82, Pica 12–72. (b) Take one carbon copy. (c) Type a C5 envelope. (d) On completion read through carefully and correct any errors.

Ref JKL/GHJ

2 June 1982

FOR THE ATTENTION OF MAIL ORDER DEPARTMENT

J Barnes & Son Ltd
Park Road
HALESOWEN
West Midlands
B63 4BB

Dear Sirs

Please send us as soon as possible, to the above address, the goods listed below:

Turn up 2 single spaces

12 pairs Nylon Sheets, Style H232, @ £6.99 each
12 Quilted Bedspreads, Style H128, @ £9.95 each

Turn up 2 single spaces

We enclose cheque for £205.88 which includes £2.60 for postage.

Yours faithfully
MIDLAND FURNITURE CO LTD

Enc

APPLICATION FORM—AP/82/K

BOULTON AND JAMES PLC
Personnel Department
57 Worcester Road
BIRMINGHAM
B29 6PB

POSITION APPLIED FOR *Shorthand-typist to Sales Manager*

SURNAME *GILSENAN*	OTHER NAMES *Gloria Bernadette*

Address *28 Broadmeadow Close Kings Norton Birmingham B30 ~~2RG~~ 2QR*

Mrs/Miss/Mr/Ms *Miss*	Home telephone number *021-472 2892*

Height *5' 8"*	Weight *9 stone*	State of health *Good*	Serious illnesses *none*

Nationality *British*	Place of birth *Dundee*	Date of birth *5 July 1962*

Living at home *Yes*	Home owner *No*	Rented accommodation *No*	Other accommodation *none*

Leisure activities *Tennis, Squash, Ballroom Dancing, Swimming*

FORMS

Business organisations have a great variety of forms which have been printed, or duplicated, with guide headings, boxes, columns, etc, and the typist has to type in additional information. When the insertion is typed on the same line as the printed heading, there are 2 clear spaces before the start of the insertion. Where the insertion comes below a printed heading, it is typed on the next line. However, if the column is deep and the information to be inserted is short, it will look better with a clear space between the printed heading and the inserted matter.

Information typed in opposite headings should be on the same line as the base of the printed heading and, therefore, it is important to know how close your typewriter prints to its aligning scale. Type a sentence and study exactly the space between the typing and the scale so that, when you insert a form and wish to align your typing with the bottom of the printed words, you will know how much to adjust the paper with the variable line spacer. When typing over ruled or dotted lines, no character should touch the ruled or dotted line. Therefore, with the variable line spacer adjust the typing line so that, when typed, the descending characters y, p, g, etc, are very slightly above the dotted line or underscore.

Practise typing information on a skeleton form

3   There is a skeleton of the above form in the HANDBOOK AND SOLUTIONS MANUAL and copies may be duplicated. Insert the form into your typewriter and then type in the handwritten words.

See **Practical Typing Exercises, Book One**, page 28, for further exercises on

COLUMN DISPLAY IN FULLY-BLOCKED LETTERS

When the matter is to be displayed in columns, 3 spaces should be left between the longest line of one column and the start of the next. The first column starts at the left margin, and tab stops are set for each of the other columns as explained on page 40 (d–h).

6   Type the following letter on A4 paper. (a) Margins: Elite 22–82, Pica 12–72. (b) Take one carbon copy. (c) Type a C5 envelope. (d) On completion read through carefully and correct any errors.

Ref PEW/PG

22 September 1982

Horizon Publishers PLC
Croesyceiliog
CWMBRAN
Gwent
NP4 2XF

Dear Sirs

CHRISTMAS ANNUALS

We have today received your latest catalogue and would like
to place the following order for children's Annuals:

12 only	TREASURE HUNTING	£5.60 each
10 only	SOCCER STARS	£5.23 each
15 only	POP IDOLS	£4.80 each

As we shall be putting our Christmas display on show in
2 weeks' time, please deliver this order by October.

Yours faithfully

> **Note about PLC.** Under the 1980 Companies Act, a public limited company must indicate on its stationery that it is a public limited company. The words may be written in full or abbreviated in upper or lower case.

7   Type the following letter on A4 paper. (a) Margins: Elite 22–82, Pica 12–72. (b) Take one carbon copy. (c) Type a C5 envelope. (d) Make your own line-endings. (e) On completion read through carefully and correct any errors.

Our Ref KB/JG   9/7/82
Miss M J Fields   20 Bath Road   Bitton   BRISTOL BS15 6HS
Dear Madam
As requested in your letter of 7 July, we have pleasure
in sending you under separate cover copies of
the books for which you ask, as follows:

STUDY NOTES ON COMMERCE	J A C Shafto	£4.25
LEGALLY YOURS	J E Montague	£4.30
USE OF OFFICE MACHINES	G Dew	£2.50

We trust you will find these of help to you
and look forward to the receipt of your order
in due course.
Yours faithfully   Miss K Baxter

See **Practical Typing Exercises, Book One,** pages 21 and 22, for further exercises on

Technique development

TYPING SUMS OF MONEY IN COLUMNS

Refer to the instructions given on page 56 with regard to the typing of decimals. Then note the following.

The £ sign is typed over the first figure in the £'s column.   Example: £
Units, tens, hundreds, etc, fall under one another.   110.05
                                                                             20.00
                                                                              0.10
                                                                             13.72

Practise typing sums of money in columns

1 Type the following on A5 portrait paper, taking care to type the decimal points, units, tens and hundreds figures under one another. (a) Centre the exercise vertically and horizontally. (b) Leave 3 spaces between the columns. (c) Single spacing.

```
    £         £         £
  146.57    358.25    216.90
  200.06    347.12    325.89
   19.55     20.75     77.00
    4.56      7.89      7.49
```

INTERLINER LEVER

The interliner lever may be found on the right or left side of the typewriter. Locate this on your machine. The interliner lever frees the platen from the ratchet control, so that the platen may be turned freely forward or backward as required. When the lever is returned to its normal position, your machine will automatically return to the original spacing.

DOUBLE UNDERSCORING OF TOTALS

If you have to type double lines underneath the totals, use the interliner. When typing totals proceed as follows:

(a) Type the underscore for the first lines above the totals. (Do not turn up before typing the first lines.) These lines extend from the first to the last figure of the longest item in each column.
(b) Turn up twice and type the totals.
(c) Turn up once, and then type the lines below the totals.
(d) Turn the cylinder up slightly by using the interliner lever and type the second lines. Then return the interliner lever to its normal position.

Practise typing double lines under totals

2 Display the following exercise on A5 landscape paper. (a) Single spacing for the main part. (b) Leave 3 spaces between columns. (c) Follow the instructions for the total figures. (d) Decimal points must fall under one another.

```
    £           £           £           £
  228.90      12.34      212.34      109.87
  404.75     566.78       33.44      654.57
  323.25      90.12      105.62    1,010.85
1,234.56      35.45    1,212.05      354.25
  789.00   1,237.95      343.18    1,213.65
  654.32     220.16      331.26      434.12 ←──────Do not turn up
                                           ←──────Turn up 2 spaces
3,634.78   2,162.80    2,237.89    3,777.31
                                           ←──────Turn up one space
                                           ←──────Use interliner
```

See **Practical Typing Exercises, Book One,** page 27, for further exercises on

Sums of Money in Columns   Interliner Lever

PRODUCTION TYPING

Job 17 Production Target—12 minutes

Type the following letter on A4 paper. (a) Use suitable margins. (b) Take one carbon copy.
(c) Type an envelope.

Our Ref LW/CC

19. 5. 82.

R W York Esq MA BSc JP
Principal
Doone Comprehensive School
North Street
POOLE
Dorset
BH 14 OLS

Dear Mr York

In July we shall have a vacancy for a school leaver, aged between 16 and 17, in our Internal Audit Department. Applicants must have a minimum of four 'O' levels, 2 of which should be English and Maths.

The post offers an excellent opportunity to a person who intends to follow an accountancy career, and day-release facilities will be available.

I am enclosing 4 application forms and should be pleased if you would be kind enough to let your pupils know of this vacancy. Completed application forms should be returned to me.

Yours sincerely

L WATSON
Personnel Officer
Encs

Check your work before
removing from machine
and correct any errors

Job 18 Production Target—5 minutes

Type the following exercise on A5 landscape paper. Centre vertically and horizontally.

NORTH SEA OIL FIELDS

Andrew	Cormorant	Maureen
Beryl	Crawford	Vivian
Brae	Forties	Piper
Brent	Heather	Tern
Bruce	Hutton	Thistle

SKILL BUILDING

Type exercises A, B and C 3 times. Keep your eyes on the copy while you type and also when returning the carriage/carrier.

Margins: Elite 22–82, Pica 12–72

A Review alphabet keys

1 As he was at the zenith of his power, the tax official began
   an enquiry into the development of this joint stock company.

B Improve control of vowel keys

2 locate unusual receiving suggestion examination distribution
3 assume anxious financial sufficient explanation requirements
4 Your suggestion has been received and we are anxious to have
   an explanation of your quite unusual financial requirements.

C Build accuracy on common prefix drill

5 pro- procure profess process protect promise prolong profile
6 con- contain confirm condemn conceal confess consist content
7 Promise that you will not prolong the process. Also confirm
   that Connie will not conceal the contents of that container.

	Accuracy/speed practice	30 wpm	One minute	Not more than one error	

A/S 42 The weather is likely to remain mild in the south, with some   12
        light rain, but in the north there may be ground frost which   24
        could cause ice on some roads. (SI 1.10)   30

A/S 43 The garage mechanics were not able to fix the valve, so they   12
        had to withdraw their car from the race. The driver did not   24
        take part in the old-car rally. (SI 1.23)   30

A/S 44 Road conditions have been quite difficult for some time, but   12
        we are sure they will improve. We share your view, and know   24
        we must be patient and careful. (SI 1.23)   30

   1 | 2 | 3 | 4 | 5 | 6 | 7 | 8 | 9 | 10 | 11 | 12 |

Record your progress   One minute

R 19 When you are asked to compile a letter, you should use short   12
      words if they express clearly what you want to state. Short   24
      sentences are easy to read and help the reader to understand   36
      what you are trying to explain. (SI 1.29)   42

   1 | 2 | 3 | 4 | 5 | 6 | 7 | 8 | 9 | 10 | 11 | 12 |

Accuracy/speed—One minute at 30 wpm
Record Your Progress—One minute

Job 19

Production Target—7 minutes

Type the following addresses on paper cut to represent C5 size envelopes. Mark the first envelope FOR THE ATTENTION OF MISS J HUGHES.

Messrs Hughes & Baxter   Solicitors   7 Fore Street   EXETER   Devon EX4 3AT
Mr James Emery MD   43 Union Street GLASGOW   G1 4PG
Ms Margaret Hatton   92 Dublin Road   BELFAST   Northern Ireland   BT2 7HF
Robert Brown Esq   56 George Street   EDINBURGH   EH2 3NS
Harris & Co plc   Heaton Road   NEWCASTLE-UPON-TYNE   NE6 5QE
Mrs J Farwell   7 High Street   LEIGH   Lancs   WN7 1BR

Job 20

Production Target—7 minutes

Type the following exercise on A4 paper. Margins: Left 2″ (51 mm), Right 1″ (38 mm).

POSTFAX

A POST OFFICE SERVICE

Postfax is a service that enables you to send an exact copy of a
document from one Post Office to another. At present the service
is available at Post Offices in the major business centres throughout
the United Kingdom.

TRANSMISSION

Hand in the document at a Post Office. It will be fed into a machine
which transmits the image via the telephone system to a receiving machine
at a Post Office in the city of destination. The receiving Post Office
will then deliver the copy to a given address or it may be collected.

SIZES OF DOCUMENTS

You can send any document up to a maximum size of 14 in × 8½ in
(355 mm × 215.9 mm).

Check your work before
removing from machine
and correct any errors

Job 21

Production Target—4 minutes

Type the following exercise on A5 portrait paper. (a) Centre vertically and horizontally.
(b) Follow layout for capitalization and the instructions for line-spacing.

ATTENTION ALL GARDENERS
(Leave 2 clear spaces)
consult us for
(Leave one clear space)
Fencing and Walling
Lawn Turfing   (Use single
Machine Digging   spacing)
Landscaping
(Leave one clear space)
Quotations on request
(Leave one clear space)
A1 Gardeners Ltd   (Last 2 lines in single
Derby Road, Kegworth, Derby   spacing)

ENUMERATIONS USING ROMAN NUMERALS

When Roman Numerals are used for enumerations they may be blocked at the left.

eg (i)   Surname   Leave 4 spaces after right bracket
   (ii) Christian Name Leave 3 spaces after right bracket
   (iii) Address   Always leave 2 spaces after the right bracket in the longest
                        number.

Practise typing numbered items

2   Type the following exercise on A4 paper. (a) Margins: Elite 20–85, Pica 10–75. (b) Single
    spacing. Arabic figures in blue indicate the number of spaces to be left after the Roman
    numeral

DEMAND FOR FLATS

It would appear that the market for flats has expanded considerably during the last 5 years, as hundreds have been and
are still being built for sale or to let by private developing
companies.

I⁴   DEMAND

There is a good demand for flats in residential areas, and the
best sellers are said to be those in blocks which are not more
than 3 storeys high.

II³ MARKET VALUE

It is a fact, however, that the value of flats does not increase
to the same extent as that of new houses, though new flats have
a higher market value than second-hand ones.

III² MORTGAGE

Another hindrance to the sale of flats is that some large building societies, who would be prepared to lend money on a house,
are reluctant to do so for flats.

3   Type the following on A5 landscape paper. (a) Double spacing. (b) Margin: Elite 22–82,
    Pica 12–72. NOTE: The text must always start at the same point on the scale.

    HINTS ON TAKING DICTATION AND ON TRANSCRIPTION

        (i)⁵   Keep your notebook handy.

        (ii)⁴   Put an elastic band round used pages.

        (iii)³   Keep your pen filled.

        (iv)⁴   Have in reserve a pencil sharpened at both ends.

        (v)⁵   Date each page at the top and bottom.

        (vi)⁴   Rule a left margin of about 2.5 cm.

        (vii)³   Use asterisks and footnotes for long substitutions.

        (viii)²   Draw a line across the page after each letter.

See **Practical Typing Exercises, Book One,** page 26, for further exercises on

Type the following letter on A4 paper. (a) Use suitable margins. (b) Take one carbon copy. (c) Type a C6 envelope. (d) Leave 3 spaces between each of the columns in the display portion. (e) Make your own right margin.

Our ref DC/AB

25 February 1982

Mrs T Groves
12 West Avenue
ROCHESTER
Kent
ME1 1DZ

Dear Mrs Groves

RIGHTIME WATCHES

We recently became agents for RIGHTIME wrist watches, and, when next you are in town, we hope you will visit our store and see for yourself the good value we are offering.

The following are only 3 of the wide price range:

Gold Plated	Expanding bracelet	17 jewel	£150
Self-winding	Water-resistant	21 jewel	£165
Self-winding	Day and date	21 jewel	£155

These watches are all fitted with incabloc shock-protected fully-jewelled lever movement and guaranteed for 2 years.

From the enclosed brochure you will see that we offer a great variety of jewellery at reasonable prices.

Yours sincerely   Check your work carefully
                                                       before removing from
                                                       machine and correct any
                                                       errors

DOUGLAS CARSON
Manager

Enc

Technique development

ROMAN NUMERALS

Use of Roman Numerals

(a) For numbering Tables or Paragraphs instead of using ordinary (Arabic) figures
eg, Chapter IX   Table XIII

(b) Sometimes to express the year
eg, 1980 MCMLXXX

(c) For designation of Monarchs, Forms and class numbers
eg, George VI   Form V   Class IX

(d) Small Roman Numerals are used for numbering prefaces of books, or sub-paragraphs or sub-sections.

Examples of Roman Numerals

Study the following table. Note the 7 symbols, I (one), V (five), X (ten), L (fifty), C (one hundred), D (five hundred) and M (one thousand). Note also that when a smaller numeral precedes a larger one it is subtracted, eg, IX = 9; but when a smaller numeral follows a larger one it is added to it, eg, XI = 11.

Roman numerals may be typed in upper or lower case. It is important to remember to use a capital or small I (i) to represent the figure one.

Arabic	Capital Roman	Small Roman	Arabic	Capital Roman	Small Roman
1	I	i	20	XX	xx
2	II	ii	30	XXX	xxx
3	III	iii	40	XL	xl
4	IV	iv	50	L	l
5	V	v	60	LX	lx
6	VI	vi	70	LXX	lxx
7	VII	vii	80	LXXX	lxxx
8	VIII	viii	90	XC	xc
9	IX	ix	100	C	c
10	X	x	500	D	d
			1000	M	m

Note: In the above example the Roman numerals are blocked at the left.

Practise typing Roman Numerals

1   Type the following exercise on A5 landscape paper. (a) Margins: Elite 22–82, Pica 12–72. (b) Double spacing.

Refer to Section IX, Chapter II, Page 340, Paragraph 2(iii).

Read parts XVI, XVII, and XVIII, sub-sections ii, vi, and x.

The boys in Forms VI and IX will take Stages I, II, and III.

Charles II, Henry VIII, George IV, James VI, and Edward III.

See **Practical Typing Exercises, Book One,** page 25, for further exercises on

Type the following exercise on suitable memo paper. (a) Take one carbon copy. (b) Use suitable margins.

FROM J HAYWARD

TO MISS S JACKSON (Personnel)

9 AUGUST 1982

SECRETARY TO MANAGING DIRECTOR

Further to my telephone conversation on Tuesday last, I confirm that Mr J L Howard-Smith's Secretary will be leaving at the end of September and that a replacement will be required at the beginning of October.

The person appointed should be over 25 years of age and should have the following qualifications:

1 LCC Private Secretary's Diploma
2 GCE 'A' Levels (preferably English and German).

When you have short-listed 3 suitable candidates please let me know, and I will arrange for Mr Howard-Smith to interview them.

WF/JH

Job 24   Production Target—6 minutes

Type the following exercise on A4 paper. (a) Suitable margins. (b) Double spacing.

THE RECEPTIONIST

The receptionist is the first person a caller will meet and the impression created is important.
What qualities should a receptionist have? The following are a few suggestions:

(a) Pleasant appearance, dresses attractively and speaks clearly and quietly.

(b) A pleasant disposition and the ability to put people at their ease.

(c) She should like meeting people.

(d) Courtesy is essential at all times, whatever the provocation. Therefore, patience and self-control, together with a friendly smile, are ideal qualities.

Check your work before removing it from machine and correct any errors

SKILL BUILDING

In exercises A, B and C, type each line or sentence 3 times. If time permits, complete your practice by typing each group of lines as it appears. Keep your eyes on the copy while you type and also when returning the carriage/carrier. Use single spacing with double between exercises.

Margins: Elite 22–82, Pica 12–72

A Review alphabet keys

1 Joan Faith quickly jumped over the burning boxes, and walked away from the scene of the disaster with dazed feelings.

B Speed up carriage/carrier return

Type the following lines exactly as shown. Repeat the exercise 3 times.

2 I will.
I will go.
They may go today.
Ask them to go with you.

C Build skill on word-family drill

3 nip lip hip gip rip tip dip sip van can ban ran pan fan man.
4 bold cold fold hold gold sold told full dull hull bull pull.
5 The man told us that he ran to stop the van as it moved off.
6 He sold a full can of ice-cold orange to that happy old man.

Accuracy/speed practice   29 wpm   2 minutes   Not more than 2 errors

A/S 40 The rain poured down and it was too wet to go outside so the   12
2 girls had to play in the house, and they were quite bored.   24
At last they found a case which had no top, and they planned   36
to make a lid for it, but could not do this without a hammer   48
and nails which they could not see in the tool box. (SI 1.16)   58

A/S 41 One of the great problems of today is the pressure of noise: 12
noise in the streets, in the home, by day, and sometimes far   24
into the night. Are buses and lorries the chief cause? No.   36
As we hear these all day, we get used to them. So it is the   48
infrequent sounds, such as those made by jet planes. (SI 1.16)   58

1 | 2 | 3 | 4 | 5 | 6 | 7 | 8 | 9 | 10 | 11 | 12 |

Record your progress   2 minutes

R 18 Many people who pay rent are eligible for rent allowances or   12
rebates — an allowance if you are a private tenant or rebate   24
if you are a council tenant.   29

You should write to your local council. Then they will need   41
to know your income. The bigger your family the better will   53
be your chance of getting help, and the sooner you apply the   65
more quickly will you get help. (SI 1.36)   72

1 | 2 | 3 | 4 | 5 | 6 | 7 | 8 | 9 | 10 | 11 | 12 |

Type the following exercise on A4 paper, using margins of Elite 22–82, Pica 12–72. Take a carbon copy.

```
THE MAIL ROOM

Opening and Distributing the Post

Each organization has its own particular method of dealing with incoming
mail, and you MUST follow exactly the system employed.  The following
points are those used in many offices when dealing with incoming mail.

1 Letters addressed to individuals or departments are not opened before
being distributed.  This, of course, includes letters marked PERSONAL
and PRIVATE.

2  Open envelopes carefully with letter opener or with letter-opening
machine.

3  Take out documents and check to see that any enclosure(s) is there.

(a)  Clip letter and enclosure(s) together.
(b)  Retain envelope.
(c)  If an enclosure is missing, check that it is not in the envelope,
and make a note on the letter to say that it is missing.

4  Stamp all documents with date and time of receipt.

5  Sort documents into trays or other containers for each person or
department.

6  Registered letters should be entered in a special register and a
signature obtained from the person to whom they are delivered.
```

Check your typing and correct any errors before removing the paper from the machine

---

Job 26—Spot the errors

Read the following passage carefully. Each line contains an error that may be spelling, spacing, line-end division, hyphenation, etc. When you have found and marked the errors, type the corrected passage using margins of Elite 22–82, Pica 12–72. Do not type the figures on the left-hand side.

Line
Number

```
1       Our Managing Director, Mr john R Pritchard, says it will be
2       all right for us to buy new chairs for our typists. He is
3       well aware that poor posture impedes breathing, hampers ci-
4       rculation and interferes with muscular action,  Therefore,
5       it will be permissable for you to choose your own chair.  He
6       points out that many clarks in the open-plan office have
7       benefitted from the posture chairs bought last February.  If
8       your would like to see the new chairs, ask the Office Manager.
```

Key on page 172

See **Practical Typing Exercises, Book One,** pages 67–69, for a further exercise on

Proof-Reading

5 Type a copy of the following on A4 paper. (a) Make all the necessary corrections. (b) Margins: Elite 22–82, Pica 12–72. (c) Double spacing. (d) Take one carbon copy.

Telephone Services ← —— *Caps please*

1 Morning and Alarm Calls

lc/ uc/ You shd make Arrangements w the telephone exchange f early

morning calls/at specific times during the day.   *or calls*

2 Personal Calls

Shd you wish to make a long-distance/call to a ~~particular~~ /stet *Certain*

person, it is often better to book a personal call. The

call/ timing f the/does not begin until the person required has

NP/ answered. [A small ~~change~~ *charge* has to be pd f the service in

NP/ addition to the normal charge/for the call. [It is cheaper   *wh is made*

to make yr telephone calls fr 6 pm to 8 am.

6 Type a copy of the following on A5 portrait paper. (a) Make all the necessary corrections. (b) Margins: Elite 13–63, Pica 6–56. (c) Double spacing.

FILING AND INDEXING

l.c./ *DEPARTMENTAL FILING* ✓ *2 clear spaces* *Each dept or Section*

all/ *within a dept wl retain copies of / documents*

usually/ *recd + sent out. Sections wl / adopt a suitable*

system to meet their own needs.

CENTRAL FILING ✓ *2 clear spaces* *Used mainly by large*

Filing/ uc/ *firms w specialists in charge of the / section.*

N *It is ~~difficult to get copies~~ economical of*

space, but sometimes it is difficult

Stet. *to get copies of ~~documents~~ letter wh are*

urgently required

See **Practical Exercises, Book One**, page 24, for further exercises on

SKILL BUILDING

Type exercises A, B and C 3 times. Keep your eyes on the copy while you type and also when returning the carriage/carrier.

Margins: Elite 22–82, Pica 12–72

A Review alphabet keys

1 If he makes a determined and zealous effort, I am quite sure
  Robert will very quickly join the top-ranking experts.

B Improve control of special characters

2 "2" 3 is/was 4 @ £5 6 & 7 "8" 9 (9 — 8) Mr & Mrs one's £102.
3 They asked, "Will you both come to Jim's party on March 14?"
4 Mr & Mrs J Burgess (address below) paid £34 for the antique.
5 He/She requires 20 only @ £5 each, and 18 only @ £5.50 each.

C Improve control of word division

6 mis-take, com-mand, dis-pose, feel-ing, fic-tion, care-less.
7 suc-cess, mil-lion, con-nect, traf-fic, les-son, sup-ported.
8 home-made, bed-room, trade-mark, under-take, self-possessed.
9 prob-able, chil-dren, knowl-edge, resig-nation, pref-erence.

Accuracy/speed practice   29 wpm   One minute   Not more than one error

A/S 37 We hear that you plan to buy new desks, chairs and files, so | 12
       we are sending you a copy of our price-lists which will give | 24
       you a wide range of choice. (SI 1.07) | 29

A/S 38 In the spring we like to go to a farm where we are made most | 12
       welcome. We all have a very happy time as we are allowed to | 24
       do more or less as we like. (SI 1.14) | 29

A/S 39 Against the clear blue morning sky, the white sails of their | 12
       graceful yachts made an ever-changing pattern as they danced | 24
       and swayed in the breeze. (SI 1.21) | 29

   1 | 2 | 3 | 4 | 5 | 6 | 7 | 8 | 9 | 10 | 11 | 12 |

Record your progress   One minute

R 17 It may be next October before I can be certain of the number | 12
     of guests we shall have for the Dinner. I feel sure that it | 24
     will be greater than it was last year as members have bought | 36
     a hundred or more tickets already. (SI 1.28) | 43

   1 | 2 | 3 | 4 | 5 | 6 | 7 | 8 | 9 | 10 | 11 | 12 |

Accuracy/speed—One minute at 29 wpm
Record Your Progress—One minute

LONGHAND ABBREVIATIONS

In a rough draft certain longhand words may have been abbreviated, but these must be typed in full. Some of these abbreviations are given below.

Abbreviation	Word in full	Abbreviation	Word in full	Abbreviation	Word in full
bn	been	co	company	dept	department
f	for	fr	from	hv	have
recd	received	rect	receipt	ref	reference
sec	secretary	sh	shall	shd	should
th	that	togr	together	w	with
wd	would	wh	which	wl	will
yr	your	yr	year		

Note: & (ampersand), Co, and Ltd, are only abbreviated in the names of companies; the & may also be abbreviated with figures.

Practise typing from abbreviated typescript

3 After studying the above abbreviations, read the following passage to see that you understand it, and then type a copy on A5 landscape paper. (a) All abbreviations to be typed in full. (b) Margins: Elite 22–82, Pica 12–72. (c) Double spacing.

YOUR ORDER PURCHASE/12/82

Thank you f yr letter wh we hv recd today. I hv asked our Despatch

Dept about the goods wh you ordered last week and find th they hv bn

sent to you. I shd be pleased if you wd let us know as soon as they

arrive.

May I point out th you hv not pd our Invoice Number 2345 wh shd hv bn

pd at the end of last month.

4 Type the following exercise on A5 portrait paper. (a) Margins: Elite 13–63, Pica 6–56. (b) Single spacing.

VACANCY FOR JUNIOR TYPIST

We hv recd yr application in reply to our advertisement in the POST f
a Junior Typist. We note th you wl be 18 years of age in a month's
time and th you hv obtained 'O' Levels in 6 subjects.

We think you wl be suitable f the vacant position & shd be pleased to
see you on Wednesday next at 2 pm. We wd like you to bring w you yr
references togr w any certificates wh you have.

CORRECTION SIGNS

When alterations have to be made in type-written or handwritten work of which a fair copy is to be typed, or in copy for printers, these are indicated in the original copy by 'Correction Signs'. These signs are recognised and understood by all who are concerned with this type of work. To avoid confusion, the correction sign is placed in the margin against the line in which the correction is to be made, with an oblique line placed after it to show that it is the end of the particular correction. Study and learn the use of the following Correction Signs.

Sign in margin	Meaning	Mark in text
l/c or lc/	Lower case = small letter(s)	— under letter(s) to be altered or / struck through letter(s)
u/c or uc/ or Caps/	Upper case = capital letter(s) When a word(s) is underlined Caps is written in the margin this means type the word(s) in capitals; DO NOT underscore the word(s) unless specifically asked to do so, when the instruction would be Caps and u/s (underscore)	= under letter(s) to be altered or / struck through letter(s)
ჟ	Delete (take out)	— through letter(s) or word(s)
NP or //	New paragraph	[placed before first word of new paragraph
Stet/	Let it stand, ie, type the word(s) that have been crossed out and have a dotted or broken line underneath	- - - - under word(s) struck out
Run on/	No new paragraph required. Carry straight on	⟿
⋀	Caret—insert letter, word(s) omitted	⋀ placed where the omission occurs
◡	Close up—less space	◡ between letters or words
trs/	Transpose, ie, change order of words or letters as marked	⊐⊏ between letters or words, sometimes numbered.
#	Insert space	⋀
CLARKE	If a word is not clear in the text, it may have been written in the margin in capitals in a ruled box. The word should be typed in lower case, or as indicated in the original script.	

Practise typing from typescript with simple correction signs

1 Type a copy of the following exercise on A4 paper. (a) Make all the necessary corrections.
(b) Margins: Elite 22–82, Pica 12–72. (c) Double spacing.

CHEQUES ← *Spaced caps*

lc   A Cheque is an order in writing addressed to a bank by a customer

H   directing payment to self or to ~~one~~ another person. There are

usually 3 parties to a cheque — the person who draws the cheque,

Caps   called the Drawer; the bank on which the cheque is drawn, called

Caps/   *toλ*   the Drawee; the person whom the cheque is to be paid, the Payee.   *Caps/*

Stet   ADVANTAGES The main ~~advantage~~ *benefit* of having a bank account is that

you can make payments by cheque, thus avoiding the necessity to

of money λ   carry with you a large sum when you go shopping.

WRITING A CHEQUE When you make out a cheque, be careful to see

Stet   that the ~~sum~~ *amount* in figures agrees with the written words. Any altera-

NP   tion made must be initialled by you. [Keep your cheque book

trs   in a safe place at all times.

2 Type a copy of the following exercise on A5 portrait paper. (a) Make all the necessary
corrections. (b) Margins: Elite 13–63, Pica 6–56. (c) Single spacing.

Trade Descriptions Act ← *CAPS + UNDERSCORE*

Every care is taken to ensure the accuracy of all
trs   descriptions and specifications at the time of going to
uc   press. We must, however, reserve the right to alter prices
stet/ ⊃   as circumstances ~~require~~ without notice in advance. [Where   *NP*
such alterations in price take place, customers be given   *λwill*
the opportunity to amend their order.

Run on   Similarly, we reserve the right to ~~change~~ *alter* specifications   *or cancel*
stet   without prior notification. [If you require further   *NP*
uc   information please write to the editor.

NOTE:
Certain words which have
been inadvertently
omitted from the original
text may be inserted in
the margin and encircled
in a balloon. The words in
the balloon must be typed
where indicated by the
caret sign.

See **Practical Typing Exercises, Book One,** page 23, for further exercises on

UNIT 40   **Correction Signs**   **92**